BONDS OF THE DEAD

BUDDHISM AND MODERNITY
A series edited by Donald S. Lopez Jr.

RECENT BOOKS IN THE SERIES

The Holy Land Reborn: Pilgrimage and the Tibetan Reinvention of Buddhist India
By Toni Huber (2008)

Buddhism and Science: A Guide for the Perplexed
By Donald S. Lopez Jr. (2008)

In the Forest of Faded Wisdom: 104 Poems by Gendun Chopel, a Bilingual Edition, edited and translated
By Donald S. Lopez Jr. (2009)

Shots in the Dark: Japan, Zen, and the West
By Shoji Yamada (2009)

Locations of Buddhism: Colonialism and Modernity in Sri Lanka
By Anne M. Blackburn (2010)

Introduction to the History of Indian Buddhism
By Eugène Burnouf (2010)

BONDS OF THE DEAD

Temples, Burial, and the Transformation
of Contemporary Japanese Buddhism

MARK MICHAEL ROWE

THE UNIVERSITY OF CHICAGO PRESS
CHICAGO AND LONDON

MARK MICHAEL ROWE is associate professor of religion at McMaster University.

The University of Chicago Press, Chicago 60637
The University of Chicago Press, Ltd., London
© 2011 by The University of Chicago
All rights reserved. Published 2011.
Printed in the United States of America

20 19 18 17 16 15 14 13 12 11   1 2 3 4 5

ISBN-13: 978-0-226-73013-4 (cloth)
ISBN-13: 978-0-226-73015-8 (paper)
ISBN-10: 0-226-73013-1 (cloth)
ISBN-10: 0-226-73015-8 (paper)

Library of Congress Cataloging-in-Publication Data

Rowe, Mark (Mark Michael)
    Bonds of the dead : temples, burial, and the transformation of contemporary
Japanese Buddhism / Mark Michael Rowe.
      p. cm. — (Buddhism and modernity)
    ISBN-13: 978-0-226-73013-4 (cloth : alk. paper)
    ISBN-10: 0-226-73013-1 (cloth : alk. paper)
    ISBN-13: 978-0-226-73015-8 (pbk. : alk. paper)
    ISBN-10: 0-226-73015-8 (pbk. : alk. paper) 1. Buddhist funeral rites and
ceremonies—Japan. 2. Buddhism—Japan. I. Title. II. Series: Buddhism
and modernity.
    BQ5020.R69 2011
    294.3′43880952—dc22

                                                                2011009198

FOR MIK, MASAKO, AND TANEO

下駄も仏も同じ木の切れ

Clogs and Buddhas are both carved from the same tree.

CONTENTS

List of Illustrations   *xi*

Acknowledgments   *xiii*

Introduction   *1*

1.   The "Death" of Japanese Buddhism   *17*

2.   Avoiding Abandonment   *44*

3.   Challenging the Status Quo—Myōkōji   *69*

4.   Limitless Connections—Tōchōji   *112*

5.   Scattering Ashes   *152*

6.   Sectarian Researchers and the Funeral Problem   *178*

Conclusion   *221*

Appendix: Jōdo Sect Survey of Funerary Buddhism (1994)   *231*

Works Cited   *235*

Index   *249*

ILLUSTRATIONS

Figures

1   The Bone Buddhas at Isshinji   *49*

2   The Eternal Tomb   *50*

3   Individual graves at Kuonbo   *57*

4   Wakamiya Mausoleum   *66*

5   The Annon grave site   *72*

6   An Annon forest grave   *73*

7   Close-up of Annon gravestones   *74*

8   Schematic of an Annon grave   *99*

9   Tōchōji's water garden   *116*

10   The Rakandō   *117*

11   The precept ceremony at Tōchōji   *124*

12   Dainichi Nyorai   *215*

Tables

Table 1.   Religious affiliation of 328 eternal memorial graves   *64*

Table 2.   Sectarian research centers   *181*

ACKNOWLEDGMENTS

I had initially thought to make some clever point here about how so many books on Buddhism, regardless of time period or approach, carry acknowledgments explicitly referencing doctrine, usually codependent origination (*pratītya samutpāda*). By opening my own book with a common aphorism about the shared origins of lowly footwear and resplendent Buddhist statues and thus situating Buddhism in the mundane, I had planned to signal a different set of commitments. Of course, as readers of this book will soon realize, employing codependent origination as a way to explain the many relationships and bonds necessary to getting a book to print represents precisely the everyday use of doctrine that I explore in these pages.

This book could not have reached this point had it not been for the help of many incredible people. First and foremost, Jackie Stone is quite simply the best advisor on the planet. Her diligence, attention to detail, breadth of knowledge, and kindness appear limitless. My sincere gratitude goes also to Stephen "Buzzy" Teiser and James Boon for all their support, suggestions, and brilliance. I hope they will recognize some manifest traces of themselves in these pages.

There are far too many friends, colleagues, and associates who had a hand in this to thank them all properly here, so their names, listed in no particular order, will have to suffice: Kevin Osterloh, Paul Copp, Stuart Young, Levi McLaughlin, Joshua Dubler, Lisa Cerami, Reggie Jackson, J. D. Ullrich, Steve Covell, Alex Vesey, Andrea Jones, Asuka Sango, Lori Meeks, Sakura Handa, Heather White, Patty "PB" Bogdziewicz, Lorainne Fuhrmann, Kerry Smith, Yasuko Makino, Erik Rutherford, and John S. LoBreglio.

In Japan, I am also indebted to many amazing people. Shimazono Susumu has been a fantastic mentor and colleague over the years. Murakami Kōkyō provided countless hours of invaluable conversation. I would also like to thank Soda Yumiko, Fujii Masao, Himonya Hajime, Inoue Haruyo, Teshima Jirō, Koyama Shōji, Matsushima Ryūkai, Kotani Midori, Awaya Ryōdō, Tomatsu Yoshiharu, Ogawa Nagisa, Okamoto Wakō, Sugawara Toshikiyo, Chisaka Genbō, Takeda Dōshō, Hirose Kōjirō, Kikuchi Hiroki, Shannon Parker, Christopher Isherwood, Allison Alexy, and Ryan Ward.

I owe a particular debt to Takizawa Kazuo, Ogawa Eiji, and Yasuda Mutsuhiko for allowing me the opportunity to learn from their life labors. Sadly, Takizawa Jūshoku passed away before I finished the project, but even in death he had much to teach me. To all those who took the time to speak to me about the most intimate aspects of their lives, but whom I am prohibited from naming directly, I hope that this book will in some way serve to indicate my most profound gratitude. Thank you.

I could not have finished this book without the invaluable support of my colleagues at McMaster University. In particular, James Benn and Shayne Clarke went over several drafts and buoyed my spirits up when things looked bleak. Anders Runesson kept me sane by agreeing to train through several Hamilton winters. There's nothing like a fifteen-kilometer run in minus twenty degrees Celsius to make chapter revisions seem like fun. Sheryl Dick, Doreen Drew, and Jennifer Nettleton have helped me in more ways than I can say.

The original research for this book could not have occurred without generous funding from Fulbright, the Social Science Research Council, and a Whiting Fellowship. I also received generous support from the Arts Research Board of McMaster, which allowed me to go back to Japan during summers both to conduct new research and to tie up all the loose ends on this project.

The improvement in this book that came from William Bodiford's careful reading of the manuscript cannot be overstated. It is still a far cry from what he envisioned, but I hope that he will like what he reads. Bill Kelly provided shrewd and powerful suggestions—the conclusion, in particular, was dramatically improved by his insight. To the anonymous "Reader #2," who meticulously slogged through the manuscript not once, but twice, I hope you will allow me to buy you dinner someday. I would also like to thank Donald Lopez, Alan Thomas, and Elissa Park at the University of Chicago Press for their interest in the manuscript and their efforts to get it to publication.

My mother, Jean Rowe, has read through countless drafts of the book. I simply could not have done any of this without her support and guidance. My wife, Junko, has gamely supported me from the early days of my academic career. Hopefully now she thinks it was worth it. My son, Cyrus, will also be happy that the book is done so we can finally get back to more important things like fishing, badminton, walking the dog, and PlayStation 3.

This book is for all our family ancestors, near and distant. May it in some way alleviate their thirst.

WATER AND STONE

The dead in Japan thirst. This is something I learn early on as a member of my wife's family, visiting her ancestral grave in rural Tokushima in the stifling August heat. We attend first to the grave itself, filling plastic buckets with water and grabbing ladles, coarse *tawashi* brushes, and the rags that are available at nearly all Japanese graveyards. I start at the top, climbing on the stone base to pour water over the peak of the gravestone. I then work my way down, scrubbing away dirt and dust to the incessant rhythm of cicadas in full chorus. I pay special attention to the deep indentations where the family name is engraved in oversized characters. Along the side, I come across the names of my in-laws, but it is not yet time to visit those memories: First we must clean. I clear out the incense holder and from the two vases at the front of the stone remove the brown, desiccated leaves, a stark reminder that no one has attended this grave in a while. When my mother-in-law was alive, she visited as part of her daily exercise. She would change the water and leaves as she told her deceased husband and the other relatives about family news. Now she waits to hear from us. I scour out the crusted mud in the basin between the vases. The small green frogs that were always here when there was a daily visitor have moved on to damper climes. By the time I am done, my wife and son have cleared the base of cobwebs and the remnants of a wasps' nest. Finally, we pour several buckets onto the granite base to clear away any remaining dirt, refill the vases with water and new branches of *shikimi* leaves, and place a fresh cup of water next to the family crest.

We then attend to those within. The Japanese dead not only thirst for the cool water, cans of beer, or cups of convenience-store sake that the living provide, they also hunger for the grains of raw rice, bags of crackers, and sweets that we pile up for their immaculate consumption. They crave incense as well, which we offer, always after a long battle with the wind and uncooperative matches. Most of all, though, the Japanese dead thirst for conversation, for visits by family and updates on our goings on. They thirst, I imagine, for attention and remembrance.

My son goes first. Still unsure of what is expected, he exaggerates his movements, clapping his hands together loudly before throwing his head down and making some shushing sounds as though he is speaking under his breath. I go next, inwardly saying hello to my wife's parents and then acknowledging the grandparents and elder brother whom I never met. I address my thoughts to those I knew, telling them that their grandson is almost as tall as his mother and that I am optimistic about getting a job, though I have no idea where it might be. The family, I assure them, is doing well, but as always, I ask them to look out for us. After several years of doing this, I no longer ponder whether or not, if they are always watching over us, they actually need to be told what we are doing. My son and I step away as my wife moves forward, offers some grains of rice, and clasps her hands together in silence. She is there for a long time, communing silently with her parents. Though she speaks to them every day at our small, makeshift altar in New Jersey, it seems that there is much to catch up on.

As my son and I return the buckets and brushes to the small shed in the middle of the graveyard, we pass a number of graves that have clearly been abandoned. On one, the stone is slightly askew and the water basin has cracked along the side. At another, someone has placed plastic *shikimi* branches in the vases to keep up appearances, but even these have somehow turned brown. Behind the grave, an old wooden memorial tablet, its writing bleached out by the sun, has cracked and tipped over onto the stone. Now that there are only daughters left in my wife's family, each married and living elsewhere, I wonder what will happen to her family grave. Will it too dry out and collapse? Will her parents not feel abandoned and forgotten? Who will attend to their needs? Who will slake their thirst?

TEMPLES AND GRAVES

This is a study of contemporary Japanese Buddhism and the care of the dead; of how religious, political, social, and economic forces over the course of the twentieth century led to the emergence of new funerary practices in Japan and how, as a result, the care of the dead has become the most fundamental challenge to the continued existence of Japanese temple Buddhism. This challenge extends beyond the economic, demographic, and social forces of change into the realm of more existential doubts about the role of the tradition and the true meaning of Buddhist understandings of death.

Therefore, secondarily, this is a study of the primary overseers of shaping tradition within Japanese Buddhism today; of the interplay and tensions between Buddhist ideals, as reflected in the activities of Buddhist intellectuals, and the often conflicting practical needs of temple priests in the context of their daily responsibilities as caretakers for the dead.

In Japan, 90 percent of all funerals are Buddhist, and the majority of all temples derive their primary income from maintaining graves and providing mortuary services for parishioners.[1] At the same time, most Japanese see temple priests less as representatives of a distinct Buddhist lineage than as ritual specialists and caretakers for the family ancestors.[2] Buddhism, as it is lived in Japan today, is intimately tied to the family, and it is the multigenerational ancestral graves, maintained at temples, that serve as the central locus of this relationship. This lifelong, hereditary, and increasingly onerous bond of obligation has its roots in the temple parishioner system (檀家制度 *danka seido*), which began in the seventeenth century, and, despite its legal end in the late nineteenth century, continues to set the tone for temple/family dealings up to the present day. A person's identification with one of the traditional Buddhist sects is not necessarily based on particular doctrinal positions but rather centers on loyalty and obligation to the temple where one's family ancestors are interred.[3] Today

1. Since most Japanese consider themselves as both Buddhist and Shinto, surveys of Japanese religious affiliation notoriously produce totals nearly double the actual population of the country. The government religious survey for 2007 found that 84 percent of Japanese identify as Shinto, and 70 percent are Buddhist (Bunkachō 2008, 31). At the same time, data from the early 1980s showed that roughly 65 percent of all Japanese also consider themselves nonreligious (Swyngedouw 1993, 50). These numbers speak to the contextual nature of religious practices in Japan as well as the association of the term religion (宗教 *shūkyō*) with Western notions of weekly worship and exclusive devotion. For more details on the contextual nature of Japanese religious affiliation, see Reader 1991; Swyngedouw 1993; and Roemer 2009.

2. The term *sōryo* 僧侶 can be translated into English in a number of ways, all of which carry some Christian connotation. I have chosen "priest" because these people are ordained members of the clergy who can perform certain rites and administer certain sacraments. At times, I use the term abbot (住職 *jūshoku*) to refer to priests who are abbots of temples.

3. Throughout this book I use the term "sect" to refer to different Buddhist denominations. At the risk of evoking negative connotations in the minds of readers, I think this usage is justified because it emphasizes the institutional distinctiveness of these organizations in the modern period. The main Buddhist sects in Japan today include True Pure Land (浄土真宗 Jōdo Shinshū), Sōtō Zen (曹洞宗 Sōtōshū), Pure Land (浄土宗 Jōdoshū), Rinzai Zen (臨済宗

it is almost a cliché in Japan that the younger urban generation will only learn of their particular sectarian affiliation when there is a death in the family and they have to find a Buddhist priest for the funeral.[4]

As the composition of Japanese households has changed due to drastic demographic shifts in the postwar period, the extended household—the bedrock of temple Buddhism—has become more of an ideal than a reality.[5] Nevertheless, multigenerational, extended-family values are still a powerful force in contemporary Japanese society, sustained through modern laws, popular nostalgia, and extensive advertising. While certain scholars have focused on the vanishing hometown (故郷 furusato) as a central discourse in modern Japanese identity,[6] I believe the crucial apparatus for imagining the "perfect Japanese family" continues to be the extended-family grave, passed on through first sons and housing, in supposed perpetuity, the family ancestors, wives, and male heirs.

As this study will show, the ideal of the family grave, like the very stone itself, is no longer able to weather contemporary realities. Urbanization, depopulation in rural areas, smaller family sizes, an increasing number of people who do not marry, a rising divorce rate, the aging of the baby boomers (団塊の世代 dankai no sedai), and a growing number of women who are no longer satisfied with the patrilineal-burial status quo have all created a demand for new burial forms more in line with current social realities. In turn, these new forms of interment have given rise to new types of relationships with temples, relationships based on individual choice rather than inherited obligation.

JAPANESE BUDDHISM AND BURIAL

In order to investigate what changing burial forms reveal about the state of temple Buddhism in contemporary Japan, this book will explore a new type of eternal memorial grave (永代供養墓 eitai kuyōbo) that emerged in

Rinzaishū), Tendai (天台宗 Tendaishū), Nichiren (日蓮宗 Nichirenshū), and Shingon (真言宗 Shingonshū). Many of these sects are further divided into different lineages (宗派 shūha).

4. Ian Reader recalls one such story (Reader 1991, 3). While conducting research on Japanese funeral companies between 1997 and 1999, I heard many accounts from funeral directors of families that needed to call parents or grandparents in rural hometowns in order to find out their own sectarian affiliation.

5. I borrow the expression "temple Buddhism" from Stephen Covell, who defines it as "Buddhism as lived by the members of those sects of Japanese Buddhism that were founded ʃoos" (Covell 2005, 4). In other words, the activities and institutional structures of hose sects listed in note 3 above. See also Covell and Rowe 2004.

for example, Ivy 1995, chapter 4.

the late 1980s and early 1990s.[7] As with their extended-family-grave pre-decessors, these new burial forms offer unique insights into family structures, social norms, and religious affiliation in Japan. By allowing individual, single-generation membership, with no requirement to become a temple parishioner (檀家 *danka*), these eternal memorial graves represent a radical departure from the traditional obligation to support the temple that houses one's ancestors—an obligation that, until now, had to be passed on from generation to generation, carrying with it a significant financial commitment.[8] Once people are able to choose a gravesite at a temple they like and one that places no burden on their children, the whole dynamic of relationships to temples changes from one of obligation to one of choice, potentially signaling the end of the parishioner system itself and the beginnings of a post-*danka* Buddhism. Since most eternal memorial graves do not require one to become a member of the temple's sect, they represent a profound challenge to the current norms of temple affiliation and sectarian identity. Will sectarian distinctiveness weaken, leading to more transsectarian forms of Japanese Buddhism, or will it become more entrenched as one of the few ways to distinguish between temples? Or will other, more commercial, factors become determinative of temple affiliation, or even replace it?

As much as changing burial practices tell us about Japanese society, they also offer critical insights into the ways in which temple Buddhism is perceived, propagated, and contested in contemporary Japan. Historian Tamamuro Taijō's 圭室諦成 1963 *Funerary Buddhism* (葬式仏教 *Sōshiki Bukkyō*) traced the historical circumstances by which Japanese Buddhism came to be associated with the physical and spiritual care of the dead. The

---

7. The generic term used for these new graves, "eternal memorial" 永代供養, though appearing similar to expressions such as 永代経 *eitaikyō* or 永代読経 *eitai dokkyō*—permanent chanting of sutras on the death anniversary (命日 *meinichi*) or every month on the day of death (忌日 *kinichi*) in order to generate merit for the deceased—is actually very different. The latter terms have a long history in Japan, describing a practice that has traditionally been used for temple parishioners who were already deceased (Mochizuki 1954–1963, vol. 1, 256–57). Furthermore, that practice did not involve a new style of burial, nor did it necessarily allow one to have rites performed at a temple from a different sect. As we shall see, the more recent term that is being applied to new grave forms describes a very different burial phenomenon.

8. Although translating *danka* as "parishioner" runs the risk of importing certain Christian ideas of church membership, I feel that a more direct rendering, such as "temple donor family," would prove unnecessarily cumbersome. The important distinction to be made is the sense of moral and fiscal obligation on the part of the *danka*, both in the present and for future generations, to one's home temple as the place where one's family ancestors are interred—obligations not imposed by eternal memorial graves. The *danka* system will be addressed in chapter 1.

expression "funerary Buddhism" has since become pejorative, synony-
mous with the supposed decline of Japanese Buddhism. The most common
perception is that of wealthy temple priests profiting handsomely from the
misfortune of others. Yet at the same time, for most Japanese it is entirely
natural to turn to temples when there is a death in the family or for annual memorial services. Yearly anniversaries of deaths, the summer festival of the dead (お盆 o-bon), and the spring and autumn equinoxes (彼岸
higan) are all times for visiting temples to request memorial services to
benefit the spirits of family ancestors and the newly dead.[9] Surveys consistently reveal that most Japanese visit temples primarily for memorial
services and funerals. In fact, it was the realization (during my early visits
to temples in western Japan) that most Buddhist priests seemed far more
concerned with memorializing ancestors than attaining enlightenment
that led to my current research.

Anyone familiar with the Buddhist tenet of no-self (refutation of any
immutable metaphysical essence) may find it contradictory that Buddhist
priests spend so much time and effort generating merit on behalf of individual spirits, but this has never represented much of a problem on the
ground, either in Japan or in other countries where Buddhist memorial services are performed (Cuevas and Stone 2007, 7). This is not to say that certain Buddhists are unconcerned with what they see as clear contradictions
between doctrinal tenets and actual practices. Concomitant with the public discourse on funerary Buddhism in Japan has been an effort by intellectuals, researchers, and leaders within the various sects to deal with the
so-called "mortuary problem" (葬祭問題 sōsai mondai).[10]

The sōsai mondai is a catchall term for a broad range of doctrinal, historical, social, institutional, and economic issues confronting the tradi-

9. *O-bon*, also referred to as the "ghost festival," is the time when ancestral spirits are
called back into homes, feted, and then sent off again. Families visit graves and may also purchase wooden memorial tablets from temples upon which a priest has written a short prayer
and the name of the deceased. Aside from New Year's celebrations, this is one of the only
times in the year that family members return to their hometowns. For the Chinese origins of
the ghost festival, see Teiser 1988.

10. Used as a synonym for "*sōshiki*" 葬式 and "*sōgi*" 葬儀, or "funeral," *sōsai* brings to
mind the term *kankon sōsai* 冠婚葬祭, or "the major ceremonies of life," such as coming of
age, marriage, funerary, and ancestral rites, and thus reinforces the positive images of family and the life cycle. By evoking the term *sōsai*, Buddhists are able to downplay the image
of an overpriced, inscrutable, antiquated ritual (the funeral proper) so as to emphasize the
more traditional and "Japanese" ideas of ancestor worship and services for departed spirits.
In publications and conferences, sectarian scholars seem to take pains to use the term *sōsai*
exclusively.

tional sects of Japanese Buddhism. While these issues are clearly interrelated, this "problem" signifies different concerns to different groups and is a source of ongoing debate within each Buddhist organization. Intellectuals, researchers, sect leaders, and local priests in every sect all have different ideas about how best to situate "funerary Buddhism" in relation to the no less nebulous and diversely conceived category of "Buddhism."

For sectarian scholars who study both doctrinal texts and their respective sects as organizations enmeshed in contemporary society, funerary Buddhism represents a crucial intersection of sectarian ideals and local temple realities. If, for example, Buddhist sects emphasize a normative stance on the doctrine of no-self or codependent origination, how is this to be reconciled with a temple economy that is built almost entirely on conducting rituals to help the individual spirits of deceased family members? Although this sort of question may not trouble temple parishioners or even priests, it is of ongoing concern to Buddhist leaders and researchers, as evidenced by the numerous surveys, conferences, pamphlets, and books on the mortuary problem being produced by every major sect. In addition, then, to including the voices of temple priests, parishioners, and those seeking new types of graves, this study will also analyze the writings of sectarian scholars charged with surveying and maintaining both the teachings of their respective organizations and the institutions that propagate those teachings.

THE STUDY OF BUDDHISM AND DEATH

One obstacle to the study of contemporary Japanese Buddhism, and one that I believe has done much to deflect scholarly attention, is the widespread opinion, both popular and academic, that contemporary Buddhism in Japan has compromised its doctrinal underpinnings and no longer holds any spiritual potency or social relevance. The perception of Japanese Buddhism as a tradition in decline has a long history, one that is in large part due to the intimate connections between Buddhism and death.[11] This study, however, uses funerary Buddhism to argue for a more complex vision of the tradition.

The scholarly study of funerary Buddhism is currently undergoing a boom of sorts, with two edited volumes on the subject and several other

11. For details on the "corruption" of Japanese Buddhism, see Covell 2005, 14–18; and Watt 1984, 188–90.

related works in English already published.[12] In addition to promoting studies of Buddhism that combine the examination of doctrinal texts with research into art, relics, archaeology, ritual, and other material aspects, these collections further validate the importance of ethnographic approaches to the question of how different Buddhist groups care for the dead. Such research shows that, far from being a compromise of fundamental doctrinal tenets, funerary Buddhism reveals the tradition at its most vibrant: rituals, cosmologies, hagiographical accounts, and doctrinal explanations ranging from the sublime to the mundane, all serving to help the living help the dead.

Emphasizing the positive aspects of mortuary Buddhism is not meant to downplay the considerable financial benefits that temples derive from their monopoly on mortuary ritual. On the contrary, the study of Buddhism and mortuary practices is most illuminating precisely when it treats both the ideals and the realities of temple life as "Buddhist." The attempt by temple priests to see to both the emotional needs of their parishioners and the financial requirements of their temples, often at the cost of maintaining doctrinal orthodoxy, should not be taken as an indicator of Buddhist decline, but rather as Buddhism in action, as an example of Buddhists confronting changing social practices and modern concerns over the fate of tradition. The discourse of Buddhist decline is also a Buddhist discourse.

Despite broader calls within the field of Buddhist studies for more ethnographic studies of Buddhism that are doctrinally and historically attentive, there is still a surprising dearth of such scholarship, particularly in Japan.[13] Robert Sharf has identified what he calls an "unfortunate division of labor" that keeps Buddhologists from studying contemporary

12. Strong 2004; Williams 2005; Covell 2005; Bernstein 2006; Langer 2007; Cuevas and Stone 2007; Hur 2007; and Stone and Walter 2008.

13. I would argue that 1995 was a watershed year for both critical self-reflection in Buddhist studies and calls for ethnographic work to counter textual and elitist biases in the field. Examples include Lopez 1995, Sharf 1995, and an issue of the *Journal of the International Association of Buddhist Studies* 18, no. 2 (1995) devoted to methodological issues in the field. Significant works that take Buddhism as their primary ethnographic object include Stanley Tambiah (1970, 1976, 1984) and Melford Spiro (1970). More recent studies include Cadge (2005); Leve (1999); Klima (2002); Kitiarsa (1999); and Seneviratne (1999). Contemporary Japanese Buddhism has started to receive some attention in the last few years with Jørn Borup's overview of Rinzai Zen Buddhism (2008), Stephen Covell's book-length treatment of contemporary Tendai Buddhism (2005), Nakajima Takanobu's *Temple Economics (Otera no keizaigaku)* (2005), Ueda Noriyuki's popular *Hang in There Buddhism! (Ganbare Bukkyō)* (2004), and a special issue of the *Japanese Journal of Religious Studies* 31, no. 2 (2004) on traditional Buddhist sects in the contemporary period.

forms of Buddhism and has anthropologists producing synchronic ethnographies of new religious movements that fail to adequately consider historical and doctrinal forces (Sharf 1995, 452–53).[14] A key aspect of Sharf's
critique of a philological/ethnographic split in studies of Japanese religions
is the very reification of categories such as doctrine and practice. Regardless of whether these divisions are seen as heuristic markers, emic categories, or tiresome binaries, their unchallenged installment as oppositional
pairs deflects critical attention away from the disciplinary logic according to which they have been accepted as distinct entities to begin with.
The present study seeks not merely to counter the prevailing emphasis
on doctrine with thick descriptions of temple life, but rather strives to explore in detail the manner in which Buddhist teachings are discussed and
implemented, that is, in other words, "practiced," in a variety of settings.
The particular forms of the tradition that temple priests learn at training
monasteries and sectarian educational institutions are often vastly different from those forms they encounter when inheriting a temple. The "mundane" concerns of maintaining temple property and keeping parishioners
and family members happy on an unstable income from irregular funeral
and memorial rites often supersede any study of other "higher" forms of
the tradition. Furthermore, for the average parishioner, Buddhism is usually not seen as a collection of doctrinal teachings, but as a set of practices
that are considered "traditional" rather than "religious" per se. As a result, for those exploring new burial possibilities, the range of responses to
Buddhist teachings and temple practices as evincing noticeably religious
significance can run from curiosity to outright indifference.

The study of contemporary Japanese Buddhism cannot limit itself to
what occurs behind the temple gate. Therefore, in addition to examining
the myriad ways in which priests and parishioners negotiate their relationships, their interpretations of doctrine, and their roles within the various
sects, I have also made a point of addressing how sectarian researchers and
intellectuals study and propagate Buddhist teachings. Individual temples
belong to larger institutional organizations (sects), and it is through that
often contentious and troubled relationship that the scholar is able to grasp
the broader picture of how sectarian ideals and social realities intersect.
Among the activities of these researchers we again encounter a multiplic-

14. While it is true that scholars of Japanese religions focus on new religious movements
rather than the traditional Buddhist sects, there are many studies that take the doctrinal and
historical underpinnings of these groups seriously. See, for example, Davis 1980; Hardacre
1984 and 1988; and Earhart 1989.

ity of Buddhisms: doctrinal texts and sect history; contemporary social issues and Buddhist responses; and those institutional forms of Buddhism that are surveyed and analyzed using social scientific methods.

As Timothy Brook reminds us, "Factoring the concrete sociality of religious life into the study of Buddhism opens the analytical possibility that what goes on is not incidental to Buddhism but constitutive of the historical practices to which we, and those who have done them, assign its name" (Brook 2005, 146). Writing about multiple Buddhisms is not to argue that there is no such thing as "Buddhism"; such a postmodern deconstruction does not interest me. The question addressed in this study is not simply whether scholars can meaningfully speak about a single, unified Buddhism, since clearly we cannot and, just as clearly, that inability in no way keeps us from our work. The question, then, is not "Is there such a thing as Buddhism in Japan?" but rather, "Why are we not including all of these different things that happen at temples, graves, and sectarian research centers as legitimate elements of that larger thing it still seems to make sense to call 'Japanese Buddhism'?"

ETHNOGRAPHIC DETAILS

Much of the research for this project was carried out during an eighteen-month period from the summer of 2003 to the end of 2004. During that time I visited approximately fifty sites, including temples, shrines, and municipal graveyards, all of which maintained eternal memorial graves. My primary areas of research were in the Kansai (mainly Kyoto, Osaka, and Kobe) and Kantō (Tokyo, Chiba, Shizuoka, and Saitama) areas, but I also visited graves in Kyūshū, Shikoku, Tōhoku, and Niigata. At my main field sites, Myōkōji 妙光寺 in Niigata and Tōchōji 東長寺 in Tokyo, in addition to regularly attending temple functions, I used a combination of formal and informal interviews with burial society members (people who have purchased plots in the eternal memorial graves), parishioners, temple staff, volunteers, temple families, and priests. At both temples, I conducted extended, formal interviews with between twelve and fifteen burial society members. I then chose several of those members for a second round of extended interviews.

I conducted most of my research on the Grave-Free Promotion Society (chapter 5) during summer visits to Japan from 2000 to 2003. Here too I made use of formal interviews with approximately fifteen Society members as well as regular meetings with the head of the society, Yasuda

Mutsuhiko 安田睦彦. I also took part in an ocean scattering ceremony and surveyed society members via the organization's newsletter. I received roughly three hundred responses out of a potential ten thousand members (based on the unlikely assumption that every single society member receives and reads the newsletter). The low response rate dissuaded me from formal presentation of the results in the present study. Nevertheless, the personal narrative answers of many respondents allowed me to extrapolate, to a certain degree, to the membership at large.

For my study of sectarian research centers I focused primarily on the Research Center for Sōtō Zen Buddhism (曹洞宗総合研究センター Sōtōshū Sōgō Kenkyū Sentā), the Nichiren Contemporary Religion Research Center (日蓮宗現代宗教研究所 Nichirenshū Gendai Shūkyō Kenkyūjo), and the Jōdoshū Research Institute (浄土宗総合研究所 Jōdoshū Sōgō Kenkyūjo). I chose these centers primarily because they are the most active in terms of research and textual production, but accessibility, location, and serendipity also played a part. I made regular visits to the centers, attended conferences, spoke with researchers, and went through the material each center produced for temple and public consumption. My conversations with researchers occasionally put them in the position of having to be critical of their organizations; I have thus avoided presenting any information that might identify my informants. In the case where the information was already published, I felt it responsible to identify the person.

During my six years as a graduate student at Kyoto University in the 1990s, I also had countless opportunities to visit temples throughout Japan, from the very wealthy to the nearly abandoned, from rural to urban, and in every major sect.[15] Home stays at temples, casual conversations, formal interviews, and yearly interactions with the priests at my wife's family's home temple in rural Tokushima have all helped me develop a sense of the different realities facing temple priests and parishioners. During my main research phase for this study (2003–4), I interviewed approximately thirty temple priests of varying ages and levels of formal training. In addition to questions about how they ran their temples and their temple graveyards, I also asked them about how they saw their relationships with their respective sects and what issues most troubled them when thinking about the future. Though these conversations are not presented in any formal way, they do form the background for the image I portray of contemporary Japanese Buddhism.

15. The only area of Japan in which I have yet to visit a Buddhist temple is Hokkaidō.

OVERVIEW

Chapter 1 sets the background for this study by tracing key historical factors in the modern period that have led to the current state of Japanese Buddhism. Although numerous studies treat the relationship between Buddhism and death in the premodern and modern periods, the contemporary role of Buddhist temples as landlords for the dead has yet to receive significant scholarly attention. Chapter 1 will thus trace the development of so-called funerary Buddhism by focusing on four main themes: (1) the modern emergence of funerary Buddhism; (2) ongoing critiques of funerary excess and, by extension, of funerary Buddhism; (3) the rise of the professional funeral industry; and (4) the effects of Japanese Buddhism's encounter with Western modernity.

Chapter 2 begins by introducing the concept of *muen* 無縁. With its connotations of dying alone or being abandoned after death, *muen*, or the lack of human connections, is the engine that is driving the demand for new burial options. This chapter then outlines the current state and limitations of traditional temple graves in the face of *muen*. Beyond its symbolic and ritual functions, the grave is also a physical presence on temple grounds, one that is both a source of temple revenue and a burden on temple resources. When family members no longer visit or pay for the maintenance of the grave, it becomes abandoned (*muen*) and thus ceases to produce any revenue until it is reclaimed.[16] Legal requirements for declaring a grave abandoned in order to reuse it have been relaxed, but the time and money required to recover an abandoned grave are still substantial. Furthermore, each grave takes up a certain amount of the finite space available on temple grounds, placing a constraint on the total number of parishioner families the temple can accommodate. The best way to attract new parishioners is through graves, but many temples simply do not have the land for additional burial plots. The development of eternal memorial graves provides an opportunity for temples to bring in a significant number of new people, offer care for parishioner families with no one left to maintain their graves, and significantly improve temple income.

Chapter 3 provides the first of two in-depth case studies of temples running successful eternal memorial graves. As arguably the first true

16. Average costs for grave maintenance vary greatly, but are not particularly high. My informants generally noted a range from four thousand to ten thousand yen per year, about what someone would pay on a monthly cell phone bill.

eternal memorial grave in Japan, the Annon 安穏, or "peace and tranquility" grave at Myōkōji, a Nichiren temple in rural Niigata, is crucial to our understanding of how this new burial technology emerged and spread throughout the country in a relatively short time. Much of Annon's success is due to the temple's abbot, Ogawa Eiji 小川英爾, a Nichiren priest who is very vocal about the problems facing local temples dependent on what he sees as outmoded views of the temple/parishioner relationship. His desire to create a radically new type of grave based on individual membership rather than formal parishioner status in his temple, along with his media savvy and unconventional methods, helped create a watershed moment for modern Japanese burial in the early 1990s.

In addition to detailing the development and growth of the new gravesite, this chapter will also provide several ethnographic narratives of Annon grave members, as well as Ogawa himself. These accounts serve to clarify common reasons for choosing such sites, detail ways in which these new graves respond to the *muen* problem, and implicate scholarly models for conceptualizing religious affiliation in Japan. They also demonstrate the ways that these new burial sites both register changes in contemporary society and offer an arena in which to challenge established social norms. For example, the patrilineal basis of the extended-family grave has often meant exclusion for unmarried or divorced women. Those unable, or unwilling, to enter their husbands' family graves were, until the development of eternal memorial graves, excluded from having their own graves or individual memorial services and would generally end up in communal graves. Chapter 3 presents two such narratives of women who use the Annon grave to assert control over various facets of their current lives and their posthumous fates. Finally, chapter 3 provides a narrative of Ogawa's views of temple Buddhism and his goals for Annon. In his frank assessment of the parishioner system and the Nichiren sect as an organization, we are offered a detailed account of both local (temple) and institutional Buddhism in Japan.

In dramatic contrast to the rural location and smaller scale of Annon, the eternal memorial grave at Tōchōji, a wealthy Sōtō temple in central Tokyo, forms the subject of chapter 4. Within eleven years of founding the new grave and its En no Kai burial society in 1996, membership had reached capacity at ten thousand. A second site has been completed at a Sōtō temple in rural Chiba, two hours outside of Tokyo, and a third at a Nichiren temple in Tokyo. Like Annon, the eternal memorial grave at Tōchōji offers avenues for moving beyond traditional bonds so that one can be memorialized by friends, acquaintances, and even strangers. Tōchōji's innovative reimagining of *muen* as a way to transcend the restrictions of tradition and "connect to people without limitations" demonstrates the significance of these new sites both for temples and Japanese society as a whole.

Unlike Annon, which derives much of its success from Ogawa's personal charisma, the startling growth of En no Kai can be attributed in part to its office staff, who are actually employees of the commercial company that helped design and promote the new grave. Though not ordained into the Buddhist priesthood, these workers represent the main interface between the temple and burial society members and have taken on many of the roles traditionally carried out by temple priests. Tōchōji's highly successful mix of business and religion suggests ways in which the scholar of religion might see their combination as not necessarily indicative of Buddhist decline or commercialization, but rather as aspects of negotiations that naturally occur at all temples and thus act as legitimate manifestations of Buddhism. In addition to exploring this mix of venture capital and proselytization, chapter 4 also addresses the relationship between burial society members who have joined the temple in the last ten years and traditional temple parishioners, many of whose families have been connected to the temple for much longer periods of time. Not surprisingly, there is some evidence of parishioner resentment toward the burial society members, who join the temple out of choice, pay a single set fee for all of their services, have no obligation to help pay for temple upkeep, and never have to worry about abandoned graves.

Chapter 5 shifts the attention away from temples to the Grave-Free Promotion Society, a civic group with a membership of over ten thousand that promotes the scattering of ashes in nature. Although interment of one's ashes in a family grave is still the predominant form of burial in Japan, this group has generated a surprising amount of press and is clearly affecting the way people think about burial. The public discussion and debate regarding scattering reveals significant shifts in conceptions of family, social norms, and memorial rites. In eschewing family graves and a fixed location for memorial services, however, the society is also presenting an implicit challenge to Buddhist mortuary rites and temple income. This chapter examines in detail the wide variety of Buddhist responses to the economic and philosophical threat posed by this emerging trend and explores what those responses—from outrage, to grudging acceptance, to temple adaptations of scattering practices—reveal about the relationship among Buddhist doctrine, burial, and Japanese families. In arguing the necessity of memorial rites for family members, priests reinforce the fact that, far from being conditioned by ideals of nonattachment, temple Buddhism in Japan is fundamentally dependent on the maintenance of bonds (縁 en), of the critical ties that bind family members, ancestors, and temples. Thus as much as the lack of bonds (muen) implicates contemporary burial practices and broader societal shifts, the reliance on en to defend Buddhist mortuary practices reveals the intimate connections, and potential tensions, between Buddhist doctrine and the ways in which Buddhism is lived and propagated in Japan.

Chapter 6 considers the doctrinal implications of funerary Buddhism by expanding the scope of this study to include the voices of scholarly priests working in sectarian research centers. How exactly do sectarian researchers, working on behalf of the sect's hierarchy, understand the mortuary problem? How do their understandings differ from those of temple priests? What are the mechanisms by which sects survey temples and disseminate results, and how do local priests respond? These centers represent an important, but previously overlooked, site in the maintenance and production of Buddhism in Japan. Exploring the methods, frameworks, and assumptions employed by these researchers to understand and influence temple priests provides key insights into the intersection of doctrinal orthodoxy, temple realities, sectarian identity, and institutional forces. I argue that the activities of these researchers serve to interpret the material forces affecting funerary Buddhism (changing family structures, loss of parishioners, and the pervasive influence and authority of the funerary industry) as signs of deeper existential questions about the significance of Buddhist funerary rites, the role of Buddhism in contemporary Japanese society, and the self-perception of temple priests.

The disposition of a corpse involves a broad spectrum of practices that cannot be neatly divided into categories of doctrine/custom or secular/religious. The study of mortuary rites and burial, therefore, challenges the scholar of religion to engage with a variety of sources and approaches that range from doctrinal texts, ritual practices, and popular narratives to ethnographies, legal studies, land use issues, and the intersection of relig⸱ and consumer culture. Funerary Buddhism provides a unique and cor hensive frame for understanding religious political, economic, le⸱ artistic aspects of Buddhist organizations (Rowe 2009, 27). Suc⸱ ranging approach allows scholars to comprehend religious deeply embedded in the fabric of everyday life. On the oth⸱ tion to the doctrinal and sectarian forces that help shape to individual temples allows us to view local realities and practices as part of a broader institutional context; in other words, temples as profoundly involved in the world while situated within a specific Buddhist lineage. As such, this book does not place doctrinal ideals and economic realities into opposition but situates them as mutually constitutive ingredients in the broader field of Buddhism.

CHAPTER ONE

The "Death" of
Japanese Buddhism

What meaning does a temple hold for people? What meaning does a
temple hold for priests?
—Nichiren sect booklet

In the early 1980s, researchers at the Nichiren Buddhism Modern Religious
Institute (日蓮宗現代宗教研究所 Nichirenshū Gendai Shūkyō Kenkyūjo)
undertook a project to explore troubles facing temples in depopulated areas. The project team visited temples across the country and conducted
detailed studies of ten geographic regions. Initial reports were published
in the center's journal, but as the researchers were keenly aware, this did
not mean that anyone would read them. A simplified version of their findings was printed in the form of a booklet for all Nichiren temples, and
the booklet soon spread beyond the sect with requests for extra copies
coming from other Buddhist groups and the Ministry of Culture (Nichirenshū Gendai Shūkyō Kenkyūjo 1989).[1] Though generally approving of
the research, Nichiren leaders complained that sharing it outside the sect
amounted to airing dirty laundry.[2]

The booklet itself, though academic in approach and tone, was intended to be provocative. Its layout hints at a kind of discourse outside the
usually conservative writing of the research center, with the cover page
almost screaming the title: "Do you know what's going on at temples in

1. When I called the research center to ask for a copy of the almost fifteen-year-old report,
the young staffer, at first doubtful that he could help me find back issues of anything, when
told the title, immediately said, "Oh, *that* report," and sent it to me the same day.

2. This booklet and the history surrounding it were introduced to me by one of the primary researchers on the original project, Ogawa Eiji 小川英爾. He is also the abbot of Myōkōji,
the Nichiren temple that is the subject of chapter 3.

17

depopulated regions?" in a large, tabloid-style font. Opening the booklet, the reader is immediately confronted with the following question: "Are temples becoming extinct?" with "extinct" (崩壊 hōkai) suggesting both the physical collapse of individual temples and the general disintegration of the entire temple system.

The introduction, arranged like a poem in short, one-line sentences and written by then head of the research center, Akahori Shōmei 赤堀正明, is translated here in full because it so clearly introduces the central themes of this chapter.

> Are temples becoming extinct?
> A temple has been left behind.
> Deep in the mountains at the end of a winding road stands a temple with a small thatched roof.
> Three years ago, the old priest passed away and now there is no one there.
> When someone dies, the priest from the next village will come and chant sutras.
> Until the postwar land reforms, a few acres of rice fields provided for the land tax.
> Even after that, the villagers would offer enough to the Buddha for the priest to live on.
> After the war, the young people gradually left for the cities.
> Only old people remained in the village.
> Even now, with no priest, they gather once a month at the temple to continue the "Confraternity of the Lotus Sūtra."
> Two years ago, the temple living quarters collapsed from rot.
> The pillars in the temple are warped, and the screens do not fully open.
> No repairs can save it now.
> Years from now, perhaps all that will recall the history of this place will be overgrown graves.
> What meaning does a temple hold for people?
> What meaning does a temple hold for priests?
> What meaning did a temple hold for Śākyamuni and Nichiren?[3]
> Originally for Śākyamuni, a temple was a monastery (精舎 shōja) where the dharma was taught and where disciples were trained.
> A temple is a place where people pursue the Buddha's teachings.

3. Nichiren 日蓮 (1222–82), also referred to as Nichiren Shōnin 日蓮上人 or 日蓮聖人, was the founder of the Nichiren sect.

Nichiren Shōnin said, "Since the Dharma is sacred, the person [who pursues/upholds it] is noble. Since the person is noble, the place [where that person pursues the Dharma] is sacred."[4]

The abode of those who study the *Lotus Sūtra* is pure, and it is taught that those who gather there are also purified.

This is the meaning of a temple.

And so we will ask again, why was this temple built here?

Is it simply that a building, which happened to be a temple, grew old and decrepit?

Is it that there were no longer kind-hearted people to take care of it?

Is this temple today no longer of any use?

In a changing world, was the temple unable to keep up?

Was it a problem not with the temple itself, but rather with the priest?

We want to know who or what did this.

We fear that if we cannot find out, we will no longer be able to speak of the future of the Nichiren sect.

This small, dilapidated temple vividly captures the issues confronting contemporary temples and their organizations: rural temples abandoned for lack of a successor or maintained only through irregular visits by a priest from a neighboring village,[5] loss of temple income[6] and support since the redistribution of temple land in postwar land reforms, and a parishioner base diminished by age and rural depopulation.[7]

---

4. 法尊とければ人尊とし、人尊とければところ尊とし。 This passage is from Nichiren's letter to Lord Nanjō. For a translation of the entire letter, see Yampolsky 1996, 502–3.

5. Numbers vary greatly depending on the geographic area, but the most recent Sōtō sect-wide survey found that nearly 20 percent of the 14,052 temples surveyed were being run by a priest from another temple (兼務 *kenmu*), whereas 2 percent were without any priest at all (Sōtōshū shūmuchō 2008, 177–78). For the Jōdo sect in the late 1980s, 12.8 percent of temples were run by outside priests and 1.3 percent had no priest (Jōdoshū shūsei chōsa kekka kenkyū iinkai 1991, 17). Of Shingonshū Chizanha temples, 29.4 percent were run by an outside priest, but there are no numbers for abandoned temples (Chizan Denbōin 1994, 20).

6. Depending on the types of jobs that are included in the category of "outside work," sectarian surveys over the last thirty-five years regularly show that between 20 and 40 percent of priests take on additional jobs (兼業 *kengyō* or 兼職 *kenshoku*) (Chizan Denbōin 1994, 28; Nichirenshū Shūmuin 1974, 78–84; Shingonshū Buzanha Kyōka Sentā 2003, 7; and Sōtōshū Shūmuchō 1987, 53–55).

7. The problems facing temples in depopulated areas (過疎地寺院 *kasochi ji'in*) have occupied researchers from Buddhist sects since the 1950s. The Nichiren sect has revisited the issue several times since the early 1980s, most recently in an ongoing research project on temples in under- and overcrowded areas. See the center's research journal for details (*Gendai Shūkyō Kenkyū* 2004, 2005, and 2006). For a sociological study of different types of depopulation and the effect on temples, see Inoue 2003.

Equally significant, however, are the more abstract questions posed in this passage that relate to the deeper meaning of temples in contemporary Japan. How do temples get left behind? What exactly is the role of a temple, or Buddhism for that matter, in a rapidly modernizing world?[8] Although the passage speaks of the purificatory power of the *Lotus Sūtra* as the "meaning of a temple," it is the wretched image of a temple graveyard overrun with weeds that both reminds us of the central place of death and burial to the continued existence of Japanese temples and hints at a potentially bleak future for Buddhist sects. The "death" of Buddhism thus covers three related connotations: the fundamental and long-standing relationship between Buddhist temples and death rites, the negative perceptions of this funerary Buddhism, and, finally, the fear, expressed so plainly in the introduction to this pamphlet, that the tradition may not merely be dying but may be going extinct.

The goal of this chapter is to trace the main historical circumstances— from the Tokugawa period (1603–1867) up to the present day—that have led to this dire assessment of Japanese Buddhism. What factors gave rise to funerary Buddhism? How have critiques of funerary excess and Buddhism evolved over time? How did the professional funeral industry grow to be so powerful? How has the encounter with Western modernity transformed Japanese Buddhism?[9] The answers to these questions will provide important background for what follows in later chapters.

Much of this historical overview focuses less on the explicitly "Buddhist" aspect of mortuary practices than on the social, economic, and legal developments that have had the greatest impact on temples. My intention here is not simply to decenter Buddhist sectarian or doctrinal history but rather to consider equally relevant forces such as changes in the civil code, postwar land reforms, new family structures, and the perennial desire for social status. I am particularly interested here in demonstrating the ways in which funerary ritual and graves act as important sites of status and control, be it social, economic, legal, or cultural. Furthermore, as I hope to show both here and throughout this book, not only are graves and funerals reflective of the status quo, of social norms, and of various technologies

8. The ongoing struggle by sectarian researchers to locate Buddhism within Japanese modernity as well as fashion a response to contemporary problems from the thought of Śākyamuni and sect founders will be taken up in chapter 6.

9. For those interested in the connection between Buddhism and death in earlier periods, see T. Tamamuro 1963; Ebersole 1989; Bodiford 1993; Haga 1996; F. Tamamuro 1999; Hur 2007; and Stone and Walter 2008. The best English overview of modern death rites in Japan remains Bernstein 2006.

of control, but they are also sites where people challenge those norms and test the limits of that control.

THE EMERGENCE OF FUNERARY BUDDHISM

Although Buddhist mortuary rites had been performed in Japan since the early eighth century, it was the changes in the Tokugawa period that brought families, temples, and death together in the way that we see them today. Ironically, it was the introduction of another religion, and the subsequent reactions to it in the seventeenth century, that began the process.

Beginning in 1613 with bans on Jesuit padres and gradually expanding to include all Christians, a progressively more pervasive system of investigation, rewards for information, and certification served not only to increase the shogunate's reach but also to establish the role of temples in matters of local governance.[10] A key element of the shogunate's anti-Christian campaign involved employing local temples to essentially monitor the populace.[11] Under the temple certification system (寺請制度 *terauke seido*), each household had to receive proof every year from its temple that it was not Christian.[12] Anyone branded a Christian faced a gruesome death. With the spread of this system in the second half of the seventeenth century, the relationship between temples and commoners became decidedly more coercive. Ostensibly implemented to counter the perceived threat of Christianity, this policy transformed temples and priests into organs of the state, giving them an inordinate amount of control over the lives of their parishioners, who were beholden to local priests for certifying them as non-Christian.[13]

As several scholars have shown, temples were not shy about using their position as identifiers of heterodoxy to build and maintain temple

10. Also referred to as the *bakufu* 幕府, or "tent government," the term shogunate can refer to any of the military governments ruling Japan from the twelfth through nineteenth centuries. Here, I use the term to refer to the Tokugawa rulers.

11. According to Duncan Williams, by 1671, "the practice of temple investigation and registration had become nearly universal" (Williams 2000, 214–16). For more details on the shogunate's anti-Christian activities, see Williams 2005 and Hur 2007. For a book-length treatment of Christianity during the Tokugawa, see Elison 1991.

12. After 1669, certification also included the Nichiren *Fuju fuse* 不受布施 sect, which had been banned in that year (Williams 2000, 219–20). For a more detailed treatment of this group, especially its persecution in the early Tokugawa era, see Miyazaki 1969.

13. Tamamuro Fumio has done extensive work on the abuses of the certification system, which includes cases of priests who extorted sexual favors from parishioners by threatening to brand them as heretics (F. Tamamuro 1999). Nam-lin Hur colorfully describes putting temples in charge of certification as akin to "throwing meat to a hungry tiger" (2007, 87).

membership. The bond between the local populace and temples thus became formalized into the so-called parishioner system (*danka seido*). Though the *danka* system did not constitute official government policy, the Buddhist sects attempted to make it appear as such, locking the populace into a multigenerational, obligatory relationship with temples.[14] Parishioners were expected to provide financial support for temple construction and repairs, as well as to hold all funerals and memorial services at their home temples. Temples were so successful in their efforts that the *danka* system would go on to define the relationship between the Japanese and temples right up to the present day.[15]

The emergence of the parishioner system in the Tokugawa period, especially with the spread of the temple certification program, also had considerable impact on how the dead were buried. While previous generations of commoners would have built communal monuments, in the seventeenth century we begin to see stones dedicated to individuals and couples.[16] In the centuries that followed, these graves expanded to include families. Tokugawa period grave excavations reveal a significant mid-eighteenth-century surge in family-centered graves in Edo and surrounding areas.[17] These new styles of gravestones "represent the heightening of a family-centered consciousness—a shift in thinking in which the modern extended family (*ie*) became the central unit of society, and for which memorial services for the dead became prevalent" (Tanigawa 1992, 288–89).

By the end of the Tokugawa period, several historical trends had coalesced to provide the first foundations of the modern relationship between temples and households, namely, Buddhist funerals and memorial

---

14. For a specific example of Buddhist regulations written to look like a government decree, see Williams 2005, 24.

15. The parishioner system also marks an important benchmark for those who favor a decline model of Buddhism in Japan. Tsuji Zennosuke (1877–1955) may be the most famous proponent of this approach, but it certainly appears in more recent scholarship, most notably in the work of Tamamuro Fumio and those scholars indebted to him. Alex Vesey has offered some important correctives to this view (Vesey 2003, 386–88).

16. Rather than the extended-family graves we see in the modern period, the earliest gravestones were constructed by couples who, worried about what would happen to them in the next world, decided to be buried together near a temple (Shintani 1997, 142). In the eleventh and twelfth centuries, married couples were buried separately back with their respective families, but this custom gradually shifted over the next two centuries so that women would be buried with their husbands' families (Glassman 2001, 37–38).

17. Tanigawa warns that his findings hold only for the warrior and farmer classes, but are not conclusive in regards to the merchant class (Tanigawa 1992, 293).

rites for all levels of society, grave sites for the general populace, and an emerging ideal of the extended-family household.

Meiji Period—Graves and the *Ie* System

The transition to the modern period was not a smooth one for the Buddhist sects. Beginning in 1868, a series of separation edicts (神仏分離令 *shinbutsu bunrirei*) attempted to disassociate all aspects of Buddhism from Shinto shrines and worship in order to advance Shinto as the state creed. The resulting suppression of Buddhism (廃仏毀釈 *haibutsu kishaku*) entailed the destruction of tens of thousands of temples, the laicization of thousands of priests and nuns, and the loss of countless objects of Buddhist art. So devastating and widespread was this disassociation, that it has been compared to China's cultural revolution (Grapard 1984).[18] Once Shinto was "purified" of Buddhist accretions, it could be put to work.

To further integrate Shinto into people's lives, the government shifted various ritual and bureaucratic responsibilities from temples to shrines. For example, it mandated household registration at Shinto shrines (氏改め *uji aratame*), criminalized cremation (seen as a Buddhist practice), and took steps from 1872 to pave the way for Shinto funerals.[19] But Buddhist mortuary rites could not be simply legislated away, and the ban on cremation was lifted after two years (in 1875). Only a few years later, in 1882, Shinto priests would in turn be banned from officiating funerals.

Other attempts at social engineering in Meiji had similarly mixed results. The family registration law (壬申戸籍 *jinshin koseki*), which took effect in 1872, officially abolished temple certification and thus moved families outside the reach of temple control.[20] Subsequent legal changes,

18. The definitive study of this period in English remains Ketelaar 1990. See also, Grapard 1984 and Collcutt 1986. In Japanese, see Yasumaru 1979.

19. The first step was an 1872 decree limiting the period of impurity (the time before someone could visit a Shinto shrine after attending a funeral) to one day rather than one month for priests officiating a funeral. This legislation, which flew in the face of long-standing views of what was needed to overcome death impurity, was intended to allow Shinto priests to pull double duty at funerals and state functions at shrines. Later in the same year the Ministry of Doctrine put out a manual for Shinto funerals that followed from earlier Tokugawa texts and that outlined every step of the mortuary process in Shinto and Confucian terms (Bernstein 2006, 41–66). For more details on Shinto funerals in the Tokugawa period, see Kenney 2000.

20. In its place, the Meiji government promoted a policy that was designed to accurately count the number of households and gather other census information to facilitate nationwide taxation and the creation of a modern army. By removing temples from their place in the chain

however, transformed the very nature of families in ways that would bind them to temples across generations. In 1898, with the promulgation of the Meiji Civil Code (民法 minpō), the extended Japanese household, or ie, was codified as law. This law was intended to project and maintain an elite, idealized vision of family that, though based on actual family structures dating back to the late Tokugawa period, was quite alien to most Japanese (White 2002, 8). In addition to acting on families locally, the extended-family ideal was to act nationally to help form the basis of a family state with the Emperor as the symbolic father.[21] This family ideology, premised on a hierarchical Confucian model, was part of a broader attempt to create a unique Japanese culture that could stand up to the pressures of modernization and state formation.[22]

The civil code attempted to homogenize not only families but also disparate burial customs.[23] Under the Meiji government, the wide variety of burial practices that existed throughout the country were quickly brought under government control.[24] In the years leading up to the 1898 promulgation of the Meiji Civil Code and within the code itself, a single unified framework of burial and ancestor-based ritual was mandated to rationalize the process and promote the concept of the extended family and ancestor worship as the cornerstone of the Emperor system.[25]

In addition to codifying the ie, the civil code also addressed issues of succession. The most significant aspect of the civil code for our purposes is clause 987, the right of household succession (家督相続の特権 katoku

---

of government bureaucracy, this law took away the obligatory hold, sustained by the power to declare someone a heretic, that priests had maintained for over two centuries. The danka system continued, but the underlying threat of certification did not. The law also abolished shrine registration.

21. Robert Smith stresses the need for a detailed study of this phenomenon in his work on ancestral tablets (Smith 1974). For a cynical account of the development of the family state, see Irokawa 1985, 280–93.

22. See, for example, Gluck 1985, 158–89. Necessary to this project of defining the traditional was a detailed survey of existing customs.

23. Ivy 1995; Gluck 1985; and others have noted how researchers were dispatched throughout the country to research local customs in order to help write the civil code.

24. For example, in 1872, the Finance Ministry put out an order banning the long-standing custom of burying corpses at the edges of cultivated fields (Mori 1993, 151). The government also banned independent funerals (自葬 jisō), in which no priest officiated, and instead required that either a Buddhist or Shinto priest take part (Y. Tsuji 2002, 178).

25. The importance of the extended-family ideal to the larger project of Japanese modernization and the cult of the Emperor has already received a good amount of academic attention in the West, but few have noted, as some Japanese scholars have, that this ideology was in part embodied in, and supported by, the extended-family grave. See, for example, Mori 2000, 216–54.

sōzoku no tokken), which stated that the "ownership of the genealogy, the ritual implements, and the grave passed to the head of the household" (quoted in Mori 2000, 219). In other words, ownership and maintenance of the family grave was both a right and an obligation, and thus fundamental to defining the *ie* as a unit and the successor as its head. Legal scholar and modern historian Mori Kenji sees this "ancestor ideology" as concrete proof that the Meiji government was fundamentally concerned with maintaining the continuity of the *ie* through memorial ritual, as well as legally establishing ancestral rites as the cornerstone of a national morality (ibid.).

This clause continued to bind temples to the family system via succession and graves right into the postwar period, despite the legal dissolution of the *ie* system in 1947. The current civil code, promulgated in 1951, reflects a compromise between those groups of legislators who wanted to abolish the household system and those who wanted to preserve it (Mori 2000, 49–51). Clause 897, covering the inheritance of ritual/religious assets (祭祀財産の継承 *saishi zaisan no keishō*) states that it is no longer the "head of the household" inheriting the grave, but rather the person whom "custom" dictates.

> The genealogical records, ritual implements, and the rights to the grave, not bound by previous statutes, shall be inherited by the person who, according to custom, should perform the ancestral rites. However, if the progenitor designates a person to perform rites for the ancestors, then this person shall be the inheritor. In the case where custom is not clear, the family courts will determine the person who shall inherit. (H. Inoue 1990, 246)

The custom that is being referred to here is the *ie*, and thus the inclusion of "according to custom" ensures that the ideals of the extended-household system remain strongly entrenched in the current code even though they are not explicitly named.

The problem is that the rapid urbanization during the twentieth century, particularly during the period of high economic growth from 1955 to 1970, has caused the actual extended-family household to largely disappear from the national landscape. Yet, despite these drastic demographic changes (or, precisely *because* of them), the extended-family ideal remains ingrained in both the popular imagination and the law. I will return to the repercussions of the postwar civil code on contemporary burial in the following chapters.

Postwar Temple Economies

In the postwar period, Japan saw the promulgation of both a new constitution and the Religious Corporation Law (宗教法人法 *shūkyō hōjinhō*). The former provided for freedom of religion and church/state separation, and the latter defined the legal requirements for an organization to be declared "religious."[26] Yet, as with the Meiji Civil Code, it was legal reforms dealing with property, as much as those explicitly treating religious matters, that had a profound affect on temples.

Though largely ignored by scholars of Japanese Buddhism, postwar land reforms dramatically transformed temple economics as they forced priests to become increasingly dependent on mortuary income. In the postwar period, Occupation and Japanese government leaders deployed numerous strategies to democratize the country's economic structures. Among the most successful was the special measure for establishing independent farms (自作農創設特別措置法 *jisakunō sōsetsu tokubetsu sochihō*), or, as it is more commonly known, the *nōchi kaihō* (農地解放 farmland release),[27] which overturned the long-standing landlord system (地主制度 *jinushi seido*) in just three years. From 1946 onwards, the government forced absentee landlords to sell their land back to farmers. Before the war, only 28 percent of farms were owned by the people who worked them (自作農 *jisakunō*), yet, after the policy was implemented, that percentage nearly doubled to 55 percent (Nojima 2005, 40). By 1950, 90 percent of all arable land was owned by the people who farmed it (Tipton 2008, 160).

Initially temples and shrines were allowed to retain one *chōbu* 町歩 (2.5 acres) of any farmland they owned, but in later reforms they also lost that land. According to a 1950 survey by the Ministry of Forestry and Agriculture (農林省 Nōrinshō), the *nōchi kaihō* had compelled religious organizations to sell just over 19,100 acres of tenant farmland (小作農 *kosakunō*), or 38 percent of the total land they owned, and 1,732 acres, or 30.5 percent of their independently farmed land (Bukkyō Taimususha 1969, 52). By one calculation, these changes meant that a temple would lose, on average,

---

26. According to article 1 of the law, its purpose is "to enable religious organizations to acquire legal ability in order that they may own establishments for worship and other properties; maintain and operate them; and carry on their business affairs and enterprises for the achievement of their purposes" (quoted in Ryūkoku Daigaku Shūkyōhō Kenkyūkai 1990, 87). For more on the effect of this law on temples, see Covell 2005, 33–34.

27. These policies are generally glossed in English as "land reform."

73,404 yen of income annually.[28] Taking the average Sōtō Zen temple earnings in 1959 to be 148,325 yen, this meant that a midsize temple could lose approximately half of its yearly income—an amount that was already lower than the average starting salary for a high school graduate (Sōtōshū Shūmuchō 2008, 4). At the lower end of the temple hierarchy, loss of income from agricultural sources meant that the lowest income temples were making less than 260 yen per day, less than a day laborer's wages (Sōtōshū Shūmuchō 1959, 20). Furthermore, rural temples would also lose the rice, wheat, and vegetables that could have been grown on those fields. Finally, since any national land that was not deemed necessary to religious activity fell under the *nōchi kaihō* measures, 1,000 acres of temple precinct land and 3,500 acres of mountain and grassland were also "released" (Bukkyō Taimususha 1969, 52).[29]

Local histories and sectarian publications from this period and subsequent histories, reveal the extent of the economic damage and its long-term effects. The 1959 Sōtō sect white paper on Sōtō sect revitalization devoted a third of its pages to charting the poor state of temple and sect economics (Sōtōshū Shūmuchō 1959). Also, according to official Sōtō sect history, one reason it was able to establish a propagation and training center (教化研修所 *kyōka kenshūjo*) in 1955, before any other Buddhist sect, was that the other sects were too impoverished by the land reforms to come up with the necessary funds (Sōtōshū Shūmuchō 1991, 336).[30]

---

28. These numbers come from a 1959 Sōtō Sect white paper (Sōtōshū Shūmuchō 1959). The calculation is premised on the assumption that one *tan* 反 (one tenth of a *chō* 町) produces one *koku* 石, or 1,000 *gō* 合 of rice. One *gō* is the equivalent of about two bowls of rice. In other words, a quarter of an acre provides five and a half bowls of rice a day, which is roughly the amount needed to feed two people for a year.

29. Of course, this was not the first time that massive amounts of temple land were "reclaimed" by the government. As noted above, the anti-Buddhist movements of early Meiji resulted in the loss of tens of thousands of temples. Unfortunately, pre-Meiji survey data are not reliable. For example, it seems unlikely that the total number of temples in Japan dropped from between four hundred sixty and five hundred thousand at the end of the Tokugawa period to under ninety thousand in 1872. Survey data from 1872 to 1876 is much more reliable and shows a loss of over fifteen thousand, or 17 percent of all temples over that five-year period. The difference is that the loss of temples in early Meiji coincided with a precipitous drop in the total number of priests. In 1872 there were about six priests for every seven temples. By 1876 that ratio had fallen to 1:4 (Collcutt 1986, 162). The postwar land reforms, by contrast, resulted in considerable loss of temple land, but not the temples themselves. There was also no forced laicization of priests in the postwar period.

30. The text does not go into details as to why the Sōtō sect had money for a research center when others did not. Presumably, the size of the Sōtō organization, at over fourteen thousand temples, was not insignificant. The other force acting on temples at this time was

In Murakami Kōshin's 村上興進 self-published history of his small Tendai temple in rural Gumma prefecture, land reforms represent the most
important change in the postwar period. Until the sudden and drastic loss
of land, the primary source of revenue for Murakami's Myōtenji temple
妙典寺 had been sericulture carried out by the family. The situation was
even worse for Enmyōji 延命寺, another temple in the area. Generally, the
government would buy the land from temples and sell it to independent
farmers, but in Enmyōji's case, the government sold the land without buying it first. In a bizarre turn, the temple retained ownership and the land
ended up having two owners. In the words of Murakami, "the enactment
of land reforms occurred without real understanding of their purpose,
leaving all kinds of problems to the present day. There is no doubt that
this was a serious blow to temples" (Murakami 2008, 36–37).

Other data suggest land reforms were also creating new economic realities for local priests. According to a 1957 Shingon Chizanha 智山派 survey, 15 percent of the sect's temples were maintained with income from
real estate and only 35 percent were able to subsist on parishioner support (quoted in Bukkyō Taimususha 1969, 53). This meant that by 1957,
half of that sect's temples could not survive on temple income alone. Only
25 percent of Sōtō priests were able to work solely within the temple while
one-third had to take outside work. Diminished temple lands were also
used to generate much needed income. In 1965, in Tokyo alone, Buddhist
organizations ran 158 parking lots, 135 kindergartens, 40 playschools, 40
apartments, 13 rental properties, and 8 medical clinics. It is estimated that
there were only seven to eight hundred temple playschools and kindergartens in the prewar period, but that number increased 400 to 500 percent
after the war (Bukkyō Taimususha 1969, 54).

The one exception to this income problem was the Shin Buddhist sect,
which had on average twice as many *danka* per temple as the other major
sects. According to a 1960 survey quoted in the *Modern Buddhist Alma-
nac*, the average Ōtani-ha Shinshū temple had ninety-five *danka* families,
whereas Tendai, Shingon, and Zen temples averaged fifty per temple (Bukkyō Taimususha 1969, 54). This is not to say that Shinshū temples were
wealthy; a survey conducted by the Honganji branch of Shinshū in 1959
found that roughly half of that sect's ten thousand temples had a yearly
income of one hundred thousand to two hundred thousand yen and 29 per-

---

the rise of the New Religions, which were seen as taking away the membership, and therefore
financial support, of temples.

cent had an income of less than one hundred thousand yen (Jōdoshinshū Honganjiha 1962, 5).

Without revenue from agricultural holdings, temples had to turn to other sources of income. In 1947, only 20 percent of Sōtō temples reported relying on income from outside work by the temple priest and the temple family. Within seven years, that number had jumped to 64 percent (Sōtōshū Shūmuchō 1959, 25–26). I would argue, however, that the most significant result of the land reforms was the increased dependence by temples on revenue from temple graves, funerals, and memorial rites.

Although we lack comprehensive data by which to compare pre- and postwar temple income across all sects, we do have numbers from the Sōtō sect to support the view of a drastic shift to funerary income in the postwar period.[31] Between the mid-1960s and mid-1970s, the average amount earned by a temple for funerary services (conducting the funeral and providing a posthumous name) increased tenfold. In subsequent decades, the increase has ranged between 150 and 300 percent: in 1975 it was 22,118 yen, in 1985 it was 72,170 yen, and in 1995 it had risen to 170,400 yen (Sōtōshū Shūmuchō 1987, 102–3; 1998, 123–24; and 2008, 102). There is no question that mortuary income is now the foundation of nearly all temple economy. Of the 13,753 Sōtō temples surveyed by the sect in 1995, approximately 90 percent were dependent on income from funerary rites (Sōtōshū Sōgō Kenkyū Sentā 2003, 385), whereas a survey of 349 temples, published in 2003, found that over 75 percent of all income was generated by funerals, memorial services, or graves (Covell 2005, 144).[32]

But it was not simply an increased dependence on funerary income that plagued temples and helped give rise to the negative image of funerary Buddhism. Less quantifiable, but equally problematic for priests, was the increased commercialization and formalization of that funeral income in this period of economic growth. As prices for different funeral packages became fixed, problems arose regarding appropriate amounts to "donate"

31. In fact, we do not even have access to data from the early postwar period, before the other sects started extensive surveying in the late 1950s and early 1960s. In the immediate postwar period, the Supreme Command of Allied Powers (SCAP) conducted surveys of temple holdings, but this data, which resides somewhere in the depths of the University of Tokyo, has yet to be studied. This is in large part due to its potential use in lawsuits over land ownership.

32. According to a Sōtō sect survey from the early 1980s, 78 percent of the 1,800 parishioners questioned responded that their main reason for visiting a temple was for funeral or memorial rites (Sōtōshū Shūsei Chōsaiinkai 1984, chart 27). A 2002 survey of Shingon Buzanha priests found that the most common rituals performed were memorials for ancestors and funerals (Shingonshū Buzanha Kyōka Sentā 2003, 12).

to temple priests for their role in funerals and memorial services. In Japan, one does not "pay" the priest for services; instead, one offers alms (布施 *fuse*). Seen as one of the six perfections (六波羅蜜 *rokuharamitsu*) in Mahāyāna Buddhism, giving alms produces merit for both parties. Furthermore, that merit can be transferred, via the priest, to the deceased. Although tradition describes three classes of offerings—material gifts (財施 *zaise*), gifts of teaching (法施 *hōse*), and delivering people from calamity and fear (無畏施 *muise*)—the actual amount of the gift is not defined. *Fuse*, then, is something that by definition is not quantified. In contrast, the formalization of the funerary economy meant that people were becoming increasingly accustomed to fixed prices—to specific amounts exchanged for various services. The pressure both from funeral companies and mourners to be provided with a clearly stated, commodified form of donation came into tension with the priests' desire and need to keep *fuse* in the realm of religious offering.[33] Beyond the high price of funerals, it is the perception of *fuse* as an expected but unspecified expense that has done so much to propagate a negative view of funerary Buddhism. In the following chapters, we will have several occasions to revisit the tensions resulting in pressures to move *fuse* into the sphere of the general commercial economy.

The formalization of funeral pricing was not solely due to land-reform policies or the funeral industry; it also came as a result of broader forces acting on the Japanese economy as a whole. In 1960, Prime Minister Ikeda Hayato 池田勇人 (1899–1965) unveiled a plan to double private incomes within twenty years. This policy aimed to mobilize the entire country in developing industry, increasing capital, modernizing farming, and developing infrastructure. Within eight years, Japan had achieved the second highest gross national product in the world, hosted the summer Olympics (1964), and built the world's fastest train. Within ten years, the average household income had doubled and 90 percent of the populace considered itself part of the middle class (Tipton 2008, 187). Known as the period of high economic growth (高度経済成長期 *kōdo keizai seichōki*), the 1960s in Japan occasioned drastic changes in how the Japanese lived and spent money.[34] Between 1960 and 1964, the percentage of Japanese homes with

33. Another aspect of this issue relates to the desire on the side of priests to keep funerary ~~me firmly in the realm of religious activity lest it be open to taxation.

iod of high economic growth begins in the late 1950s and ends with the oil rly 1970s.

televisions went from 54.5 percent to 93.5 percent in the cities and from 11.4 percent to 81.7 percent in the countryside. By 1975, 97 percent of all homes had an electric fridge and 98 percent had an electric washing machine (Nojima 2005, 66–67). A major factor in the drive for the so-called Three Cs—car, cooler (air conditioner), and color television—was the "2DK revolution," that is, large-scale public housing projects (団地 *danchi*) that saw huge numbers of families moving into apartments that were usually less than 40 m², made up of two bedrooms, a dining room, and a kitchen (2DK). This living space, as well as the appliances that filled it, came to define the new nuclear family.

This new family, isolated from traditional support networks, and far removed from hometown temples, grew ever more dependent on the services of funeral professionals who could provide introductions to priests and advice on the amount to donate in exchange for mortuary services. In this interaction, Buddhist priests would come to be seen as sutra-chanting employees of the funeral companies; in other words, just one ingredient in a set funeral package.

CRITIQUES OF FUNERARY EXCESS

Beginning in the Tokugawa period, external critiques of the connection between Buddhism and death ritual generally took two forms. Buddhist priests were painted as defiled, black-clad practitioners of a foreign religion,[35] or, more commonly, denigrated for the extravagance, high cost, and lack of decorum of their funerary rites.[36] But what would eventually result in backlash from officials was the all-too-important link between burial and status. The growing popularity of posthumous status markers in the first half of the eighteenth century, for example, led to government crackdowns on mortuary excess, lavish gravestones, and elaborate posthumous Buddhist ordination names (戒名 *kaimyō*).[37] Many of the posthumous names that are still common today date back to this time, despite the 1831 ban on the use of the high-status honorifics *koji* or *ingō* for farmers and

35. See, for example, Watt 1984, 190; and Ketelaar 1990, 40.

36. I will deal with more explicit attacks on Buddhism during this period in the following section on Japanese Buddhism's encounter with Western modernity.

37. In descending order of perceived status (and in male/female pairs), these include *ingō* 院号, *koji* 居士/*daishi* 大姉, *shinji* 信士 /*shinnyo* 信女, *zenjō-mon* 禅定門/*zenjō-ni* 禅定尼, and *zenmon* 禅門/*zenni* 禅尼. Children's posthumous names such as *dōji* 童子 and *dōjo* 童女 also began at this time (Tanigawa 1992, 291–92).

townspeople. In the same year, the shogunate also placed a four-*shaku* 尺 (121 cm) height limit on gravestones (Bernstein 2006, 39).[38]

MEIJI FUNERAL PROCESSIONS

The legal end of the Tokugawa class system in the Meiji period transformed everyone into subjects (臣民 *shinmin*), ostensibly with equal rights. Of course, class distinctions and economic disparities persisted, and one way high status could be expressed was by an expensive, ornate, public funeral. A steady increase in the urban population and the professionalization of most common services helped to create the commercial funerary industry, which in turn provided the middle and lower classes with the opportunity to mourn beyond their means. To best illustrate this intersection of class consumption, ritual transformation, and social critique, it will be helpful to join a Meiji funeral procession.

Tokugawa-era burial provided a potential venue for expressing status aspirations, but from the Meiji period onward, the funeral procession increasingly became the central opportunity for displaying (not to mention exaggerating) one's wealth. Inevitably, such extravagance evoked an assortment of negative responses. In a 1903 article "Funerary Improvement," the well-known socialist Sakai Toshihiko 堺利彦 (1870–1933) complained that the processions—held in the daytime to better display one's wealth—blocked the streets, caused disruptions, and gave rise to pointless expense.[39] More to the point, daytime processions had lost the sincerity of past rites and were now nothing more than falsehoods and affectation (虚偽虚飾 *kyogi kyoshoku*) (Sakai 1903). Essays in the popular illustrated magazine *Fūzoku gahō* 風俗画報 joined the condemnation, calling these practices both unnecessary and unbecoming. An 1898 article on funerary reform also targeted daytime processions and offered three reasons why they should be held at night: first, to show proper deference to the dead; second, to curb the pride of extravagant displays; and third, to follow the practices of the past (Yamashita 1898, 1).

In "Bad Funeral Customs Should Be Reformed," artist Noguchi Katsu'ichi 野口勝一 (1848–1905) noted that in the Tokugawa period there was a strict division of classes, ensuring that in weddings and funerals

---

38. In fact, the association between burial and status was certainly not new to the early modern period. Tamamuro Taijō summarizes edicts limiting burial and memorial excess (薄葬令 *hakusōrei*) dating from 646 (T. Tamamuro 1963, 94–95).

39. Prior to the mid-1880s, those of lower social status generally avoided daytime processions and instead transported the body silently at night (Hiraide 1902, 205).

"the merchants have the methods of the merchant class and the samurai have the methods of the samurai class," but as these divisions break down, "Thrift is no longer a virtue and the vice of luxury is accepted" (Noguchi 1898, 1). Historian Hiraide Kōjirō 平出鏗二郎 tells us in his 1902 description of funerals that "Until the start of Meiji, even the upper middle classes did not use palanquins, but gradually extravagance spread so that now even the lowest classes use them" (Hiraide 1902, 205–6). In fact, the middle and lower classes were now participating in all the trappings of funeral extravagance: carts of fresh and artificial flowers, large banners bearing the name of the deceased, lanterns, cages of birds released (放鳥 hōchō) to generate karmic merit, and musicians playing flutes and drums (ibid.).

An even more striking example of processional posturing came in the form of uniformed nurses. Folklorist Yanagita Kunio 柳田国男 (1875–1962), writing about the participation of these nurses in processions from the middle- to late-Meiji period, saw them in a glorious light. "The nurses, dressed in white like martyrs from another age, follow behind the one who died in their arms" (quoted in S. Inoue 1990, 83). Other commentators were less generous and saw the nurses as poseurs (見得坊 miebō) who were not there to care for the sick but rather to serve as status symbols. Either way, this new custom gradually became an established part of funerals, so much so that excluding a nurse meant one had "fail[ed] to keep up appearances" (S. Inoue 1990, 84).[40]

The same could be said of the very expensive custom of handing out sweets or other thank-you gifts (引き物 hikimono), a practice that could make or break a funeral. A record of the 1889 funeral for painter Kawanabe Gyōsai 河鍋暁斎 (1831–89) indicates that the single largest expense was some six hundred sweet buns (饅頭 manjū) that were handed out to guests (ibid., 73). The widespread practice gave birth to a subindustry—otomurai kasegi[41]—in which people pretended to be funeral guests in order to receive gifts (manjū or other sweets) that could then be resold or traded to stores. Yamamoto Yūzō's 山本有三 (1887–1974) famous novel, A Stone by the Roadside (路傍の石 Robō no Ishi), takes place just before the turn of

40. Inoue does not clarify how widespread this practice of including nurses was through all levels of society, but the fact that it was being criticized in papers suggests that it was fairly common. Soldier deaths in the two major wars of the Meiji period (1894–95 with China and 1904–5 with Russia) likely would have fueled this trend, as would the rise of Western medical practice.

41. Literally "making money mourning," this expression is a compound of nouns derived from the verbs for mourning (弔う tomurau) and earning a living (稼ぐ kasegu).

the century and follows a young country boy as he goes to Tokyo.[42] He is aided by an old woman who asks him for help with her job as an *otomorai kasegi*. According to the woman, "If you do well you can hit three or four funerals in a day. . . . As women's work it's fairly lucrative" (quoted in S. Inoue 1990, 68). Apparently it was good to have child helpers, as they could quickly find out where funerals were taking place and were often given extra portions of sweets.

Another *Fūzoku gahō* article provides insight into the economic conditions of the time, noting the increasing diversity of those asking for funerary handouts. "In the past, the fellows who came to ask for food were all outcasts and beggars. Now it is not beggars but neighborhood poor, elderly, infants, and sons acting together and coming up in turns" (Hōsunsha 1898, 17). The author noted that if the sweets ran out, those waiting for handouts would often cause trouble and hurl abuse at the organizers, a concern that often led organizers to order perhaps more than was needed. This practice also entailed additional expense since more people had to be hired to hand out sweets.

This kind of phenomenon provided an easy target for the *Fūzoku gahō* writers, who denounced the emptiness of the ritual exchanges and the wastefulness of the unnecessary expenditure.

> Since a funeral is the end of a person's life, it is only natural that dutiful children and grandchildren should try as much as possible to give the deceased his due. But all things have their limits and today's funerals have crossed that line. These days one must provide food and drink for all the guests, and if you do not offer gifts worth more than the incense money received to all those who paid their respects at the thirty-fifth and fiftieth-day rites, then you are said to be someone who does not know the obligations of respect. (Noguchi 1898, 1)

Noguchi goes on to attack the funerary industry for producing nothing while simultaneously exploiting people's misfortune. He warned that any middle-class family that had to hold two funerals in one year would be ruined.[43]

---

42. The novel was published over three years from 1937 to 1940 in the *Asahi Shinbun* 朝日新聞 and *Fūfu no tomo* 夫婦の友.

43. Murakami Kōkyō 村上興匡 has pointed out that this was a period of growing nationalist sentiment and increased concern with thrift, when higher taxes and the printing of national bonds were employed to strengthen the economy. Intriguingly, Murakami finds a parallel between Meiji arguments for thrift and attacks on Buddhist funerals of the Edo period

Several themes should be clear at this point. First, graves provided a cornerstone of the Meiji government's policy for constructing an ideal household as part of a national family under the guidance of the Emperor. Second, families, with the help of an emerging funeral industry, used funeral processions to express social aspirations and overcome (at least temporarily) class divisions. Third, these expressions and aspirations were the source of extensive criticism in the popular press. These issues remind us of what has long been self-evident for anthropologists: mortuary ritual and graves are central sites of social expression and negotiation for the living, not the dead.

POSTWAR REJECTIONS OF BUDDHIST FUNERALS

The critiques of funerary excess in the popular press during the Meiji period foreshadowed many of the complaints about funerals and burial that have emerged since the 1960s. In both cases, ostentatious display and unnecessary expense have been cited as a way to chart social decline and moral decay. In the postwar period, these critics began to forcefully question not only the general expense but also the very necessity of a Buddhist funeral.

The economic and social changes of the postwar period that led to new funerary practices and increased commercialization also provoked renewed criticism. Several publications appeared during the economic boom of the early 1960s that served to reinforce and further popularize the idea of Buddhism as an exploitative force profiting off the dead. The memorable title of historian Tamamuro Taijō's book, *Funerary Buddhism* (1963), gave the public and the media a catch phrase that could encapsulate this negative image.[44] Buddhism was dealt a further blow over the next few years with the formation of the Association to Reform Funerals (葬式を改革する会 Sōshiki o Kaikaku Suru Kai). The association originated in 1964 with a column by Kyoto University Professor Inada Tsutomu 稲田務, in which he announced his decision to forego his own funeral: "I have decided against a funeral; just notices of my death will be sent out." The message apparently resonated with readers—the newspaper received only one negative letter in response, and that from a Buddhist priest (Inada

---

by the Zhu Xi school (朱子学 Shushigaku) of Confucian scholars (Murakami 1997, 113). For more details on Confucian critiques of Buddhism, see Nosco 1984 and Ooms 1985.

44. For some details on the book, see Stone and Walter 2008, 1–2; and Covell 2008, 296–97.

and Ōta 1968, 5). The next year, Inada and former National Diet Member Azuma Shun'ei made a public call for an end to funerals, and in 1967, in the journal *Miyazu*, they published their "Declaration of Nonreligion" (Murakami 1997, 114). In 1968, the association published *A Treatise on the Uselessness of Funerals* (葬式無用論 *Sōshiki Muyōron*), which included a piece by coeditor Ōta Tenrei 太田典礼 in which he stated his own desire "to die peacefully with no help from buddhas or kami" (Inada and Ōta 1968).[45] Although the book was not meant as an attack on Buddhism, it reprinted the nonreligion declaration, along with many letters from the general public complaining about the Buddhist aspects of funerals and their cost and extravagance.

Religious studies scholar Murakami Kōkyō 村上興匡 has argued that the criticism and privatization of mortuary rites from the 1960s were related to numerous forces, such as the declining significance of the household (*ie*), the medicalization of death, and an increased emphasis on individual choice over communal expectations. For Murakami, one important consequence of this individualism was a shift in the way funerals and burials were perceived. Instead of a necessary step toward pacifying the spirit and transforming the deceased into an ancestor, a Buddhist funeral became an opportunity to express the individual life of the deceased (Murakami 1997, 117–19). Particularly, since the late 1980s, given the choice in the matter of funerals, individuals have, in many cases, reduced the Buddhist aspects of the funeral or cut them out altogether, opting instead for musical funerals (音楽葬 *ongakusō*) or the increasingly popular direct burial (直葬 *chokusō/jikisō*), in which no ritualist is involved. Another choice, which also emerged at the end of the 1980s, involves scattering ashes in the ocean or mountains. These "natural funerals" very often exclude Buddhist ritual in favor of short, nonreligious ceremonies. Moreover, scattering ashes reveals a second front in the critique of Buddhist deathways, the rejection of the grave itself and thus the regular Buddhist memorials that occur there.[46] Here too, price is a factor (graves in Tokyo average roughly thirty to fifty times the cost of a scattering), but equally important is the possibility for personal expression. Another popular form of burial, which began in the latter half of the 1990s, is the so-called cherry blossom burial

45. In January 2010, religious studies scholar Shimada Hiromi 島田裕巳 published a book titled *Funerals Aren't Necessary* (葬式は、要らない *Sōshiki wa, iranai*), that billed itself as "A Treatise on the Uselessness of Funerals for the Great Funerary Nation of Japan." In less than \nths the book was in its eleventh printing and had sold over a quarter of a million copies da 2010).

Scattering ashes will be taken up in chapter 5.

(桜葬 *sakurasō*), where people buy tiny plots in a designated grassy area of a graveyard under a cherry tree.[47] Though these examples do not necessarily represent explicit critiques of Buddhist graves and funerals, I include them under the rubric of antifunerary Buddhism discourse because of their rejection of extended-family graves, formal ancestral worship, and Buddhist world view.

THE RISE OF THE FUNERAL INDUSTRY

As suggested above, central to the development and expansion of funeral styles in the Meiji period was the consolidation of previously disparate goods and services into a fledgling funerary industry around the end of the 1880s. In urban centers, funeral companies (葬儀社 *sōgisha*) began to rent and sell funerary implements, such as banners, carriages, and flowers that in the Tokugawa period had been sold by craftsmen and local cooperatives (葬式組 *sōshikigumi*). The ready availability of what would have previously seemed an extravagant luxury, coupled with the weakening of class divisions, led to fancier funerals and processions among the middle and lower classes.[48]

The Tokyo Funeral Company (東京葬儀社 Tokyo Sōgisha), established in 1886, was the first to use the term funeral company (*sōgisha*) in its name (Murakami 1997, 98), but by the latter half of the 1890s, funeral companies were already openly promoting the reform (改良 *kairyō*) of their industry, which, in less than a decade, had already gone to the "extremes of spectacular luxury on the one hand and the rejection of ceremony on the other" (Bernstein 2006, 139). At the beginning of the twentieth century, the funeral industry was "firmly established and ready to defend its interests" (ibid., 140). Indeed, according to an etiquette manual of the period, by 1905 it was simply assumed that one would hire a funeral company to take care of all the arrangements (ibid.).

POSTWAR PERIOD GROWTH

The funeral industry in Japan today is worth between 1 to 1.6 trillion yen (USD$1.1–1.76 billion) annually,[49] and despite economic setbacks, such as

47. For details in Japanese, see http://www.endingcenter.com/sakura/. Last accessed April 25, 2010.

48. For details on the emergence of the Japanese funerary industry, see S. Yamada 2009.

49. For contemporary yen amounts, I am using an exchange rate of 100 yen = ℃ US. The discrepancy in industry value results from which calculation formula is ᵘ⁻

the 1970s' oil shock and the bursting of the economic bubble in the late 1980s, it has continued to grow at a steady rate right up to the present day (Himonya 2008, 27–40). The trends that began in the Meiji period quickened with the postwar changes in urban living and always to the advantage of the funerary profession. The nuclearization of families meant a loss of multi-generational knowledge and practical expertise in all areas of life, including funerals and memorials; smaller apartments meant that wakes and funerals could no longer be held at home, requiring rented funeral halls. These halls, previously seen only in urban settings, are now present throughout Japan and host 65 percent of all funerals nationwide (Zenni-hon Sōsaigyō Kyōdō kumiai Rengōkai 2007, 6).

As mourning has increasingly become commercialized, critiques of funerary Buddhism have become more vocal and rigorous. The single most prevalent complaint about funerals is the cost; with an average price tag of 2.3 million yen (USD$25,300), it is one of the most expensive outlays in the life of a Japanese consumer (ibid., 26).[50] Naturally, as the public face of 90 percent of all funerals, the Buddhist priest is commonly cast into a cynical light as the one who profits financially from the grief of others, and it does not help that priests receive tax breaks for religious practices.[51]

Understandably, the temple priests themselves are among the most vociferous critics of the funeral industry, specifically of the undue influence of the sōgisha. As I have argued elsewhere, the funeral director's consolidation of every element of the funeral process has expanded into the realm of ritual authority (Rowe 2000). With the director instructing participants not only on their ritual duties but also on the meaning and significance of those duties, priests have been largely displaced. Many priests have complained to me that they feel much like actors on a stage or like "chess pieces" for the funeral companies. As I will demonstrate in chapter 6, temple priests, as well as sect researchers and leaders, have sought ways to reassert their ritual and spiritual authority in the face of the disproportionate control exerted by funeral directors over the entire mortuary process.

tails, see http://www.jetro.go.jp/en/reports/market/pdf/2006_13_p.pdf. Last accessed August 13, 2010.

50. It should be pointed out that some of the funeral cost is offset by the custom of incense money (香典 kōden), which is a cash gift from funeral guests to the mourning family. For details, see Tsuji 2006.

51. For more details on taxes and temples, see Covell 2005, 151–55.

JAPANESE BUDDHISM MEETS WESTERN MODERNITY

To this point, I have primarily focused on Buddhism as it pertains to funerals and graves, but to provide proper context for understanding the full range of discourses relating to funerary Buddhism in the present, we must attend to the broader forces acting on Buddhist institutions and thought in the modern period.

MEIJI PERIOD BUDDHIST STUDIES

The legal changes that came as a result of the Meiji restoration were aimed at marking a decisive break with Tokugawa-era policies. Most significant, this period saw the end to the class system, temple certification, and the unique status of priests. Forced to take regular names, free to marry, grow their hair, and eat meat, Buddhist priests found their new status as citizens reflected a diminishment in their standing as renunciants. Richard Jaffe has argued that their incorporation into the *koseki* system meant the priests lost much of their exceptional *shukke* (出家), or renunciant, status as they became subject to the same legal treatment as other citizens and saw the redefining of religious life "as an occupation rather than an estate" (Jaffe 1997, 670). That priests were no longer central to governing the public would have been made particularly clear during the separation edicts of the 1860s and the subsequent anti-Buddhist attacks of the early 1870s. Although Buddhist institutions survived this early assault and came back to thrive, the repercussions of those attacks and the various Buddhist responses to them continue to reverberate today.

Equally, if not more significant over the long term than the physical damage to temples during the period of *haibutsu kishaku* was the general trend toward modernizing Japanese Buddhism in the late nineteenth and early twentieth centuries. Two components of this modernization require attention. First, there was the move to send intellectuals of all sorts abroad to study Western forms of government, education, philosophy, and science. Part of this wave included priests such as Nanjō Bun'yū 南条文雄 (1849–1927) and Kasahara Kenju 笠原研寿 (1852–83), who went to England in 1876 to study Sanskrit and then studied under Max Müller (1823–1900); Shimaji Mokurai 島地黙雷 (1838–1911), who traveled with the Iwakura mission to Europe and India; Kitabatake Dōryū 北畠道龍 (1820–1907), who traveled and studied for several years in Europe and the United States in the early 1880s and then in South Asia in the latter half of the decade; and

Shaku Sōen 釈宗演 (1859–1919), who was one of several Japanese to deliver a speech at the World Parliament of Religions in Chicago in 1893.[52] These thinkers, along with the next generation of Buddhist intellectuals, went on to various posts in public and sectarian universities, where they began training the next generation of thinkers to approach Buddhism in light of newly imported Western philosophies and scholarly methods.[53] Unlike the priestly academies (檀林 *danrin*) operated by different Buddhist groups in the Tokugawa period, these new universities were "modeled after those in the West, with curriculums that were far broader than the sectarian and exegetical studies of the old academies" (Foulk n.d., 8).[54] This importation of ideas and approaches marks the period when Japanese Buddhism became, for many scholars, "modern," which is to say, historical. Within the broader national attempt to modernize Japan and catch up to the West, these intellectual developments cast a new gaze upon Japanese Buddhism, transforming how Buddhists saw themselves.

As Japanese Buddhists negotiated with modernity, a second concomitant and equally significant trend toward defining Buddhism came from Buddhist leaders and intellectuals wanting to promote a pure Buddhist philosophy that could stand up to Western religious traditions. They viewed the daily mix of Buddhist texts, rituals, and local customs occurring at nearly every temple in the country as superstitious and thus not "true" Buddhism.[55] Although the phenomenon of a Buddhism split into ideal and practical strands is as old as the tradition itself, certain factors of modernity made this division qualitatively different. The ideal/practical binary now had institutional relevance. Increasingly, training of priests included

52. Famous Buddhist teachers of this period also include Inoue Enryō 井上円了 村上専精 (1858–1919), Murakami Senshō 村上楠梢 (1851–1929), and Takakusu Junjirō 高楠順次郎 (1866–1945). For a study of Inoue, see Staggs 1983. For more on Kitabatake, as well as the remarkably high number of Jōdo Shinshū priests who made up these early cosmopolitan Buddhists, see Jaffe 2004.

53. For Hayashi Makoto, the division of labor in the study of Buddhism in early twentieth century Japan was, and is still today, one of the unique peculiarities of Japanese Buddhist studies. He points out that while Buddhism was being studied in Imperial University philosophy departments under the rubric of Indian Philosophy, Buddhist monks were being trained at private institutions run by the various sects. In 1918, the government officially recognized private universities, beginning what Hayashi calls the "dual system" of Japanese Buddhist studies that culminated in the formation of the Japanese Society for Buddhist Studies in 1928 with members from both the Imperial Universities, as well as from Taishō, Komazawa, Ryūkoku, Ōtani, and Risshō universities (Hayashi 2002).

54. According to Foulk, by 1904, Buddhist denominations were operating over one hundred schools for over seven thousand students (Foulk, unpublished manuscript, 8).

55. See, for example, Ketelaar 1990 and Josephson 2006.

study at sectarian universities, where the new Buddhism, inflected with western Buddhological notions, had become part of the curriculum.

POSTWAR PRODUCTION OF EXPERTISE

In the postwar period, new sectarian institutions, a surge in sectarian publishing and survey activity, and the national rush toward becoming an economic superpower further institutionalized the ideal/practical split. A key development in postwar Japanese Buddhism was the creation of research organs by each of the major sects. Examples include the Nichiren Buddhism Modern Religious Institute, Divisions for Sōtō Zen and Sōtō Zen Missionary Studies, and Ritual, Missionary, and Doctrinal Research divisions of the Jōdo sect, all established in the 1950s and 1960s.[56] Charged not only with historical and doctrinal studies of their particular sects, these centers were also established to find ways of engaging their organizations with a rapidly industrializing and increasingly global Japan. However, these groups of experts, tasked with identifying and finding solutions to sectarian problems, have emphasized a type of Buddhist subjectivity often at odds with that of local priests. Not surprisingly, they have imported various Western notions into a view of Buddhism that they actively promote to the rest of the sect, serving to further the practical/ideal division and thus alienate temple priests.[57] Nowhere is this tension more clearly discernible than in the various discourses surrounding funerary Buddhism.

CONCLUSION

The *danka* system of the Tokugawa period, though no longer carrying the weight of temple certification in the modern era, has continued to define interactions between Japanese families and temples. Meiji-era attempts to create a family state served to solidify the place of the extended-family grave in household rituals, further tying families to temples through funerals, graves, and regular memorial services for ancestors. Although there were extensive critiques of funerary extravagance in the Meiji period (and earlier), it was the postwar shift to an entirely funeral-based temple economy coupled with the complete professionalization of the funerary industry that cemented the pejorative view of temples as part of a highly

---

56. These research centers are the subject of chapter 6.
57. For a related argument, see Tanabe 2008.

profitable death industry. Popular critiques of the cost and commodification of burial from the Meiji period have continued to the present day but
now include doubts about the need for any Buddhist involvement. Complaints about funerary Buddhism extend beyond economics to include a
questioning of the tradition itself.

Significantly, much of this questioning is being vigorously carried out
by those inside the Buddhist organizations. As an amalgamation of extensive research into temple realities across Japan, the abandoned Nichiren temple that opened this chapter offers a stark symbol of one possible
future for Japanese Buddhism. As notable as the findings summarized
in that pamphlet were, to understand the full scope of forces acting on
temples, we must also consider the historical and institutional forces that
produced the pamphlet in the first place. Thus, a study of funerary Buddhism ought to include not only temples, society, and politics but also the
institutional side of Buddhism, specifically sectarian researchers tasked
with developing responses to these very real problems. The study of those
researchers must begin in the Meiji period, when new ways of conceptualizing Buddhism were imported into Japan. Indeed, the major transformations of Japanese Buddhism in the Meiji period, so well documented by
Ketelaar, Bernstein, Jaffe, and others, are essential to understanding the
contemporary situation.

Intriguingly, much of the scholarship on modern Japanese Buddhism
hints at the contemporary implications of the drastic changes that occurred during the Meiji period, but, for obvious reasons, does not fully explore their ongoing effects.[58] A detailed analysis of the postwar impact of
Meiji-period transformations, both institutional and ideological, tracing
the ripples from that drastic encounter with modernity, has yet to be done.
Extending that analysis into the present is precisely one of the things this
book attempts, and marks what I hope is the beginning of a new subfield
in Japanese Buddhist studies that focuses on the contemporary period.
Such a study depends on but also effectively complements and extends the
focus of scholarship of the late nineteenth and early twentieth century on
modern Buddhism. As with other forms of modernity, Buddhist modernity
did not simply end at some point in the twentieth century.

In the following chapters, I will return to many of the themes outlined
in this chapter—the role of the *danka* system amidst drastic demographic
changes, the commercialization of death, ongoing critiques of funerary

58. For example, consider the choice of a contemporary Buddhist wedding as the cover
photo for Richard Jaffe's *Neither Monk Nor Layman* (2001).

Buddhism, and, most important, the ways in which mortuary practices and graves serve to mediate between the living and the dead as a key arena for negotiating social norms and Buddhist identity. That identity holds not only for temple parishioners and priests but also for entire Buddhist organizations that are still very much working out the implications of modernity.

CHAPTER TWO

Avoiding Abandonment

Those who had bonds (縁 *en*) in the past are now abandoned; those who have bonds today, will be abandoned in the future.
—Hosono Ungai

This chapter takes up the difficulties of finding a grave in contemporary Japan and the dangers inherent in not finding one. It begins by introducing the concept of *muen* 無縁 (to be without bonds), a multivalent term that encapsulates the fears of Japanese who do not have graves, as well as those who lack relatives to maintain their graves into the future. Although the fear of dying alone, without anyone to care for your grave, is certainly not limited to the modern period, demographic, social, and economic shifts have recently pushed the problem of *muen* into the national spotlight. A 2010 NHK (日本放送協会 Nihon Hōsō Kyōkai) documentary boldly declared that Japan is now a society of no bonds (無縁社会 *muen shakai*) (Nihon Hōsō Kyōkai 2010). News outlets, editorials, academics, and opinion magazines have since taken up the issue of *muen shakai* focusing in particular on the thirty-two thousand people who died anonymously (無縁死 *muenshi*) in Japan in 2009. *Muen*, then, implicates twenty-first century Japan as a society that not only is incapable of caring for its dead but also cannot even identify them.

To illustrate how graves become abandoned, this chapter will outline the different types of graves currently available and the groups that manage them. We then turn to the central topic of this book—a new style of grave that emerged at the end of the 1980s in response to calls for forms of burial that were no longer premised on the extended family and thus would not be abandoned. These eternal memorial graves appear at temples, shrines, municipal graveyards, and commercial sites.[1] On average they are approximately one-eighth the cost of a traditional grave and they vary in style from simple group ossuaries to automated, high-tech buildings, to massive elaborate statues.[2]

Initially aimed at families without sons to maintain the family grave, these new sites, like any new technology, produced unexpected consequences. Soon they were attracting families who had sons, but who did not want to burden them; married women who could not stand the thought of spending eternity in their husbands' family graves; and those people who were looking for a way out of obligations to their home temples. Temple priests, as well, saw numerous possibilities in these new graves: from an easy way to generate additional income, to the only viable solution to an overcrowded temple graveyard, to the foundation of a radically new type of relationship with the public. As I will argue, in addition to combating the problem of *muen*, these graves potentially represent the first signs of a post-*danka* Japanese Buddhism.

MUEN

Every system is in part preserved by its opposite. Mary Douglas's insight into the boundary-marking function of dirt inspires us to look for that dangerous "other" against which the extended-family grave defends (Douglas 1966). Built, as it is, on the maintenance (or production) of family bonds both within and across generations, the natural enemy of the family grave is the dissolution of those ties. The term for these bonds (*en*) in colloquial Japanese signifies connections, both concrete and mysterious. To have *en*

---

1. In terms of regional distribution, just under half the graves in the 2003 edition of the *Eternal Memorial Grave Guidebook* are in the Kantō region. Hokkaidō and Tōhoku represented 8 percent of the sites, whereas Kyūshū had only 4 percent (Butsuji Gaido 2003). These numbers, however, represent only the 411 sites covered in the guidebook, and experts such as Inoue Haruyo 井上治代 and Himonya Hajime 碑文谷創 estimate that the number of eternal memorial grave sites throughout Japan is closer to one thousand (personal communication, April 2010).

2. Traditional family graves average from three to five million yen, or the price of a new, midsize car. Because of the wide variety of factors that make up the price of a grave, it is impossible to provide a more precise figure. This price includes the rights to the plot and the cost of the gravestone. Although the average price for an eternal memorial grave is approximately five hundred thousand yen, costs can range from less than a hundred thousand to more than three million yen (Butsuji Gaido 2003, 35). According to the editor in charge of the *Eternal Memorial Grave Guidebook*, of the 411 sites surveyed, just over half fall between two hundred thousand and six hundred thousand yen. Prices also depend on the number of people being interred (personal communication, July 2004).

(縁がある *en ga aru*) is to be linked by fate or destiny. To bind *en* (縁結び *en-musubi*) is to marry (or, more recently, to find a partner). Regional *en* (地縁 *chien*) refers to the connections with those in one's village or hometown, while families are connected by blood bonds (血縁 *ketsuen*).

En also represents a fundamental tenet of Buddhist doctrine, signifying the conditional nature of existence. It is used, for example, to translate the quintessential Buddhist theory of codependent origination (縁起 *engi*; skt. *pratītya samutpāda*) whereby everything in the universe, both physical and mental, is linked by complex chains of causes and conditions. This view, which "could well be considered the common denominator of all Buddhist traditions throughout the world," is thus tied to concepts commonly seen as fundamental to Buddhism: causality, suffering, and the potential end to that suffering (Boisvert 2004, 669–70). All these varieties of *en*, then, refer in some way to connections, to bonds with others. Indeed, in both the doctrinal and cultural connotations of *en*, the independent identity of the individual is subsumed, if not denied, within a network of interconnections. Bonds, in both the doctrinal and societal sense, are thus both positive (underlying links between everyone and everything) and negative (fetters and attachments that prevent us from true insight or freedom). As will become apparent, the multivalence of *en*, its encompassing of both doctrinal and cultural significance, makes it an ideal arena for understanding the interactions of temples and parishioners, as well as temples and their organizations.

While the presence of these connections in Japan is spoken of in terms of the living, the absence of such bonds is almost exclusively used to speak about the dead. *Muen*, or the absence of bonds, commonly brings to mind the abandoned dead (無縁仏 *muenbotoke*), who no longer receive visits from living descendants. These "hungry ghosts" (餓鬼 *gaki*) populate Buddhist hells, graveyards, and even the spaces of the living.[3] As potentially dangerous entities, they must be pacified and assisted every year at temple ceremonies (施餓鬼会 *segakie*) held both for those who have no one to care for them and those who died under bad circumstances.

The other common use of *muen* comes in reference to abandoned graves. In all graveyards there are mechanisms in place to protect against the abandonment of graves, but eventually there will be no family members left to maintain them. With no one remaining to care for them, these graves without bonds (無縁墓 *muenbo*), like the one mentioned in the introduction to this book, are left to dry up and fall to ruin. In so doing, they

---

3. For a detailed description of hungry ghosts in China, see Teiser 1988, 124–30.

offer a stark condemnation of the timelessness implicitly promised by the extended-family grave. Unless torn down and removed from the memorial cycle, these abandoned graves trouble all sorts of systems, from the ancestral to the economic.[4]

Whether or not contemporary Japanese believe that if no one tends to their graves then they will end up wandering the earth as haunted and haunting spirits, unable to find peace and rebirth in a Buddhist pure land, it is nevertheless clear that to become *muen* is still considered to be a most ignominious end. This fear is even more acute in those responsible for a family grave. The only thing worse than becoming *muen* oneself, my informants consistently told me, is to be the one who allows this fate to befall the family ancestors.

The problem of *muen* is also a financial one. For temples, particularly in urban areas where space is limited, abandoned graves mean lost revenue.[5] Temples keep track of graves through the collection of nominal yearly maintenance fees. Depending on the site, nonpayment for an extended period will result in loss of the grave. The law requires temples to place notices in official gazettes (官報 *kanpō*) and put up a large notice board in the graveyard for one year asking family members to come forward to claim graves suspected of being abandoned. In almost every graveyard one can find stones that have a plastic tag tied to them, indicating that the temple is looking for living relatives. If no one comes forward within one year, the grave is considered abandoned and may be emptied, torn down, and the site resold (Fujii and Hasegawa 2001, 287–90). The contents are then moved to a group ossuary and mixed with other anonymous remains. The fact that these legal requirements for cleaning out a grave were severely relaxed in 1999 is further proof of the extent to which this is seen as a national problem.[6]

It is not only the remains and spirits of the dead that are abandoned, but

---

4. The fact that I differentiate ancestral and economic systems for heuristic purposes is in no way meant to question Mauss's insight that religion, economic exchange, and kinship should not be considered separate spheres (Mauss 1954).

5. Municipal graveyards, despite a poor supply-to-demand ratio, are also plagued by the problems of abandoned graves.

6. Under the previous laws, the temple or management company had to make efforts to find the owner by contacting the local ward office and by posting a minimum of three advertisements in at least two daily newspapers. If no one contacted the temple within two months of the last advertisement, the grave was considered to be abandoned; Scholars estimate the total cost to temples at one million yen per grave (Fujii and Hasegawa 2001, 287). Since the cost for placing the advertisement in a gazette is generally less than ten thousand yen, the cost to temples under the new laws is reduced approximately a hundredfold.

often the gravestones as well. In every temple graveyard that I have visited there is always a spot, usually in one corner, where the stones from derelict graves have been collected, sometimes in striking numbers. At Dairenji 大連寺, a Jōdo temple in Osaka with two eternal memorial graves, there is literally a mountain of these gravestones, numbering in the hundreds and reaching to several meters high. Myōrakuji 妙楽寺, a Shinshū temple in Aichi Prefecture, actually collects these abandoned stones from other temples and, for between seven thousand and twenty thousand yen, will offer yearly memorial services for them (*Jimon Kōryū* 2007–8, 63–66).[7]

That these forsaken stones symbolize the potential end of temples was compellingly narrated in a 1988 NHK special "The Disappearance of Temples." The opening scene shows an elderly woman relocating her rural grave to the city. As she stands with hands clasped, the old stone mason methodically chisels out the names carved into the face of the original gravestone. After carefully removing the remains of the family members interred within, he unceremoniously dumps the stone into the vacated hole and covers it with dirt (NHK 1988). The use of this scene to frame a documentary on the loss of rural temples brings home the reality that all of the Buddhist sects are facing: where goes the grave, goes the temple. And of course, where goes the temple, goes the sect.

MODERN AND CONTEMPORARY RESPONSES TO *MUEN*

Despite attempts by the Meiji state to create a sense of nationhood and permanence around ancestral worship and the extended family, the problem of abandoned graves was apparent early on.[8] Isshinji 一心寺, an extremely popular Jōdo temple in Osaka, began collecting anonymous remains in 1887.[9] The ashes were ground up, combined with concrete and molded into life-sized, seated Bone Buddha (骨仏 *kotsubotoke*) statues (fig. 1). By the time Isshinji was burned to the ground by firebombing during World War II, the remains of nearly one million people, abandoned and otherwise, had been entrusted to the temple. Fragments of the first six statues were combined into the seventh statue in 1947 (Fujii 1982, 292). Since that

7. For more on memorial services for inanimate objects, see Kretschmer 2000.
8. For more on the centrality of family rites and graves to the creation of a national ideology in the Meiji period, see Mori 1993; Mori 2000; Hozumi 2003; Smith 1974; and Tsuji 2002.
9. I have had numerous occasions to visit the temple and it is always alive with activity. During *o-bon* お盆 week in 2003, the temple grounds were completely packed as people waited for over five hours in forty-degrees Celsius to receive memorial tablets and have prayers chanted.

Fig. 1. The Bone Buddhas at Isshinji

time they have been built every ten years, with each statue made up of the powdered remains of between one hundred fifty thousand and two hundred thousand people. The thirteenth statue (the seventh erected since the war) was enshrined in spring 2007.

THE ETERNAL TOMB

Concern over abandoned graves was also the impetus for the *Eternal Tomb* (不滅の墳墓 *Fumetsu no funbo*), a fascinating work written in 1932 by Hosono Ungai 細野雲外. Hosono terrifies the reader with countless newspaper accounts of the defacement and robbing of graves. He then attributes the problem to family graves that will all inevitably become abandoned. As Hosono puts it, "Those who had bonds (*en*) in the past are now abandoned; those who have bonds today, will be abandoned in the future. This is the

Fig. 2. The Eternal Tomb. The writing on the side of the
illustration reads: "The Eternal Tomb—to be erected in
flat areas—flooded by the gratitude of the people as they gather to
worship the ancestors. Artist's rendition by Hosono Ungai."

essential characteristic of graves built and maintained by individuals" (Hosono 1932, 2). His solution, born of the modernization, rationalization, and nationalism of the period, was to construct giant cenotaphs that would hold the remains of millions of people and serve as cultural and ritual centers for the nation. The eternal tombs built in cities would include parks and airports with electrical lighting so that planes could land at night. Those eternal tombs in coastal areas would include lighthouses.

Hosono also included a series of striking illustrations, going so far as to provide a detailed electrical blueprint for the airport lighting system. In two other dramatic images, Hosono provides us with a glimpse of the grand ritual events that would take place at the tomb. In one drawing, priests walk in procession as people crowd around a large cenotaph with the word "Coexistence" (共存 kyōzon) emblazoned on it as overhead a zeppelin trails nationalistic slogans such as "Social Service = Coexistence and Co-prosperity" (社会奉仕即共存共栄 shakai hōshi sunawachi kyōzon kyōei) and "Coexistence and Co-prosperity = Loyalty and Love of the Nation" (共存共栄即忠君愛国 kyōzon kyōei sunawachi chūkun aikoku; see fig. 2). In a second image, the zeppelin is gone, but in its place one can make out in the clouds an image of a Buddha smiling down on the procession. Though the tombs Hosono called for so passionately were never built, the book provides a vivid perspective on grave issues in the interwar period. Hosono was clearly ahead of his time in predicting the burial problems of late-twentieth-century Japan.

BUYING A GRAVE IN CONTEMPORARY JAPAN

When one buys a grave in Japan today, one is in fact leasing the land in perpetuity (永代使用権 eitai shiyōken). One does not actually "own" the grave but rather maintains it. When there is no one left to keep up a plot and pay the yearly fee, it eventually reverts back to the owner of the graveyard (e.g., temple, company, or municipality) for reuse. This system of ostensibly perpetual maintenance, then, is premised on the idealized concept of continuous descent within a localized family, a concept that is still implicitly enshrined in civil law. The Meiji civil code's institutionalization of the grave as fundamental to the definition of household succession continues to demarcate its role to the present day. Family graves are still most commonly passed down through the eldest son, who is expected to maintain the grave, carry out yearly memorial rites, and visit the grave during the equinoxes and the summer festival of the dead (o-bon), held in mid-July or August. Cremated remains are placed in urns that are usually interred in the family grave forty-nine days after a death, when the traditional Buddhist liminal period ends.[10] The deceased then receive individualized yearly memorial services on the anniversary of death for usually thirty-three, but sometimes fifty or even one hundred years, at which point they join the ranks of anonymous ancestors.

As noted, changing demographics and the rise of the postwar nuclear family have meant that the extended-family ideal has become simply that, an ideal. As described in the previous chapter, however, this ideal is still maintained in the current civil code under the guise of "custom." It also appears in all kinds of advertising campaigns, which tout the extended family and the traditional (read: bucolic) hometown (ふる里 *furusato*).[11] On the other hand, discourses surrounding burial paint a decidedly different image of current family realities. Newspaper reports bemoan the high costs of urban burial plots, television programs cover abandoned graves and temples, national magazines advise readers on methods to avoid dying without a grave, Buddhist altar makers advertise graves for individuals, and successful advertisement campaigns mock "the family grave in the sticks."

TYPES OF GRAVES

In order to situate eternal memorial graves in the context of contemporary burial, it is necessary to first outline the types of burial currently available. There are three categories of graveyard in Japan: the publicly managed graveyard, the privately managed graveyard, and the temple graveyard. The central differences among them concern management, costs, convenience, and requirements for purchase.

Publicly managed graveyards (公営墓地 *kōei bochi*) exist throughout Japan and are run by the local municipality. Graves at these sites are relatively cheap; secure (since such graveyards are run by the government, they are expected to last); and have no restrictions based on religious affiliation. Examples range from the large municipal sites in Tokyo such as Aoyama Reien 青山霊園 and Tama Reien 多磨霊園 to smaller rural cemeteries. The drawback to public graves is that in order to purchase one you must live in the assigned district (much like a catchment area for a public school), and even if one meets residency requirements, the demand, particularly in cit-

10. For details on the Chinese development of the forty-nine day rites, see Teiser 1994, 20–30. As with all of the customs described here, there are regional variations.

11. Ivy 1995, chapter 4.

ies, overwhelmingly outstrips the number of available plots. In the case of the eight public graveyards serving the Tokyo metropolitan area, the four that are within the city limits are no longer accepting applications. Despite a leveling off of applications over the last several years, the remaining four graveyards still receive about ten thousand applications per year; an average of thirty applications for every plot. The ratio runs over 50:1 for the more popular graves (Sōgi Reien Bunka Kenkyūkai 2000, 272). Furthermore, municipal graves offer only a limited range of gravestone styles and locations within the graveyard.

The category of privately managed graveyards (民営墓地 *min'ei bochi*) covers a broad range of styles that includes communal village graves, graves on private property (such as an individual family's grave plot, often located in or beside a household's rice fields), temple graveyards, and those run by corporations. The first two types represent the lion's share of graves in Japan and reflect traditional, long-standing practices, but they will be left out because they can no longer be built and thus do not impact the present discussion. I will deal with graveyards in temple precincts as a separate category below, but it needs to be pointed out here that temple graves are legally defined as a subset of graveyards run by religious corporations (宗教法人営墓地 *shūkyō hōjin'ei bochi*). Also included in this category are graveyards that, though registered through temples and thus ostensibly owned by a religious corporation, are in fact managed by a company to which the temple has lent its name (名義貸し *meigikashi*) in return for help with the setup costs and a share of profits.[12] Such sites proliferated in the period of high economic growth and again during the bubble of the late 1980s, but not without strong criticism. Since the private stonemasons and real estate companies that most often end up running these graveyards are primarily concerned with generating profits, a potential conflict of interest develops between their bottom line and the best interests of the people purchasing the graves.

The issue of commercial ownership of graves garnered official concern both in a 1998 government roundtable on burial issues (discussed in more detail in chapter 5) and a 1999 communication from the Environmental Health Bureau (生活衛生局 *Seikatsu eisei kyoku*). Chief among government officials' worries was the long-term viability of the companies running these graveyards, particularly after the economic bubble burst in the

12. Since 1968, regular businesses were no longer allowed to manage graveyards. Those that had received permission before this date still exist, but according to one source there are only nine left in the entire country (Intārokku 2002, 67).

early 1990s. What would happen to the graves if the management company went bankrupt? Another problem for consumers was the tendency
for these sites to package the sales of gravestones with the rights to the
gravesite (墓地使用権 *bochi shiyōken*), thus limiting consumer choice
and leading to unfair business practices and inflated pricing. The desire
to bring in additional customers also led some management groups (both
with and without the express support of the temple involved) to include
the promise of an elaborate posthumous name as part of the grave package.
Finally, there were the environmental and land-use issues that came when
companies started creating massive grave parks thoughout the Japanese
countryside.

Also contained in the category of privately managed graveyards are
those run by corporations for public good (公益法人営 *kōeki hōjin'ei*). These
include both incorporated foundations (財団法人 *zaidan hōjin*) and corporate juridical persons (社団法人 *shadan hōjin*). These graveyards, which began around the mid-1960s, and which often take the form of large grave
parks, all share certain characteristics. Generally they are more expensive;
around Tokyo they can average anywhere from three to twenty times the
cost of a public grave, with yearly maintenance costs reaching two to ten
times as high as a regular public grave (Sōgi Reien Bunka Kenkyūkai 2000,
246–72). Ironically, the higher price does not include greater security. Like
the graves run by companies "borrowing" the name of a temple, privately
managed graveyards are considered to be risky since their continued maintenance depends on the financial stability of the group managing them.
In terms of benefits, these graves offer the total freedom of any high-end
consumer item; as long as payment is received, there are basically no other
restrictions.

The final type of graveyard, and the one with which we are primarily concerned in this study, is the temple graveyard (寺院墓地 *ji'in bochi*).
In addition to being potentially very expensive, purchase of this grave requires that one become a parishioner of the temple, with all the costs and
duties that this membership entails. These obligations include participation in yearly services and regular donations to the temple to help pay for
upkeep and repairs. Although characterizing the activities of donation and
participation in temple services as "obligation" may seem to imply a certain cynicism, as we shall see, the extent of potential parishioners' responsibilities to a temple is often *the* biggest worry of those looking for temple
gravesites. In the 1998 comedy, *I Have No Grave!* (お墓がない *O-haka ga
nai*), Iwashita Shima 岩下志麻 plays a famous actress who, after becoming

convinced that she is about to die, searches all over the greater Tokyo area for an appropriate grave, even going so far as to rent a helicopter to fly over ancient imperial tombs (古墳 *kofun*). At one point she is introduced to the head abbot of a large temple who tells her he cannot accept members of other sects and that she must become a parishioner first. When she tells him that she cannot do this and that she is nonreligious, the priest asks "But you want a grave, right?" "But," she replies, "I don't need religion." The implication is that the costs of becoming a *danka* are not worth the benefits of a temple grave (Hara 1998).

Each type of graveyard has its benefits and its drawbacks. For some Japanese, the low cost of a municipal grave is the biggest draw; for others, commercial graveyards offer the opportunity for an elaborate or individualized grave that would be impossible to find in an urban setting; whereas others insist on the security, whether financial or spiritual, of a temple graveyard. In all three cases, however, the overriding concern is finding a grave that will be maintained after one is dead.

Although the Ministry of Health, Labor, and Welfare (厚生労働省 *Kōsei rōdōshō*) puts out yearly statistics on the number of graves in Japan, the categories used by the ministry are slightly different from those outlined above. Nevertheless, one can draw a general picture of where the Japanese are interred. In 2008, there were 884,701 graveyards in Japan. Of these, 32,379 (3.7 percent) were local community cemeteries (地方共同団体 *chihō kyōdō dantai*), 686 (less than 0.1 percent) were run by corporations (民法法人 *minpō hōjin*), 58,127 (6.6 percent) were owned by religious groups (宗教法人 *shūkyō hōjin*), 686,107 (78 percent) were individual sites (個人 *kojin*), and 107,402 (12 percent) fell into the category of "other," which unfortunately offers no other specifics.[13] Also illuminating for the present discussion is a survey regularly carried out by the All Japan Funerary Professional Cooperative Association (全日本葬祭業協同組合連合会 *Zennihon Sōsaigyō Kyōdō Kumiai Rengōkai*). In 2007, the survey found that two-thirds of respondents owned a grave. Of that group, 52.4 percent had a temple grave, 26.8 percent had a plot in a publicly managed graveyard, 10.5 percent were in a commercially managed site, and just under 10 percent were in local community graves (*Zennihon Sōsaigyō Kyōdō Kumiai Rengōkai* 2007, 96). No matter the graveyard, however, all rely on descendants to maintain them.

13. See http://www.mhlw.go.jp/bunya/kenkou/seikatsu-eisei21/pdf/03–08.pdf. Last accessed May 2010.

ETERNAL MEMORIAL GRAVES

For many commentators, Japanese burial underwent a revolution in the late 1980s with the emergence of a new solution to the *muen* problem. This would not be a state-sponsored response, such as that envisioned by Hosono, but was instead begun at a few individual temples in Kyoto, Niigata, and Tokyo. Initially conceived of as responses to public concerns over the fate of family graves and the *muen* problem, these eternal memorial graves soon spread throughout Japan, offering new opportunities for those individuals and couples unable or unwilling to buy traditional graves, as well as for temples that could no longer exist given their dwindling parishioner base.

Until these graves were built, people without descendants had few viable burial choices. In most cases, temples would find ways to deny graves to those who could not prove they had someone to maintain them. Even when they could purchase a grave, either at a temple or some other site, singles, divorcees, and childless couples had no way to ensure continuity and had to face the fact that the graves would soon become abandoned. In the late 1980s and early 1990s, a number of new options emerged. One of these, scattering ashes in the ocean or mountains, offered the drastic solution of forgoing a grave altogether.[14] For most Japanese, however, this implicit rejection of memorial rites proved far too radical an idea. The second type of solution addressed the problem of *muen* directly by offering various ways of maintaining graves through a third party.

Most scholars trace the modern emergence of the eternal memorial grave to 1985, when the Kuonbo 久遠墓, or "Eternal Grave," was added to the massive Mount Hiei Enryakuji Grave Park (比叡山延暦寺大霊園 Hiei-zan Enryakuji Dairei'en) (H. Inoue 1990, 12–14).[15] By 2004, Kuonbo held approximately seven thousand eternal memorial graves. Although originally aimed at individuals and childless couples, spots for families were soon made available. In addition to two types of individual graves (costing 550,000 or 780,000 yen) and one for couples (costing 1.1 million yen), Kuonbo offers the Merciful Eye (慈眼 *jigen*) grave for up to four people (2.15 to 2.6 million yen), the Kannon 観音 grave (2.1 million yen), and the deluxe An'nyō 安養 grave for two or more (4.06 million yen for the first two

14. Scattering ashes will be discussed in chapter 5.
15. At the time, the graveyard, which lies on the Shiga side of Mount Hiei, had sixty-five thousand graves in total. For more details on Kuonbo, see http://enryakuji-daireien.co.jp/index.html. Last accessed October 14, 2010.

Fig. 3. Individual graves at Kuonbo

and five hundred sixty thousand for every additional person).[16] Costs include the gravestone, engraving, the rights to the plot, and memorial services throughout the year. Memorials for most members are conducted by Enryakuji priests at the on-site Memorial Hall (回向堂 ekōdō), with those in the deluxe grave receiving personalized memorial services in front of the grave for fifty years.

Although the high-end An'nyō graves resemble a smaller version of the traditional family grave, those for individuals and couples are uniformly designed, small, cramped together, and disproportionately sized (fig. 3).[17] They all have a small indentation for water and a flat stone upon which to

16. Kannon graves are so named for the statue of the Bodhisattva of Compassion that looks over them. An'nyō is a type of Buddhist Pure Land.

17. The individual graves are only 27 cm across, while those for couples are 33.6 cm in diameter. With a height of approximately one meter, the gravestones look gaunt and distorted.

place offerings on the ground in front of them, but most of the individual and couple graves do not have built-in vases or a spot to place incense. Instead, visitors may borrow portable sets from the main office.

When I visited Kuonbo in 2004, I found it next to impossible to stand in front of one of the graves without backing into the stone in front of it. In the rare cases where someone had put flowers at the grave, they only served to make it look all the more cramped. It would be almost impossible, in fact, to offer incense without lighting the flowers on fire as well. All of this served to reinforce the impression that these graves are not meant to be visited. Like a cheap imitation of a classic designer brand, or a one-room condo in the suburbs, these graves seem to offer only an allusion to the golden days of (mortuary) luxury and an illusion of community.

It is tempting to view these stones, arranged in tight rows and lacking any variation, as "the McDonald's of graves," but such a dismissal misses how revolutionary they were when built and why they continue to sell. According to my interviews with those on the management staff, Kuonbo's popularity was due primarily to the fact that they offered individualized memorial services by an Enryakuji priest and the ostensible guarantee that they would never be abandoned. Further adding to the appeal of these graves is their low price, the lack of restrictions based on religious affiliation, the location on one of the most celebrated mountains in Japan, and the religious and cultural cachet attached to Enryakuji temple, headquarters of the Tendai sect and among the most famous temples in Japan.

By presenting the model of a grave that could be maintained and memorialized without descendents, Kuonbo offered far-reaching new possibilities for posthumous care. The national acceptance of this new approach to burial, however, required a modification of traditional concepts of bonds that would permit the possibility of being memorialized by those who were not family or friends. As I shall argue, the most important step in the development of eternal memorial graves involved an innovative reworking of traditional notions of community by certain temple priests. With the fixed social bonds of family and region rendered increasingly anachronistic by shifting demographics, the general public was not seeking to decry community, but to find it in new places. Scholars have approached the corporate family in Japan and the popularity of New Religions as variations of new communities, replacing village structures with corporate or ritual hierarchies. What is potentially most significant about several of the new eternal memorial graves is the way in which a small number of temples were able to offer people a sense of community and a set of social bonds based on choice.

It is for this reason that one of the temples most frequently mentioned as offering the first true eternal memorial grave is Jōjakkōji 常寂光寺, a Nichiren temple in western Kyoto. The temple grounds contain the grave of the Women's Monument Society (女の碑の会 Onna no Hi no Kai), founded in 1979 by Tani Kayoko 谷嘉代子. The group, initially formed for women widowed in the Second World War, erected a monument at the temple engraved with the words "As long as a single woman lives, we will pray for peace here." According to Tani, the monument expressed the sentiment that "though a woman lives alone, once she dies she wants to rest with her friends" (Tani 1994, 86).

Though the monument was erected in 1979, the actual grave was not built until ten years later. The ossuary was named the Mausoleum of Linked Intentions (志縁廟 Shienbyō) symbolizing that those interred within were joined by choice and shared intent rather than the customary bonds of family or region. I shall have much more to say in the next two chapters about this shift in the types of bonds expressed through graves and memorials.

By 2000, the Women's Monument Society had more than six hundred members, due in large part to a noticeable shift in membership that began around 1990, when young, single women began joining. Tani sees the change as part of a larger trend toward variety in funerary styles that not only allowed single and widowed women to make choices but also married women, who may not wish to spend eternity with their husband's ancestors (Tani 1994, 88).[18]

Although the Women's Monument Society was formed a full decade earlier, because the grave itself was not actually built until 1989, many commentators point to the Annon graves at Myōkōji, a Nichiren temple in rural Niigata prefecture, as the first eternal memorial grave. I will discuss in more detail the scope and significance of Myōkōji's success in chapter 3. I would argue that even if Annon was not the first eternal memorial grave, it is the most significant. Myōkōji's influence, both in terms of membership and national media attention, spawned imitators across the country and undoubtedly started the broader eternal memorial grave movement. Although Kuonbo addressed concerns over a lack of postmortem attention by offering eternal prayers and grave maintenance, there was no concerted attempt to form a community of members or draw people into a relationship with the temple. Shienbyō offered community, but only to a select group and not as a form of temple renewal. It was the combination of these

18. This trend will be discussed in detail in chapters 3 and 4.

aspects: new types of graves not bound to the parishioner system, a different conception of community, and an attempt to create a new kind of temple membership that led to the national success of Myōkōji's Annon grave. And it is these same elements that make eternal memorial graves such a potentially important source of insight into both the current realities and possible futures of Japanese Buddhism.

CHARACTERISTICS OF ETERNAL MEMORIAL GRAVES

After appearing at a small number of temples in the early 1990s, eternal memorial graves began taking off around the turn of the millennium. The growth of these sites is attested to by the publication in 2000 of a guidebook to over 225 eternal memorial graves. By the fourth edition in 2005, that number had nearly doubled (Butsuji Gaido 2005).

Eternal memorial graves encompass a wide variety of styles, from large, visually striking ossuaries, to sites indistinguishable from traditional family graves. Some sites are built around Buddhist statues and imagery, while others show no overt religious symbolism. They vary in size and orientation—above ground, underground, indoor, and outdoor. For example, the Kannon Seien grave at Hōsen'in 宝泉院, a Shingon temple outside of Tokyo, is topped by a ten meter–high Kannon statue with colored ribbons streaming down from the statue's hand.[19] The eternal memorial grave at Gokurakuji 極楽寺, a Jōdo temple in Nara prefecture, comes in the form of a colossal "fragrant" elephant (香象 kōzō)[20] lying on its side, with a small statue of Amida Buddha atop a lotus blossom on its back.

Early names for eternal memorial graves included emphasis on the collective nature of the sites (e.g., Communal Worship Grave [合祀墓 gōshibo]); the assurance of permanence (e.g., Eternal Ossuary [永代納骨堂 eitai nōkotsudō]); choice (e.g., Living Grave [生前故人墓 seizen kojinbo]); and religious themes (e.g., Grave for [those] Gathering in Amida's Pure Land [倶会一処墓 kue'isshobo]).[21] Initial reactions among the public were mixed. Since the early eternal memorial graves did not have fully developed systems in place for maintenance and memorial services, people were unsure

19. This imagery is meant to evoke traditional images of Amida and Kannon descending from the clouds to carry the deceased away to the Pure Land. See, for example, Horton 2007, 49–53; and Stone 2004.

20. Skt. gandhahastin, meaning "fragrant elephant"; one of the sixteen honored ones (bodhisattva) of the Bhadra-kalpa (Mochizuki 1954–1963, vol 2., 1065).

21. Literally "to gather together in one spot"; this is a Buddhist term signifying rebirth in Amida's Pure Land.

of how to distinguish between these graves and the ossuaries for abandoned spirits (*muenbo*) mentioned in the previous section. Like many new technologies, it took some time before the conception caught up with the form, but eventually temples began to develop both the "hard side" (the physical grave) and the "soft side" (the system of maintenance and memorial, as well as the philosophy of the site). These two aspects of eternal memorial graves help define the differences between sites. For example, although all these new graves fall under the generic name of eternal memorial grave, for many sites, such as those versions that were added to certain municipal graveyards from the second half of the 1990s, there is actually none of the merit transfer that is associated with memorial services at temple graves.[22] The grave is maintained by a third party, but not memorialized in the Buddhist idiom. Rather than eternal memorial, what one finds instead is eternal administration (管理 *kanri*).

Most of the early eternal memorial graves take the form of ossuaries with some method for displaying the names of those interred within. Some sites allow individual stones, plaques, or statues for each person, while others, such as Moyai no Kai in Tokyo, only have space for a large wall with row upon row of officelike nameplates. These graves usually include a designated spot to make offerings and pray—in the case of monuments, right in front, and in the case of buildings, often inside. Another common burial style includes indoor lockers in the form of traditional Buddhist altars. Remains are stored in the bottom half of the locker, with the top half ranging from a style indistinguishable from a household altar to modern forms in Osaka that include a video monitor offering scenes from the life of the deceased.

Hongō Ryōen 本郷陵苑, an indoor graveyard in a central Tokyo highrise, stores remains in a back room that is accessed by a computer operated system. Family members wishing to pay their respects to the deceased simply place their member's card into a slot, and within thirty seconds clear glass panels slide open to reveal an altar holding the remains and displaying the name(s) of the deceased, flowers, water, and incense.[23] Hongō Ryōen is run by Kōanji 興安寺, a Jōdo Shinshū temple that keeps

22. This does not mean that no memorial services are offered, but that they are not premised on transferring merit to the deceased. This point will be addressed later in the chapter.

23. Video demonstrations of most of the sites are available online. In the video for the Yokohama location, an elderly woman has a conversation with her deceased husband about the merits of his indoor grave. See http://www.ryobo.com/dounai/index.html. Last accessed May 7, 2009.

its main temple hall on the third floor.²⁴ The Tokyo grave has completely sold out, but a second one is planned with additional sites now open in Kagoshima, Nagoya, and Yokohama.²⁵

Another important distinction to make between different forms of eternal memorial graves concerns the method of interment. The main division in eternal memorial graves is between those sites that immediately combine the remains of all members in one large ossuary, referred to as *gōshi* 合祀 or *gassō* 合葬, and those that have a place to store the individual urns for some set period of time. Although the former style is generally much cheaper, it is still not particularly popular. The vast majority of people prefer to maintain some personal space even after death. Indeed, it was largely due to the fact that many of the first eternal memorial graves were premised on combining remains from the outset that they did not succeed. At a Jōdo temple in Tokyo, for example, the head priest built a communal grave in his temple graveyard.²⁶ Although the site generated a lot of interest and inquiries, nobody wanted their ashes mixed right from the start. Even after the priest cut the price in half, almost nobody chose this option.²⁷

In the case of individually stored remains, there are also important distinctions. In most instances, the urns are not placed in individual containers, but are stored all together, often in an underground bunker. In this case, individual tablets may be on display in the temple, such as at Tōchōji, the Sōtō temple in Tokyo that will be the subject of chapter 4. In nearly every grave, the remains will be moved into a shared ossuary after some set period of time. For most sites this occurs after thirty-three years, intentionally adopting the traditional waiting period before the individual dead become anonymous ancestors. In the case of Myōkōji, the subject of chapter 3, remains are moved to the shared ossuary eleven years after there are no longer any relatives around to pay the nominal yearly maintenance fee. A few eternal memorial grave sites even "guarantee" individual treat-

24. The fourth floor has facilities for receptions and meals. This brings up the interesting issue of having people walking, eating, and defecating above images of the Buddha in the main hall one floor below. This is also a problem at a temple I visited in Tokyo that, due to financial difficulties, had built an apartment complex on the precincts and then installed the main hall of the temple on the first floor. In addition to the "disrespect" paid to the Buddha, the junior priest also resented the fact that he could not chant or bang the drum at early morning services for fear of evoking the wrath of the tenants on the floors above.

25. The Yokohama site is now also sold out.

26. Personal communication, April 2004. Name of temple withheld at request of priest.

27. As we shall see in the next chapter, the choice to place remains directly into a communal ossuary can even be a highly effective form of revenge.

ment forever, but this is very rare.[28] Finally, there are places such as the Nichiren temple Chōshōji 長照寺 in Tokyo that divide the remains (分骨 bunkotsu), keeping a small amount intact and distinct for a set period and placing the rest in a shared ossuary (Butsuji Gaido 2005, 124). Thus, for all but a very few of these graves, the "eternal" aspect does not mean one will be perpetually memorialized as an individual. Interestingly, the shared rhetoric of permanence indicates that in fundamental ways these new graves are not new at all, but clearly duplicate the established transition from individual to ancestor.

In addition to the physical disposition of the dead, another significant way of distinguishing between different types of eternal memorial graves is in terms of the religious requirements for joining them. According to the guidebook, there are basically four categories of religious affiliation recognized by temples that have eternal memorial graves. The most common class of eternal memorial grave has no restrictions based on religious affiliation (宗教一切不問 shūkyō issai towazu). I shall return to this category shortly. The second type allows someone to join as long as he or she is a member of one of the established sects, but not of a new religion (在来仏教であれば宗派不問 zairai bukkyō de areba shūha towazu). The third kind of eternal memorial grave requires that one at least be a member of the temple's sect, but does not require you to become a parishioner of that particular temple (当寺の宗派に帰依する tōji no shūha ni kie suru), while the last category, which in this way makes it indistinguishable from a traditional family grave, requires all its members to become danka (Butsuji Gaido 2003, 38–39).[29]

The most common phrase seen in advertisements for eternal memorial graves, "We do not ask your sect" (宗派を問わず shūha o towazu), requires further consideration. Although most temples do not insist that one become a parishioner, it is certainly a desirable outcome for the temple and a central goal of creating any new type of temple grave space.

Also, even if one belongs to a different sect, the memorial rites performed on one's behalf will still follow those of the temple that is offering the eternal memorial grave. These graves, then, do not (yet) offer some new

28. Kōkenji 廣見寺, a Sōtō temple near Chichibu Shrine in Saitama, promises to keep an individual's ashes distinct forever (Butsuji Gaido 2005, 117).

29. A look at the requirements for the eternal memorial graves listed in the guidebook shows the following breakdown in terms of religious affiliation requirements: 187 sites have no restrictions, 83 ask that you belong to one of the traditional sects, 70 ask that you belong to the sect in question, 65 require you to be a parishioner, and 6 are unclear (Butsuji Gaido 2003).

TABLE I. Religious affiliation of 328 eternal memorial graves

Religious affiliation	Number (percentage)
Company	1 (0.3)
Foundation[a]	5 (1.5)
Independent[b]	16 (4.9)
Jishū	1 (0.3)
Jōdo	26 (7.9)
Nichiren	44 (13.4)
Rinzai	19 (5.8)
Shingon	67 (20.4)
Shinshū	32 (9.8)
Shinto	2 (0.6)
Sōtō	96 (29.3)
Tendai	19 (5.8)

Source: *Eternal Memorial Grave Guidebook*, 3d ed. (Butsuji Gaido 2003).

[a] A Juridical Foundation (財団法人 *zaidan hōjin*).

[b] "Independent" (単立 *tanritsu*) refers to temples that do not have, or that have relinquished, official member-ship in a given sect. For many temples, going independent is an economic move that allows them to avoid paying sect fees (宗費 *shūhi*). For more on independent temples, see Nakajima 2005, 123–27.

form of transsectarian Buddhist affiliation. What they do offer, however, is nonparishioner membership at a temple. This kind of affiliation raises a number of issues, some of which I will discuss in chapters 3 and 4. One aspect of this relationship that deserves further attention, but lies outside the scope of the present study, is the issue of the tax status of temples offering eternal memorial graves without restrictions on religious affilia-tion. If a temple graveyard is opened up to nonparishioners, it can be said to be operating for profit rather than religious goals and is thus subject to taxation. At the time of my research, none of the sites I visited had been forced to pay additional taxes, but several of the priests voiced concerns over the possibility (table I).[30]

Like eternal memorial graves at temples, those at municipal graveyards do not have restrictions on religious affiliation, but for different reasons. At these sites, which are run by the local government and thus bound by the constitutional separation of church and state, there are no mecha-

30. For more on the taxation issue, see Covell 2005, chapter 7.

nisms in place for providing religious memorial services. People are free to invite priests in to conduct rites, but there are no government-funded Buddhist or Christian memorial services. At the Kodaira Grave Park's Communal Burial Grave (合葬式墓地 *gassōshiki bochi*) on the western outskirts of Tokyo, for example, there was a desire on the part of the office running the new grave to offer some sort of service but also a concern over potential conflicts relating to government-sponsored religious services. In the end, those in charge of the municipal grave settled on a once-yearly flower offering service, not an uncommon strategy for producing "nonreligious" rites.[31] It is also worth noting that at Kodaira, the period of time that individuality is maintained in urns before the remains are poured into a communal ossuary is a rationalized twenty years, rather than the odd-numbered years consistent with traditional practices.[32]

ETERNAL MEMORIAL GRAVES AT SHINTO SHRINES

It may strike some readers as surprising that Shinto shrines, with their well-documented aversion to death impurity, would also operate eternal memorial graves.[33] Although they are not specifically referred to as such, in every significant way they are indistinguishable from most eternal memorial graves. For example, Takeda Shrine's Mahoroba ("eminent") Grave Park near Kōfu city in Yamanashi prefecture created the Shrine of Ancestral Spirits (祖霊社 Soreisha) in 1999. Like other eternal memorial graves, Soreisha provides space to inter one's remains along with the guarantee of eternal services. Those of any nationality are welcome, but they must "believe" in the tenets of Shinto—equated with joining Takeda Shrine's support society, Sūkeikai 崇敬会. The grave itself, referred to as an eternal ceremonial ossuary (永代祭祀納骨堂 *eitai saishi nōkotsudō*), is indistinguishable from a small Shinto shrine, complete with torii 鳥居 gate (Butsuji Gaido 2005, 184).

Wakamiya Hachimangū Shrine in Kōchi Prefecture is another example of the rare, but not unheard of, shrine that operates an eternal memorial

31. Moyai no Kai, one of the oldest and most famous eternal memorial grave societies, despite having its grave situated on temple grounds, also offers a yearly flower ceremony.

32. The special memorial years (回忌 *kaiki* or 周忌 *shūki*) fall on the first, third, seventh, eleventh, thirteenth, seventeenth, twenty-third, and thirty-third anniversaries of the death. As noted, in some cases, families may continue offering services for fifty or a hundred years.

33. For efforts to promote Shinto funerary rites both historically and in the contemporary period, see Kenney 1996/97 and 2000.

Fig. 4. Wakamiya Mausoleum

grave. According to the chief priest, Ōkubo Sengyō 大久保千堯, anti-
Buddhist sentiment is traditionally quite strong in Kōchi, where 5 percent
of funerals are Shinto. Ōkubo confided that though many shrines will enshrine the spirits of the dead (御霊 mitama), he finds it odd that very few
will store the actual physical remains. He recounted to me a story about
a person who had come to him in the early 1990s and asked to have his
remains interred at the shrine. When Ōkubo told him this could not be
done, the old man angrily retorted that, "Shrines must be very cold-hearted
places indeed." The situation changed a little later, however, when the precincts of a nearby temple that had been destroyed in the Meiji period and
later purchased by an individual was donated, graves and all, to the shrine.
Since he now had this temple land, Ōkubo decided to build an ossuary on
the site, which was adjacent to his shrine's precincts. After several battles
with neighbors (over a new grave) and the city office (over whether he could
accept those who were not shrine members), Ōkubo started the Wakamiya Mausoleum (若宮霊廟 Wakamiya Reibyō; fig. 4) and the Mukō Yama
[Burial] Society 向山会 in 1995. There was still the doctrinal predicament,

however, of what he considered to be the absolute necessity of separating the polluted corpse from the pure spirit. He accomplished this by storing the cremated remains in the bottom of the grave building and enshrining the spirits in the top.[34]

Unless one reads the sign plate on the roof, the grave itself is indistinguishable from a small shrine building. Under the roof there is a row of wooden tablets with the living names of those interred at the grave followed by the honorific *mikoto* 命, often seen in the names of Japanese gods, in place of posthumous Buddhist titles. As of July 2003, there were roughly one hundred sixty spirits residing in the shrine along with the physical remains of about thirty people. A yearly service (慰霊祭 *ireisai*) for the peaceful repose of the spirits takes place during the autumn equinox. Ōkubo also performs a short service before the grave every morning.

CONCLUSION

This chapter has detailed the emergence of a new form of grave that arose in response to the increasingly widespread collapse of the extended-family grave. These eternal memorial graves, with their emphasis on permanence, offered innovative solutions to the problem of disassociated (*muen*) spirits. Furthermore, by shifting the burden of grave maintenance and yearly memorial offerings to a third party, eternal memorial graves may be signaling the end of the traditional family grave and the *danka* system it supports.

By offering spaces in graves without requiring one to become a parishioner, eternal memorial graves are rewriting the types of relationships that people have with temples. These new graves require sometimes radical adaptations of existing rules and practices, and it is here that the eternal memorial graves are significant, both to temples that are struggling to find new ways to survive and to scholars interested in the state of contemporary Japanese Buddhism. The next two chapters will provide two test cases that explore the most noteworthy aspect of these graves: the use of eternal memorial graves as the basis for a new type of temple

34. At this point, the reader might be wondering about possible analogies to Yasukuni Shrine. Though the spirits of the war dead enshrined in Yasukuni could be said to be receiving a variation of eternal memorial care, it is important to note that the actual remains of the war dead are interred over a kilometer away at Chidorigafuchi 千鳥ヶ淵. For more details on Chidorigafuchi and Yasukuni, see Inoue et al. 2004.

membership, one that is fundamentally different from the existing *danka* system. By examining what these types of burial have meant to a Nichiren temple in rural Niigata and a Sōtō Zen temple in downtown Tokyo, I hope to provide insights into the current state of Japanese Buddhism and some possibilities for its future.

CHAPTER THREE

Challenging the
Status Quo—Myōkōji

Getting my own grave, being able to put myself first, this made me so
happy and let me think that now I can live.
—Naoko

In May 1989, a young Nichiren priest sent the following fax to the editors
of the popular magazine, *Asahi Weekly* (週刊朝日 *Shūkan Asahi*). The
magazine was planning a story on "How to Avoid Dying Without a Grave"
and wanted to feature the ground-breaking burial site that the priest had
built at his rural temple in coastal Niigata. For the priest, Ogawa Eiji
小川英爾, this was a rare opportunity to bring national exposure to both
his new grave and his philosophy for a new form of temple Buddhism.

Attn: *Asahi Weekly* Editor
It is certainly true that, up to this point, graves have linked together
temples, belief in the ancestors, and the extended-family system.
However, new social realities such as growing emphasis on the individual, nuclearization of families, declining birth rates, and increases
in population shifts, singles, divorce, and depopulation mean that the
form of the grave itself must change. And yet despite all of this, numerous troubles continue to arise due to the difficulty of dealing with the
grave problem.
    As an individual, I believe that we are currently in an era where
faith is fundamentally an individual choice and not something that
can be forced upon people through household succession. Graves
should of course be created for individuals as well as for couples. Since
such a step would increase the need for large-scale graveyards, it is also
necessary to consider communal graves. At the very least, there needs

to be room for choice, and the "Annon grave" represents one temple's
response to this problem.

Despite the increasing number of nameless graves abandoned because of depopulation, this problem is not being addressed. The Annon
grave is one attempt at a solution. We are going to put the income from
the grave into a separate fund and maintain the grave with the fund's ac-
crued interest. We are not trying to make a profit; we are simply endeav-
oring to maintain the temple and the grave—a local attempt at temple
renewal (寺興し *tera okoshi*). There are currently fifteen applicants for
the grave. It is my hope that as this type of grave becomes more common, the general public will accept what we are trying to do.

The resulting *Asahi* article, advertised as a "must read" for singles and
families without children, focused almost exclusively on the terrifying
prospect of abandoned graves. The article presents a unique snapshot of
burial fears at the moment that the Annon grave was established, providing a series of quotations from several "cases" identifying the types of people being excluded from the existing grave system. These stories include
a thirty-year-old housewife who found out she could not have children;
a fifty-nine-year-old housewife who was being cared for by her daughter
but could not enter her son-in-law's family grave; a woman in her forties
who was of a different faith than her husband and thus wanted to enter a
separate grave; and a woman who lost her husband at a young age and was
told by his relatives, in no uncertain terms, that she would not be allowed
to enter his family grave (*Shūkan Asahi* August 18, 1989, 124). The article
continues this focus on gendered aspects of the grave issue by citing Fujii
Masao 藤井正雄, now an emeritus professor of Buddhism at Taishō University, who conducted extensive research on mortuary trends. Fujii called
attention to the growing number of women he saw as rebelling against the
very idea of entering their husbands' graves. Unlike those women mentioned above, who were being excluded from graves or wanted a separate
spot for religious reasons, those in this second group made a conscious
choice to find their own burial spaces. Fujii summarized their sentiments
as follows: "Since I've toiled for so long on my husband's behalf, at least let
me rest in peace on my own" (ibid.).

The *Asahi* article and Ogawa's fax present two sets of important issues
for this chapter. The first concerns societal aspects of eternal memorial
graves such as lack of grave space, changing family and social structures,
and the relation between gender and burial. Here I provide specific exam-

ples of how these new burial sites offer not only a physical space for those excluded from traditional graves, but also ground for challenging tradition itself, particularly the norms of the extended, patrilineal family. Therefore, this chapter demonstrates both the ways this new burial technology serves to counter *muen* by creating new types of bonds, as well as the ways it can be used ritually to sever traditional bonds—between husband and wife, parent and child, temple and parishioner.

The second theme of this chapter concerns issues confronting temple Buddhism, specifically the need for innovative burial systems in the face of new social realities. In response, Ogawa offers a critique of the obligatory nature of religious affiliation and a staunch belief that fundamentally rethinking the traditional parishioner system is the only way to save his temple. In tracing the origins and development of the Annon grave, I identify the beginnings of what I call the contemporary grave revolution in Japan. As I shall argue, the *Asahi* article set in motion a number of events and exchanges that brought national recognition to Annon, and, in so doing, began a nationwide discussion of the postwar fissures between traditional grave ideals and modern family realities.

THE ANNON GRAVE

The original Annon site is made up of four large graves laid out in a wide grassy area three hundred meters in front of Myōkōji's main hall (fig. 5).[1]

1. In the chapter "Lifespan of the Tathāgata" (如来寿量品 *Nyōrai juryōbon*) of the *Lotus Sūtra*, Śākyamuni describes the Buddha Land as a place of tranquility. The term "tranquility," or *annon* 安穏 in Japanese, is derived from the characters for peace and tranquility. The name came to Ogawa when an elderly woman, upon joining the new grave, told him that "I have lived alone to this old age and I have long worried about what would happen when I died. Since finding my own grave I shall finally be able to live with peace of mind (心安らか *kokoro yasuraka*)" (Ogawa 2000, 71–72). Like Nichiren priests throughout Japan, Ogawa chants this chapter of the *Lotus Sūtra* as part of his morning services, first in the main hall before the image of Śākyamuni, and then again in the hall of abbots (祖師堂 *soshidō*). It seemed only natural, then, to name the eternal memorial grave Annon from the passage that reads, "The world in which the Buddha lives is a place of peace (心安らか *kokoro yasuraka*) and tranquility (穏やか *odayaka*)" (Ogawa's translation, ibid.). The relevant passage from the *Lotus Sūtra* reads:

> When the beings see the kalpa ending
> And being consumed by a great fire
> This land of mine is perfectly safe,
> Ever full of gods and men;
> In it are gardens and groves, halls and towers,
> Variously adorned with gems,
> As well as jeweled trees with many blossoms and fruits,

Fig. 5. The Annon grave site

Each of the graves is approximately ten meters in diameter and made of two concentric octagonal walls planted with bushes around a stone pagoda (多宝塔 *tahōtō*) that is inscribed on four sides with the title of the *Lotus Sūtra* (題目 *daimoku*).

The sight was designed by garden architect Nozawa Kiyoshi 野沢清 in a conscious borrowing from the design of the communal grave belonging to the Nichirenist religious group, Kokuchūkai 国柱会.[2] According to Nozawa, the intended effect of the Annon grave is to evoke a traditional Buddhist stupa as well as represent, in miniature, the mountains directly behind it (personal communication, August 2003). Built into the face of the

---

Wherein the beings play and amuse themselves;
Where the gods beat the divine drums,
Making melodies most skillfully played,
And rain down mandarava-flowers,
Scattering them on the Buddha and his great multitude (Hurvitz 1976, 243).

2. Though primarily chosen from a design perspective, it is worth noting the place of the Kokuchūkai grave in Japan's modern burial history. The Kokuchūkai communal grave was completed in 1928 by movement founder Tanaka Chigaku 田中智学 (1861–1939). Cremated remains are poured into the back of the monument to mix with those already there, including the founder himself (Tanaka 1960, 101–6). Until fairly recently, interment was restricted to members of the religion. Officials from the group told me there has been little interest from the general public since this restriction was dropped (personal communication, September 2004). For information on Kokuchūkai, see Jaffe 2001, chapter 8; Stone 1994, 251–52; and Lee 1975.

Fig. 6. An Annon Forest grave

two walls are grave stones for each of the 108 spaces in an Annon grave.[3] The individual graves, which symbolize the 108 afflictions (煩悩 bonnō) in Buddhist thought, are organized into five areas, each represented by one of the characters from the title of the *Lotus Sūtra,* further inscribing the site with Buddhist doctrine, but also evoking, through the structure's division into numbered blocks and units, an image of the ubiquitous Japanese apartment complex (団地 danchi).

The parallel between spaces for the living and the dead is even more evident in the "Annon Forest," (杜の安隠 Mori no Annon) which is arranged in a grid pattern, with the north-south streets named after various flowers and the east-west streets running from First (一条 Ichijō) to Eighth (八条 Hachijō).[4] The Annon Forest, built in 2001 after the four main Annon graves were filled, is made up of thirty miniature versions of the Annon graves, each one meter tall and holding eight plots (fig. 6).

3. The individual graves are accessed by digging up the bushes along the tops of the walls and lifting up a stone lid.
4. For a fascinating study examining parallels between spaces for the dead and spaces for the living, see Ragon 1983.

Fig. 7. Close-up of Annon gravestones

Members are allowed to have anything they want engraved on their stones, and it is here, even more than in the overall shape of Annon, that one notes the potential break with traditional family graves.[5] At Annon the inscriptions range from the traditional—simply the name of the family—to what one might term "new age" inscriptions, often with single characters for peace (和 wa) or rest (眠 nemuru); to the international, "C'est la vie" written in Japanese katakana syllabary; to the downright campy. A pair of stones, purchased by two sisters, includes one that reads "Whoever you are, go in good health. Thank you for coming today." The companion stone next to it reads, in casual, feminine Japanese, "Please come again" (see fig. 7). Although there may be an impulse, in the case of these graves, to equate new physical forms with new ways of thinking, one must be cautious. In my observations of families visiting Annon at different times of the year, there is no discernable difference between their actions and those of people visiting a traditional grave. Visitors would begin by pouring water over the stone, cleaning it, offering candles, flowers, and incense, and fin-

5. The engraving of the stone is paid for separately and costs approximately thirty thousand yen.

ish by clasping their hands together in a silent prayer or conversation with the deceased.[6] During the summer festival for the dead, despite the lack of a set place to hold them, wooden memorial tablets (卒塔婆 *sotoba*; skt. *stūpa*) were simply laid down across some of the Annon Forest graves. The external form of the graves and the bonds that maintain them may be new, but the ritual form, for now, has not changed.

THE ANNON SYSTEM

Prospective members of the Annon grave usually contact the temple by phone or email first and are then sent an information packet describing the temple's history, the Annon grave, rules and regulations, and the yearly summer festival. Each Annon grave now costs 850,000 yen. This price covers the cost of the grave, maintenance, and communal memorial services performed during the two equinoctial periods, the summer festival of the dead, and at the annual summer gathering of Annon members in late August, the Annon Festival. Once a person purchases the rights to one of the grave sites, he or she automatically becomes an Annon Society member (安穏会員 *Annon kaiin*) and is required to pay membership dues of 3,500 yen per year. This covers the cost of the quarterly temple newsletter, *Wondrous Light* (妙の光 *Tae no Hikari*), which evokes both the name of the temple and the *Lotus Sūtra*. The newsletter includes a short essay from Ogawa, news on upcoming events, a feature on local wildlife and fauna, a biographical introduction of a parishioner family, and the extremely popular "From the Temple Household" (寺庭から *Jitei kara*), a regular column by Ogawa's wife Nagisa, introducing the quotidian side of temple life.

As with traditional graves, one does not own an Annon plot; one merely rents it in perpetuity. Once there is no one to maintain the grave and a set period of time has passed, the rights to the plot are forfeit. According to Annon's bylaws, if a member dies without leaving anyone to maintain the grave, or if the membership fees are not paid for three years, then memorial rites will continue for thirteen more years. At that time, the remains are moved to the group ossuary—located in the center of each Annon grave—and the plot reverts to the temple for reuse. Since memorial services will continue to be performed for those in the communal ossuary

6. Japanese describe what they do in front of a grave in different ways, most commonly using the verb "to pray"(祈る *inoru*). In my experience, this "prayer" often takes the form of a conversation with a specific family member who has passed away. Descriptions of such prayers routinely include some mention of gratitude (感謝 *kansha*).

for as long as the temple stands, those who purchase an Annon grave are said to receive "eternal memorial rites" (*eitai kuyō*).

MEMBERS AND PARISHIONERS

The information pamphlet from Myōkōji includes two pages of frequently asked questions, beginning with, "Is it necessary to become a follower of the temple (檀信徒 *danshinto*) in order to apply for Annon?" This question speaks to the fundamental difference between eternal memorial graves and their traditional temple counterparts as well as to deep-seated concerns about what it means to have a temple grave. As noted above, in order to acquire and maintain a temple grave, one traditionally needed to be a parishioner (檀家 *danka*) of that temple. Becoming a *danka* inevitably entails a set of largely financial obligations to the temple for regular memorial services, help with temple upkeep, and support of the priest and his family. More significantly, if the grave is to be maintained, these responsibilities must be passed on to one's descendants. It is little surprise, then, that prospective Annon members are so sensitive to this point.

During Ogawa's initial interview with potential members, as well as on the application form itself, people are asked if they have any intention of becoming a *danshinto* of the temple. According to Ogawa, this question is shorthand for asking whether they intend to ask him to perform their funerals when the time comes.[7] The most common response Ogawa gets at this point is, "But *danka* is forever, right?" This, he tells them, is why he uses the term *danshinto* to refer to the way in which one relates to Myōkōji. The temple pamphlet also attempts to alleviate these concerns:

> It is not necessary to become a *danshinto* and you will not be asked to do so by Myōkōji. However, since you are creating this bond (御縁 *goen*) with the temple, we hope that our newsletter and other messages from the temple will open up your heart. Of course, those who wish to become followers of the temple will be accepted.

Ogawa understands the connection in people's minds between becoming a parishioner (*danka*) and incurring a never-ending responsibility to the temple. Once Ogawa reassures potential members that becoming a

---

7. According to Ogawa, approximately 10 percent agree to become temple followers right away, 5 percent say no, and the rest defer the decision to later (personal communication, August 2003).

danshinto in no way obligates their descendants to do so and that their children can revert to regular Annon "member" (会員 *kaiin*) status, they often decide to join. The distinction being made here, between *danka*, or "temple parishioner," and *danshinto*, "temple follower," speaks to Ogawa's attempt to rework centuries of temple tradition.[8] By allowing members the benefits of temple parishioners (having Ogawa perform their funerals) without the requirements (committing themselves and their descendants to maintaining the temple), Ogawa is drastically altering the traditional connection between temples and households. In his eyes, he is transforming the relationship from one of obligation to one of choice, from a multi-generational commitment to an individual preference. The distinction between temple parishioners and burial society members thus has profound implications for temples, as well as for what it may indicate about the future of Buddhist affiliation in Japan.

Trying to better understand the differences between members and parishioners, I asked Ogawa if the former were more enthusiastic (熱心 *nesshin*) toward the temple than the latter. He responded that, while at other temples this was apparently the case, he could not compare the enthusiasm of the two groups at Myōkōji. Instead, he told me that the Annon members were far more self-motivated (自発的 *jihatsuteki*) than the temple parishioners. According to Ogawa, this self-motivation means that the members have a strong sense of responsibility (責任感 *sekininkan*) while the parishioners have only a sense of obligation (義務感 *gimukan*) to maintain the temple. As to the distinction between responsibility and obligation, this became more apparent in later conversations.

For example, when Myōkōji was rebuilt in 2001, Ogawa decided on a distinctly modern style. He assured me that such remodeling would have been impossible without the influence of Annon members. As he put it, "Previously, the *danka* would never have let me build something like this. They would have insisted on an orthodox architectural style." Although

---

8. The *Bukkyōgo Daijiten* 仏教語大辞典 makes no distinction between these terms, conflating them along with *dan'otsu* 檀越 (skt. *dāna-pati*) (Nakamura 1975). Many of the Buddhist priests with whom I have spoken use the word *danshinto* to connote different grades of commitment to the temple. For some, *danshinto* refers to a person who belongs to the temple, but does not have a grave there. For others, the term is used instead of member (*kaiin*) to refer to those in the temple's eternal memorial grave. In this case, using *danshinto*, with its connotation of believer, is seen as preferable to the more strictly commercial implications of member. Even though this is a distinction that may be significant to Buddhist priests, judging from the frequency with which it comes up in conversations with priests running these new graves, and in the pamphlets promoting these spaces, it is not a distinction with which many Japanese are familiar.

this example may say little about member responsibility and parishioner obligation it does suggest something about the other side of the temple equation: Ogawa's obligations to parishioners—obligations that come with certain expectations. Parishioners have a genealogical and financial stake in the temple, so for some, supporting the temple means they have a say in how it is run. With the financial success, national attention, and influx of new members that came with Annon, however, Ogawa earned the right to continue his "unorthodox" management of the temple. Members, on the other hand, often do not think of the temple as "theirs" in the way that parishioners do. Furthermore, they have chosen Myōkōji precisely because it is different from other temples and because they think that Ogawa is not like other priests. In this respect, the Annon members are not the only beneficiaries of this new temple relationship; they also offer Ogawa more leeway in running Myōkōji and the potential to return to what he sees as the proper place for temples in society.

OGAWA'S BACKGROUND

To understand the origins of the Annon grave, it is first necessary to explore the background of the man who created it. The current, fifty-third abbot of Myōkōji, Ogawa Eiji, was forced to take over the temple after his father died in the early 1980s, when Ogawa was in his third year of university.[9] Until that point, he had had no intention of even becoming a priest, let alone taking over his father's temple. He dreamt of becoming a journalist or a scholar, but he could only get into the Nichiren sect's Risshō University—a fairly minor institution in his estimation. Ogawa was the youngest of three children, but by the time his father became ill, Ogawa's elder brother was already a well-established professor of Chinese culture at Tōhoku University, and the temple parishioners were pressing Ogawa to take over as abbot. His elder sister married a young priest and Waseda University graduate whom she brought into the temple, but he would not change his name or consent to becoming an adopted son (婿さん mukosan). As a result of his unwillingness to join the family, he was not allowed to take over as abbot. According to Ogawa, his sister's husband, as a zaike 在家 (householder), overidealized Buddhism and could not adapt to the realities of a rural temple.[10] Thus, although he was the youngest sibling, by

9. According to the temple pamphlet, Myōkōji was founded in 1313.

10. The term zaike is primarily used by priests from temple families to refer to those who have converted from lay status. It is worth noting that temple-born priests, most of whom have

the time his father died, Ogawa already had accepted that he would have to take over the temple.[11] He spent his fourth year of college finishing his coursework and training at the Nichiren head temple on Mount Minobu in order to take the tonsure. Ogawa was twenty-two when he took over as abbot of Myōkōji. He admits that at that time he had no idea what he was doing and that his motivations were hardly religious.

> At a minor university like Risshō, I knew that I was not going to become a top researcher anytime soon. So rather than ending up in some inconsequential position at a research center, I thought it would be more interesting to go to the temple. So it's not that I became a priest out of some religious awakening. Rather, I was interested in the kinds of human relationships that go on at the site of the temple and the role of religion there. That's the reality of how I became a priest.[12]

Conversations about Ogawa's past consistently return to the two experiences that have had the greatest impact on his views of Japanese temple Buddhism. The first occurred during his college days at Risshō University. While studying sociology, he became disenchanted with the quality of the classes and the apathy of the teachers. At that time he came across a research center near Risshō run by the well-known cultural anthropologist Kawakita Jirō 川喜田二郎 (1920–2009). Kawakita had quit his position at the Tokyo Institute of Technology and opened the Free Campus University (移動大学 Idō Daigaku) in 1969, after Japanese universities were shut down during student riots over the revision of the Japan-U.S. Security Treaty.[13]

---

families of their own, could also legitimately be considered "householders." The association of *zaike* priests with naive idealism was a near constant in my conversations with temple-born priests. The relationship between these two groups deserves a detailed study outside the scope of the present work.

11. The majority of Buddhist temples in Japan are passed down from father to son. The issue of temple succession (世襲 *seshū*) has been a problem since marriage for priests was decriminalized in 1872, and the impact of the current decline in the national birth rate has not stopped at the temple gates. For a book-length treatment of the issue of clerical marriage, see Jaffe 2001. Since temple families, following national trends, are getting smaller, it is growing increasingly difficult for temples priests, particularly at rural temples, to find a successor. For details on this problem in the Tendai sect, see Covell 2005, 82–89.

12. Unless otherwise noted, all quotations from Ogawa in this chapter are from a series of conversations that occurred primarily in 2003 and 2004.

13. Using tents for classrooms and dorms, Kawakita offered two-week courses open to anyone eighteen or over. Kawakita developed what became known as the "KJ method," which involved conducting group fieldwork, noting data on individual cards, and then figuring out how the information could best be organized (Scupin 1997). See also, Kawakita 1967.

According to Ogawa, while other Risshō students were playing mahjong in their free time, he was at Kawakita's University. There were no formal classes or assignments; rather, groups of students would get together, devise projects, gather the necessary people and knowledge, and then carry out that project. It was here that Ogawa developed the organizational skills, networks, and approach to problem solving that defined how he would run his own temple.[14] Much of Ogawa's success comes from his willingness and ability to step outside what he sees as the rather narrow sphere of the Nichiren sect to consult with priests from other sects, nonsectarian scholars, journalists, and experts in a broad variety of professions.

The second important event that laid the groundwork for Annon came ten years later, during Ogawa's tenure at the Nichiren Contemporary Religion Research Center. He was invited to join the center in the early 1980s to take part in the research project on temples in depopulated areas discussed in chapter 1. After the strong reaction caused by both the content and wide dissemination of the original report, the research team was asked to propose strategies for dealing with the problem of depopulation and temples. Their suggestions included a reconsideration of the parishioner system and, far more radical, allowed the roughly two thousand Nichiren temples across the country that had no full-time priests to collapse or merge with other temples so that the sect could focus its energy on the remaining three thousand that still had a chance.[15] According to Ogawa, the sect's leaders not only refused to follow the team's proposals or do anything to confront the issue, but also tried to suppress the team's findings. Ogawa told me on several occasions that this experience convinced him that the sect as an organization was of little help to individual temples, and that rural temples in particular faced unique issues that could only be addressed by their priests.[16] For Ogawa, the solution to Myōkōji's collapsing buildings, overgrown garden, lack of funds, and inconsistent, memorial-service income was the Annon grave.

14. Although I never saw Ogawa use note cards to organize his ideas, it was hard to miss the large whiteboard, perennially covered in crowded red diagrams, in the room where temple planning was always carried out.

15. This collapse from five thousand to three thousand temples is mentioned several times in the pamphlet and also becomes a sort of touchstone in Ogawa's later writings.

16. Interestingly, from about 2004, Ogawa began receiving numerous requests from the research center asking for the fifteen-year-old original project data. As noted in chapter 1, recent publications show that the sect is again interested in discussing the problem.

THE START OF ANNON

In addition to Ogawa's early experiences during his college years and at the Research Center, several episodes led to his creation of the Annon grave. In his book, *A Grave For Each and Every One of Us* (ひとりひとりの墓 *Hitori hitori no haka*), and other writings, he describes pivotal conversations with two female parishioners, both widows without sons, who came to him with concerns over what would happen to them when they died.[17] These concerns hit close to home for Ogawa, who, from the moment he took over Myōkōji, faced considerable pressure from parishioners to marry and produce a son to succeed him as abbot. Unfortunately for those anxiously awaiting a male heir, Ogawa and his wife stopped having children after giving birth to four daughters. As he notes in the introduction to the book, the realization that Ogawa's own family grave could end up abandoned had a profound impact on his view of existing burial norms (Ogawa 2000, 6–7).

As noted at the beginning of this chapter, the most significant factor in Annon's initial growth was that first coverage in the *Asahi Weekly* magazine. The article was crucial to the success of the new grave, both in terms of national exposure and because it caught the attention of several individuals who were to play a central role in the transformation of public discourse regarding death and burial over the next two decades. One of these was Inoue Haruyo 井上治代, at the time a self-described nonfiction writer and student of the renowned Japanese sociologist of religion Morioka Kiyomi 森岡清美 (b. 1923). Inoue's doctoral work and popular writings took Morioka's research on changing family structures and extended it into the realm of family graves. At the time of the *Asahi* article, Inoue was at work on a new book, *The Current State of Graves: Within the Destabilized Family* (現代お墓事情—ゆれる家族の中で *Gendai o-haka jijō: Yureru kazoku no naka de* 1990). In it, she argued the need for a new type of grave that would address changing family structures and social realities. Upon seeing the *Asahi* article, she immediately contacted Ogawa and urged him to widen his scope to include a national audience. They agreed to work together to promote both the book and the Annon grave at a symposium to

17. This book, published in 2000, consists of a collection of about seventy short, two- to three-page articles divided into three sections: "Changing Graves," "Unchanging Ideas," and "Simple Thoughts." It was published first as a series of fifty weekly articles in the Sunday *Mainichi Shinbun* 毎日新聞 from October 1997 to September 1998.

be held at his temple. It was this conversation that led to the first Annon Festival in the summer of 1990 and to a partnership that continues to the present day.

The first Annon Festival ran on the theme of "Creating Bonds for the Twenty-First Century" and featured Inoue as the head of the "Society for Considering Bonds (*en*) and Graves in the Twenty-First Century." The program included an introduction to the culture and history of the region, a slide presentation by Inoue comparing American and Japanese burial practices, a Buddhist ritual service, and an improvisational jam session titled "Annon Pure Land" (安穏浄土 Annon Jōdo) that included sutra recitation, synthesized avant-garde music, folk musicians, and a group of seniors chanting the *daimoku* and the *nenbutsu* 念仏. The second day included a round-table discussion with Inoue, Ogawa, the aforementioned Fujii Masao, and Tani Kayoko, the head and founder of the Women's Monument Society described in the previous chapter. Also present were two other people who would become major forces in the transformation of Japanese attitudes toward burial. The first was Himonya Hajime 碑文谷創, who, in 1989, started his own publishing company and used it to put out Japan's first professional funerary magazine, *Sōgi*. Since that time Himonya has become *the* authority on contemporary burial practices, publishing, in addition to *Sōgi*, numerous books and articles on Japanese deathways. The final participant in that first round table was Yasuda Mutsuhiko 安田睦彦, who, less than one month later would start the Grave-Free Promotion Society (葬送の自由をすすめる会 Sōsō no Jiyū o Susumeru Kai), a civic group aimed at promoting the scattering of ashes.[18] Ogawa is convinced that bringing these individuals together at the first Annon festival provided the watershed moment that loosened taboos over public discussions of burial and transformed the way the subject was talked about in the national media. The first festival attracted numerous media outlets, both sectarian and secular, including NHK (日本放送協会 Nihon Hōsō Kyōkai) television, which ended up airing four different programs on Annon in three markets: Tokyo, Niigata, and Kyoto. Despite its remote location, once Myōkōji and the Annon grave caught national attention, the plots started selling rapidly.[19] The first Annon grave was filled within a few years and three

18. In later years the festival was shortened to one day, but the basic combination of Buddhist memorial ritual, lectures, entertainment, and summer festival dance (盆踊り *bon odori*) has remained consistent.

19. To travel to Myōkōji from Niigata station you must first take a twenty-minute train ride followed by a twenty-minute taxi or thirty-minute bus ride. A direct trip by car requires approximately forty-five minutes.

more were built over the course of the next ten years. These sold out by 2001, leading to the construction of the Annon Forest in 2002 to accommodate demand. This site sold out within five years and was expanded again in 2010 to meet ongoing demand. The name "Annon" is now a registered trademark, and currently three other locations are allowed to use the brand: Myōzuiji 妙瑞寺, a Nichiren temple in Ōita, Kyūshū, that built its single Annon grave in 1998; a Nichiren temple in Kamakura where the head priest is planning to build an Annon type grave; and a Tendai temple in Shiga prefecture that advertises its own Annon grave despite the fact that it has yet to build anything.

FROM BURIAL TO DOCTRINE

Ogawa initially saw the Annon grave as a way both to support the temple into the future and to create renewed interest in Buddhist teachings. As noted earlier, the success of Annon and the influx of energy (both emotional and financial) meant that Myōkōji's parishioners were willing to support Ogawa's innovations. Ironically, this enthusiasm has not extended to that which is supposedly most fundamental to a temple priest's work—teaching and propagating (教化 kyōka)[20] Nichiren doctrine.[21] As he explained it to me in 2003, fifteen years after the start of Annon:

> There really is not any need for kyōka because the parishioners don't care for it. If I try to talk about doctrine, the parishioners say they don't want to hear such difficult talk. They want something enjoyable—a story that will please the ancestors. That's why they don't want a doctrinal talk. I certainly want to give a doctrinal talk, but they just don't want to hear it. Also, I need to prepare in order to give such talks, but I don't have any free time for study! I have to earn money. I have to burn the candle at both ends to perform memorial services, drink sake with parishioners, meet with people, and earn money for the temple to maintain all of this. I have absolutely no free time for study. This is no good. I think the ideal priest is one who can work the fields in the

---

20. Also read as kyōge. For examples of the wide range of contexts, practices and ideals that make up kyōka in the Rinzai sect, see Borup 2008, 106–7. Depending on the sect, the term 布教 fukyō, or "proselytizing," may also be used as a synonym for kyōka.

21. The Nichiren sect rules include very clear statements about the central duty of propagation for its priests. For example, see section 15, "Regulations for Proselytizing" (布教規定 Fukyō kitei), and section 18, "Regulations for Societal Propagation Activities" (社会教化事業規定 Shakai kyōka jigyō kitei) (Nichirenshū shūmuin 2004, 96–98 and 106–8).

morning and then study in the afternoon and relax playing Japanese
chess. People in trouble can come and consult, bring some vegetables,
and ask questions. The priest can then answer from his own knowledge. But I guess that's not really doctrine, is it? If you can't speak
about doctrine using your own words, it has no meaning at all. And
that's why I say that there is no need to speak about doctrine. But we
priests feel that we must bear the burden of doctrine. So in return [for
helping parishioners with their questions] a priest would receive some
vegetables, or have them plow the temple rice fields. This would be
the ideal relationship, but I can't do it. I am the chief-engineer abbot
(土木担当住職 *doboku tantō jūshoku*), the money-saving abbot. The
truth is that I want to teach doctrine. It is only because of the new
people joining Annon that I am even able to write about doctrine [in
the temple newsletter]. The *danka* are not interested in this at all.
Even if I write it, they won't read it. In the past people read it, but now
they don't. The desire for this kind of teaching started with the Annon
members. They want to study.

For those who have not spent a lot of time speaking with temple priests in
Japan, perhaps the most striking aspect of Ogawa's narrative is his conviction that the two biggest obstacles keeping him from focusing on doctrine
are his parishioners and his day-to-day responsibilities at the temple. In
fact, his belief that he was being kept from the study of Buddhism by his
regular work at the temple is one that I constantly encountered during
my research. Indeed, I would offer Ogawa's comments as highly indicative of the ways in which temple priests across all sects, in both urban and
rural locations, spoke to me of life at their temples. It is also worth noting
that Ogawa speaks of doctrine itself as an obstacle—at least the academic
study of doctrine, which he sees as divorced from the personal lives of the
parishioner and the priest himself.[22] For Ogawa, preaching doctrine means
promoting a more general interest in Buddhist teachings and practices, a
consciousness of temples as more than simply storage spaces for the ancestors and places to offer incense.

His desire to use the Annon grave as a way to generate greater interest in Buddhist teachings took concrete form in late March 2005, when
Ogawa held the first overnight training session (参籠修行 *sanrō shugyō*) for
Annon members and Myōkōji parishioners. Eleven people (seven parishioners and four Annon members) took part in the two-day event, which

22. The perceived gap between doctrine and temple realities will be the subject of chapter 6.

included basic instruction in the proper way to sit, bow, hold Buddhist ro-
sary beads (数珠 *juzu*), play the small drums (太鼓 *taiko*) used in Nichiren
services, and chant sutras. Advertised in the temple newsletter as a "mini-
training experience," the course also included copying sutras, cleaning
the temple, and attending lectures by Ogawa on the content of the *Lotus
Sūtra*, the history of incense, and the meaning of Buddhist terms such as
memorial service (供養 *kuyō*), offerings to priests (布施 *fuse*), merit transfer
(回向 *ekō*), and petitionary prayer (祈願 *kigan*). The highlight of the training was a 5:00 a.m. walk, while chanting the *daimoku*, to the famous cave
behind the temple, where Nichiren is said to have converted a serpent. In
written comments collected after the training, many of the participants
complained about the length of the sutras that had to be copied, but most
wrote that they would take part in the "advanced" training session planned
for the following year. A second training session took part in May with five
participants, and subsequent one-day sessions continue to the present.[23]

Although, by Ogawa's own admission, many of Myōkōji's *danka* are
not interested in learning about Buddhist doctrine, the fact that there were
more parishioners than Annon members taking part in the training would
suggest that the Annon phenomenon has reenergized some of the temple's
parishioner base. When I asked specifically about his goals for this type of
program, he gave the following answer, which in many ways represents a
microcosm of his aims for Myōkōji and Annon more generally:

> My goal is to have people come to the temple for more than simply
> ancestral rites and funerals. I want people to question how they should
> live and how they should open up their lives. I want them to acquire
> the power to do these things and to have confidence, wisdom, and real-
> ization so that they will not fall victims to mind control.[24] I want them
> to experience this physically, not just intellectually. I also want them
> to make connections, not only with relatives or in business, but be-
> cause they have trained together, lived together, and because they have
> shared their troubles and helped each other. In order for the temple to
> become a center where human relations are not based on self-interest
> or calculation, everyone must learn this kind of awareness. And in or-.

23. For details, see the following page on Myōkōji's Web site: http://www.myoukouji.or.jp/
topics/index.html. Last accessed March 2, 2010.

24. This is an oblique reference to new religious groups, specifically those like Aum Shinrikyō, whose members carried out the infamous sarin gas attack in the Tokyo subway in 1995.
Since the attack, most of the major Buddhist sects have put out pamphlets for their temple
priests helping them to identify signs of "cultlike activity" among parishioners.

der for that to happen, it needs to take place with the Buddha [read: at a temple].

Ogawa's desire to expand parishioners' relationships with Buddhism beyond ancestor worship speaks to the way he views the traditional relationship between parishioners and temples. Like most Buddhist priests, he understands that the formalization of the parishioner system in the seventeenth century is largely responsible for the continued existence of Buddhism in Japan. He also believes quite strongly that the sets of relationships (extended family) and types of communities (rural) upon which the parishioner system and, by extension, temple Buddhism are based are no longer functioning as they once did. For Ogawa, Annon represents an attempt to create new kinds of temple communities that are based on voluntary participation and choice rather than obligation. I shall return to the question of how Ogawa views the state of traditional Japanese Buddhism—and the potential of new burial societies to revitalize it—below.

WHY PEOPLE CHOOSE ANNON: PERSONAL NARRATIVES

Turning now to narratives of Annon members, I would like to highlight several important aspects of the Annon grave: the way the grave and temple are perceived by prospective members in terms of both burial and Buddhism; what such graves potentially offer temples in terms of attracting new types of members; and, finally, what all of this might suggest to us about changing religious affiliation in Japan.

I should emphasize that the people whom I interviewed represent neither a unified Japanese view of death nor a Rosetta stone for religious faith; they are themselves navigating a variety of social rules and symbols, and it is this negotiation that interests me. These accounts will thus be presented in different formats: as extended narratives, as dialogues that include exchanges with the author, and as shorter quotations from several people clustered around a specific theme. My goal here is to provide insight into the ways in which obligation, personal choice, and religious beliefs are playing out in the arena of ancestor worship, memorializing, and thoughts on death and the afterlife. This is necessarily a messy and often contradictory process. I should clarify, however, that I am not attempting to discover the supposed contradictions in individual stories, but rather to hint at the unstable bedrock that underlies scholarly assumptions about contemporary Japanese religions.

POSTHUMOUS DIVORCE

A central theme in the public discourse surrounding Annon centers on the opportunities these new graves provide for women, not only the unmarried and divorced but also for those married women who do not wish to enter their husbands' family graves. Although scholars were aware of this group much earlier, it was not until 1993 that Inoue Haruyo coined the term "posthumous divorce" (死後離婚 shigo rikon) to refer to the growing number of women who think that one lifetime spent with their husbands is quite enough.[25] Inoue and Ogawa have identified this group in internal surveys of Annon members and estimate that roughly 10 percent of female members enter Annon for this reason (personal communication, August 2004). Regardless of what the actual numbers are, and putting aside the question of isolatable causes for joining these graves, clearly there is a sustained discourse about posthumous divorce in temple literature, press coverage, and among the members themselves. The category appears in several of Inoue's subsequent writings, including two books, *Family Debates Surrounding Graves* (墓をめぐる家族論 Haka o meguru kazokuron), published in 2000, and her doctoral dissertation, published in 2003 under the title *Changes in Graves and Families* (墓と家族の変容 Haka to kazoku no hen'yō).[26] Ogawa has also written on the subject, telling a troubling story of a Buddhist priest he knows who works on the mediation committee at family court. The priest boasted that he talks women out of divorce by frightening them with the prospect of becoming an abandoned spirit: "If you divorce you won't be able to go back to your family, so there won't be a grave for you anywhere" (Ogawa 2000, 24).

Posthumous divorce is a catchy phrase that makes for captivating copy (scholarly as well as journalistic), but the fact remains that it still accounts for only a small percentage of those people who are entering these new graves. By giving too much weight to the phenomenon, we run the risk

25. Inoue first coined the term in her book *Funerals and Graves are Changing Now* (いま葬儀・墓が変わる Ima sōgi/haka ga kawaru). She wanted to include it among the list of new forms of divorce like "retirement divorce" (定年離婚 teinen rikon) and "Narita divorce" (成田離婚 Narita rikon) that were catching media attention at the time (H. Inoue 1993, 120–22). Honeymoon divorce in Japanese is referred to as "Narita divorce" for the airport near Tokyo where newlyweds, returning from honeymoons abroad, realize they have made a terrible mistake and decide to go their separate ways.

26. Traditionally, it is common for scholars in Japan to publish numerous articles (in some cases, books) that they later combine to form their doctoral dissertations. By my count, Inoue wrote ten books and dozens of articles before publishing her dissertation.

not only of misrepresenting the composition of burial society members but also of glossing over the complex factors involved in choosing such sites. We must also be aware of the significant role of commentators, like Inoue, who focus on this small subgroup of burial society members. This is not to say that such women do not exist or that the emergence of such a group is not significant; the fact that I am also profiling such members shows that I think they are important. We need to remain aware, however, that by focusing solely on the phenomenon of posthumous divorcées, the variety and complexity of reasons for choosing graves like Annon may be flattened into the characteristic of a single group. I have selected two narratives to help demonstrate this point.

Naoko's story is fascinating for a number of reasons. First, it has drawn considerable attention nationally and internationally, appearing in two books, at least two national Japanese newspapers, on television programs, in the *New York Times*, and, of course, in the present study.[27] Though I had asked Ogawa not to arrange meetings with anyone who had previously interviewed with Inoue, Naoko was our one point of overlap. I did not discover this until halfway through the interview and decided that it was worth continuing both because her story was so fascinating and because our conversation might provide some fruitful contrasts with Inoue's account of Naoko's story. After going over my interview notes it became clear that thinking about Naoko's story solely in terms of women's rights—something she herself was inclined to do—neglected those elements of her narrative that concerned her views on Buddhist practice and her relationship to Myōkōji.

NAOKO

"Naoko Matsuoka" is a strongly independent and confident sixty-four-year-old Tokyo housewife and mother of three daughters who works at a women's shelter three times a week. When we spoke of her life, she related the difficulties of marrying a first son and of being merely a subordinate to his mother in their household. She kept coming back to the fact that she never had the right to decide the simplest things in the household, not even what she would put in the miso soup that she had to make every night. It was not until her third daughter was in high school that she felt she could get out of the house and help other women by working at the shelter. For Naoko, who helps out with the small family scrap metal busi-

27. *New York Times*, September 5, 2002.

ness that they run out of the garage below their apartment, buying her own grave at Annon with money she had been saving on her own for years was a profoundly liberating act.

> Unlike buying a television or a fur coat, or something, buying a grave has significance because of its connection to the extended-family system. For the same 800,000 yen you could buy a mink coat, the price is the same, but to buy a grave, that's got such huge significance (意義が凄い大きくて *igi ga sugoi ōkikute*). In Japan, for the wife of a first son to enter a different grave, for her to buy her own grave is incredibly . . . what can I say, a very special thing. Reverend Ogawa told me there is space in the grave for up to eight people, so I said to my friends, "I'm going to buy this, so if any of you want to be buried separately from your husbands, I'll let you in!" I still tell people this.

By saving a little income from her work at the shelter over many years, Naoko was eventually able to pay for her spot in Annon.

> Since we are running a business, we do not have money problems. However, Japanese men think that they are supporting us or taking care of us, "Thanks to me you can eat," they think. This kind of mentality is really strong. And my husband, who was born in 1934—he's seventy now—he's got plenty of this kind of thinking, let me tell you. But I saved a little bit each month [from helping at the shelter]—about what you would get from a tax return—and had more than enough to buy the grave at Annon. So with money that had nothing to do with my husband, but with my own will, with my will alone I was able to buy that grave. It was my own decision, an expression of my will against my husband and his household. Because I was able to do this I had this great sense that "I've done it! Now I can live!" I really felt this. . . . and of course my husband's parents have a traditional grave. And it's only natural in Japanese society that the daughter-in-law, the wife of the person succeeding in the family line would, without question, take his name, join the family, and then, of course, enter their grave. I think that's something you should decide for yourself. And when I asked Inoue, she told me that none of these things are mandated by law. There's no law that says you have to enter your husband's grave. I learned this from reading Inoue's books and speaking with her. Getting my own grave, being able to put myself first, this made me so happy and let me think that now I can live. This is why Annon is so wonderful.

As Naoko's comments make clear, posthumous divorce does not imply legal annulment but rather something more significant in its symbolic and physical rejection of the extended-patrilineal-family ideal. In fact, Naoko's husband even offered to help pay for the grave with family money, and he regularly visits the temple with her for the annual summer festival of members. He has also suggested that he might like to join, but she tells him in no uncertain terms that this is a spot for her and her friends and that he should be with his mother in the next world.

> So if my husband dies, he'll go in his parents' grave. I don't know about you, Mark, but as anyone can see, all Japanese men have a mother complex. Of course, my husband was like that when his mother was alive, but even from the time she died until quite recently, he was always talking to her in his head. So he never really acquired a sense of equality, of a fifty-fifty partnership with his wife. It's too bad, really. All his decisions and actions were based on what his mother would do or say. I think most Japanese men are like this. In the Women's Center, over 40 percent of the consultations are based on spousal problems. These husbands never think in terms of equality, of meeting us half way and speaking as equals. That's what women want, but it doesn't exist in Japanese society.

The Question of Religion

Part of my strategy for interviewing informants involved not only direct questions about why people were choosing eternal memorial graves, but also about the consequences of that choice. For example, as we shall see in the next chapter, one of the increasingly common reasons for buying one of these graves, particularly among those people with descendants, is the desire not to burden (迷惑を掛けたくない *meiwaku o kaketakunai*) their children with the financial and logistical difficulties of maintaining a grave. When informants told me that they only bought the grave in order to free their children from hardship, I would then ask if that meant that they did not want the children to visit the grave to conduct memorial services. This question produced a wide variety of reactions because it brought their personal choices into contact with both established cultural norms (that children take care of their parents in old age and after death) and religious themes (performing Buddhist memorial services to benefit the deceased).

NAOKO: Since Myōkōji is far away, I told my kids that when I die I just want them to lay my bones to rest. After that they don't ever have to worry about visiting again for memorials (供養 *kuyō*).

MARK: So you don't want them to do *kuyō*?

NAOKO: [Quickly] Oh, it's not that I don't want them to do *kuyō*. But if it's going to be a burden, then it's okay if they don't come. I've got my friends at Annon who will be there with me, so I won't be lonely at all.

MARK: I'd like to follow up on that a little bit. Earlier you mentioned that one thing you liked about Annon was that you don't need a posthumous name. What are your thoughts on Buddhism, posthumous names, memorials and the afterlife and things like that?

NAOKO: [Emphatically] Oh, I don't believe in an afterlife at all. I don't have any religious feelings, really (宗教心はないんですよ、大体 *shūkyōshin wa nai-n desu yo, daitai*). [The phone interrupts our conversation. After she answers and brings me more tea, she asks if the room is too cold before continuing where she left off.] You understand why I bought the grave, right? It's not about faith or religion at all.

Naoko's repeated insistence that her reasons for joining Annon had nothing to do with religion was clearly tied to her perception of me as a scholar of religion. This view was in part intensified by the topics I was broaching: memorial rites, thoughts on the afterlife, and her activities at the Buddhist altar. She was also contrasting our conversation with interviews that she had previously done with Inoue and several major newspapers.[28] She explained, "Mark, you are interested in religion, so your viewpoint is a little different. When I get together with Inoue, we just hammer away at women's issues. For me, joining Annon was not about religion." In addition to the article in the *New York Times*, Naoko was also featured in two major Japanese newspapers. In one article, which was part of a three-part series titled "Remembering the Household (*ie*)," Naoko's decision to enter Annon is placed in the context of her ongoing independence within the household—her decision to work outside the home, renovate their apartment, and have her husband do some of the daily chores (*Chūnichi Shinbun* 中日新聞, January 4, 2001). In Inoue's book as well, Naoko is presented as a

28. Reading Naoko's interview with Inoue, I later found that Inoue and I were indeed interested in very different aspects of Naoko's story. Certain elements, however, such as the miso soup story, were featured in Inoue's narrative and also appears in the *New York Times* article.

woman who stoically bore the yoke of her husband's family for years before finally declaring her independence and buying her own Annon grave.
In none of the articles is anything written about her thoughts on joining
a new temple. My own conversations with Naoko covered similar ground,
but with an additional story that left me wondering about her actual lack
of "religious feelings."[29]

After years of trying, Naoko's middle daughter finally became preg-
nant. In 2004, at the same time that Naoko found out about the pregnancy,
a notice came from Myōkōji about extra wood left over from the carving
of the new Buddhist statue in the main hall. The letter asked if anyone
wanted to buy a small statue of Śākyamuni made from the remaining
blocks of wood at a price of six hundred thousand yen. Naoko fretted over
the expense but finally decided to go ahead and buy one in order to ensure
a safe delivery for her daughter. Once she received the statue, she prayed
before it every day for a month until her grandchild was born safely. At first
blush, this kind of ardent activity would seem to contradict her claims of
disbelief, or at least indicate a shift in her relationship to the temple in the
six years elapsing since she first joined. However, as she pulled the statue
out of its small portable altar and showed it to me, she seemed far more
excited about its craftsmanship than its efficacy.

> This is really wonderful. I totally love it. I got it so that my daughter
> and my grandchild would be able to have a healthy and peaceful future.
> This is a real masterpiece. You can't put a price on this. It's got gold
> leaf in places where you can't even see—underneath and on the back.
> It's all handmade. People who aren't interested in this kind of thing
> look at this and think, "What is that?" They don't think it's anything
> special. Of course, there are Buddhist statues for sale at shops and at
> Buddhist specialty stores for about thirty thousand yen, but those are
> Chinese and machine made. They're actually made by machines!

There are a number of things about this story that I find striking. The
first is Naoko's view of the value of this statue as stemming not from any
innate or mimetic spiritual power, but rather from its manufacture (hand-
made) and its origins (Japan). In addition, the people who do not appreciate

29. In questioning Naoko's insistence that she is not religious I am in no way implying
that I have some insight into her experience that she herself lacks. Rather, as I shall argue
below, I believe she was simply responding to what she perceives as a Western view of religion
that is quite at odds with her own.

the statue are missing its meticulous construction and attention to detail, not its religious significance. During our conversation I remember being excited at the potential fissures this story opened up between her position, reinforced through numerous retellings to journalists and Inoue, as someone who joined Annon for independence rather than for religious reasons. Going over the interview again later, however, it was not clear whether her purchase of the statue and daily prayers before it actually countered or supported her claim that she was not religious.

The disjuncture between Naoko's insistence that she was not religious and the fact that she bought and regularly prayed before a Buddhist statue in order to protect her daughter speaks to a common theme in the study of Japanese religions. Despite the fact that the majority of Japanese describe themselves as not religious (無宗教 mushūkyō), one still finds them visiting temples and shrines, purchasing votive amulets, and praying before family altars.[30] They often act, in a word, religious. This supposed contradiction cuts to the heart of this project and to any work that purports to explain some element of Japanese religion in the modern and contemporary periods. As scholars have shown, the use of shūkyō 宗教 to denote the term "religion" was a late nineteenth-century development necessitated by the renewed contact between Japan and the West after two and a half centuries of near isolation (Shimazono 2001). The lingering connection, in the minds of most Japanese, between the term shūkyō and a largely Western notion of religion as exclusive and monotheistic continues to plague the study of Japanese religions. Scholars have thus suggested models of religion in the Japanese context as "participatory" and/or "contextual."[31] More recently, Ian Reader and George Tanabe have focused attention on prayers for benefits in this world (現世利益 genze riyaku), what they have termed being "practically religious," as a useful rubric for approaching Japanese religious life and the bridge that connects Buddhist doctrine to popular practices. The authors illustrate the ways that Japanese religions focus on action over belief and how prayers that seem aimed only at material benefits actually index "spiritual states, including peace of mind and salvation" (Reader and Tanabe 1998, 16). It is within the context of these types of Japan-specific interpretations of religion that we must attempt to understand Naoko's participation in prayers for the healthy delivery of her daughter's baby.

30. For a survey of Japanese religiosity, see Swyngedouw 1993.

31. See, for example, Reader 1991, 15–22; and the debate between Reader 1991b and Anderson 1991 in the *Japanese Journal of Religious Studies*, December 1991.

The expression Naoko repeatedly returned to in our conversation was the right to decide (決定権 *ketteiken*). From taking a second seat to her brothers while growing up, to having to ask her mother-in-law what should be in the miso soup, to being able to work outside the home, Naoko's telling of her life story traces a growing desire to take control of her own life. This belief informs everything from how she chooses to be buried to whether or not her daughter should take her husband's name:

> When she married I told her to discuss the name with him. I said, "You two should discuss it—it's not the law that you take his name." She tried to talk to him, but he rolled his eyes and said, "Why are you asking me that?" Because he thinks it's only natural that she take his name. It's fine if they discuss it and agree, but for one party just to decide how it should be—that's not right. To just take the leadership, the power, the rights, that can't happen. That's why for me, buying a grave was a move against that kind of thinking. This was the clearest, easiest to understand, most concrete expression of my will (of my response to this kind of thinking) to my husband, to my children, and to others. This was easy to understand, a concrete action—not just saying it should be like this and that with words only, not ideas and principles, but doing it with actions, in a way all could understand. Inoue told me that she wanted to write about me in her book, and I said, "Go right ahead, write whatever you want." I wonder if I'm just strange? But Inoue told me that there are others. And my friends say, "Wow, that's great, your own grave. I want to do that, too." But even though lots of people may think this way, no one around me is actually doing it. Even at Annon I doubt that there are many people like me. Isn't it mostly couples without kids and single women?

As anthropologist Michael Jackson has so eloquently argued, just as all human societies have developed notions of that which is beyond human control—from destiny to the weather—so too have humans always struggled to "countermand and transform these forces by dint of their imagination and will so that, in every society, it is possible to outline a domain of action and understanding in which people expect to be able to grasp, manipulate, and master their own fate" (Jackson 1998, 19). Viewed in relation to this insight, Naoko's thoughts (and actions) regarding the statue and her impending posthumous divorce at the Annon gravesite are not contradictory impulses but rather contiguous. They are both elements of Naoko's desire to manifest control over those things that she cannot.

Though clearly about independence from her husband, Naoko's purchase of an Annon grave plot was also about trying to exert control over what happens to her after death—about controlling where and with whom she ends up. By emphasizing the posthumous divorce narrative, Inoue and journalists are able to bring to light the profound implications of eternal memorial graves for issues of gender, normative social roles, and self-determination. My concern, however, is that by placing Naoko's decisions primarily in the context of independence from her husband, we may be missing what her story tells us about less tangible attempts at autonomy. In the same way that her purchase of the statue was in part an attempt to control the myriad factors that could go wrong during the birth of her grandchild, is there not also an aspect of her joining Annon that relates to controlling her postmortem fate?

In an article on the category of death in Buddhism, Jacqueline Stone focuses on the issue of control as a way to understand the appeal of Buddhist positions at both the official and local levels. Buddhism's offer of mastery over death manifests doctrinally in the escape from *samsara* (the cycle of rebirth), and ritually through meditation or transfer of merit. According to Stone, "This promise of control over that most mysterious and terrifying realm—death—has been a chief source of Buddhism's attraction as a lived religion, and the perceived possession of such control has been one of its major sources of legitimation" (Stone 2005, 57). Naoko's story, then, encompasses several different elements of control that must be considered. This is not simply a contrast between her assertion of financial independence from her husband and a less empirically verifiable effort to ensure a healthy birth. Rather, we should consider these different attempts at control along a continuum and then ask how they inform each other and our understanding of Buddhism in contemporary Japan. Though the aspect of Buddhism with which I am dealing—new burial practices—intersects with the aforementioned forms of control noted by Stone, most obviously in the promise of continued memorial services for the deceased, there are also practical, psychological, economic, and legal issues of control to consider. In the same way that Naoko's apparent fetishization of the material aspect of the Buddhist statue complicates a strictly "religious" interpretation of its purchase, so too does the very idea that daily prayers before the statue would physically protect her grandchild trouble a strictly this-worldly reading of her posthumous divorce.[32]

---

32. Lest I be accused of a strictly functional reading of Naoko's story, I would like to clarify that this is not my intent. I am looking for a way to approach material efficacy in Bud-

In taking the statue as more than an icon of religious faith, I am trying to open some space for a religious interpretation of Naoko's desire for
postmortem autonomy. I am not conflating Naoko's independence from
her husband and her prayers for her granddaughter. Rather, I see the attempts at control over different dimensions of her life that are revealed in
her purchase of both the Annon grave and the Buddhist statue as speaking
to a concept of religion that does not allow a clear distinction between
those elements one might consider strictly religious (e.g., prayer, ritual, or
soteriology) and those that have traditionally fallen under the purview of
economists and social scientists.

Tome's Story—A Different Sort of Separation

This next narrative is helpful for thinking beyond posthumous divorce to
a different yet related form of agency, that of postmortem revenge. Tome,
who was born in 1925 in rural Niigata, not far from Myōkōji, is the youngest of six children. As she told me, her given name, literally translated,
means "Stop," as in "stop having more babies." When she was two, her
mother died and she was sent off to Tokyo to live with an uncle who had
no children of his own. Though she was close with her uncle, her aunt
treated her terribly. Tome had a suitor in Tokyo when she was young, but
he was killed in the war and she never married.

Her aunt's younger brother died without children years ago, and it was
left to Tome to find him a grave. He was initially placed in a municipal
grave in Tokyo, but later she found out about Annon on the radio and eventually bought a space there for him. When her adoptive parents both died,
she also got a space for them in a municipal grave in Tokyo, where she
was living at the time. In 2000, Tome brought her parents' remains to Annon. At that time she had the remains of her aunt's brother moved into
the communal spot in the center of the Annon grave and had the grave
redone with a new stone. This was ostensibly to clear space for her adoptive parents, but when she moved them in, rather than interring them as
a couple, she placed her aunt's remains directly into the communal grave
space, or, as she calls it, the "*muen* spot," and her uncle by himself into
the newly redone Annon grave. When she first told me this story, she explained that she had to move her aunt's brother because he was not a part

---

dhism that treats it neither as a degeneration of the teachings nor as somehow distinct from
faith.

of her uncle's family and therefore could not be placed in the same grave.[33]
As for why her adoptive mother (her aunt) was put directly into the *"muen
spot"* rather than in the grave with her husband, Tome said this would be
better since then her aunt's brother would no longer be alone—he could be
with his sister. At the time, this explanation struck me as somewhat un-
usual, but I did not pursue it. In a later conversation, however, I made sure
we came back to this point, and it was then that she admitted (with some
relish) that putting her aunt directly into the *"muen* spot" was less about
her concern for the brother than it was about revenge for years of bad treatment. In Tome's own words, "I was finally able to put her in her place!"

Though this story speaks of a different kind of postmortem separation
and agency than Naoko's case, it does point, in a similar way, to the use of
these new graves as a way to reject established behavioral norms, specifically in these two narratives—the ideal of obedient daughters and wives.
Tome's story also indicates a similarly multivalent attempt at control. Although unable to stand up to her aunt or have peaceful time alone with her
uncle while either one of them was alive, she is now able to arrange things
to her own satisfaction. Tome is very pleased that after she dies, she will
be able to enter the grave at Annon with her adoptive father, whom she
cares for very deeply and for whom she had the grave stone redone to read
"beauty and heart" (美と心 *bi to kokoro*).

> When you're going "over there," you need to purify your heart. That
> was the feeling I was trying to get at. When you have bad feelings there
> is no beauty, so I was saying, "let's always carry an untainted heart."
> Since it's only for one generation, they let you put whatever you want
> on the stone. And well, my face isn't very beautiful, so I want at least
> to have a beautiful heart!

Since Tome has no relatives who will look after the grave once she dies,
the plot will automatically revert to the temple after thirteen years, and
she and her adoptive father will be placed into the group ossuary in the
center of the grave. Tome is pleased with this arrangement and is not at all
troubled by ending up *muen* on her own terms: "After ten years or so I will
be moved in with the other anonymous dead (無縁仏様 *muenbotoke sama*)
and that's totally fine."

---

33. This speaks to the traditional view of family graves as supporting single-line, patrilineal descent.

It is fascinating to compare the way that Tome speaks of the fate of her own remains as opposed to those of her aunt. First of all, the temple does not refer to the shared ossuary in the center of the Annon graves as "*muen*," since this expression still carries a strong connotation of abandonment in Japanese. Indeed, the temple makes a careful distinction between where its members finally end up and the dreaded abandoned grave (無縁墓 *muenbo*) or monument for the abandoned dead (無縁塔 *muentō*). Instead, it is referred to as "The Central Ossuary" (中央納骨室 *Chūō nōkotsu shitsu*), or, in the case of Mori no Annon, "The General Grave" (総廟 *Sōbyō*). When Tome originally told me of putting her aunt's brother and then her aunt in with the "anonymous dead," there was, in her description and rush to explain, an implicit understanding that this was something out of the ordinary. The irregularity of putting her aunt directly into the ossuary, rather than with her husband, struck me as particularly acute since they had shared a grave in Tokyo until that point. I was also surprised that Tome seemed not to consider the inevitability of her own eventual arrival in the same spot as her aunt.

In fact, this question comes up with all Annon members as well as those of other eternal memorial graves, who will all eventually end up in some shared, anonymous space. The difference between eternal memorial graves and communal ossuaries for abandoned graves, though, is that, while anonymous, those in graves like Annon will still receive regular memorial prayers from the temple and other members. More important, they know how and when it will happen, so that it becomes a choice with positive associations, rather than a frightful and indeterminate fate. Clearly for Tome, this distinction marked the essential difference between her own future and that of her aunt. In addition to controlling what happens to her aunt, Tome is also able to determine for herself when and how she gives up her individuality and joins the anonymous dead. It is this control of when one becomes *muen* that is so crucial to the success of the eternal memorial graves.

The anxiety over one's own death manifests as an anxiety over where one's remains will end up and who will come to offer memorial rites. By arranging ahead of time where, *precisely*, one will be buried (e.g., space 32, section *myō* 妙 of Annon 4), what will be written on the stone, what one's posthumous name will be, and how many years one will be in that space before being shifted to a more nebulous status in the group ossuary, one is exerting control over certain elements of death (see fig. 8).

One is extending, past the line of death, one's intent and will, one's identity. This is the element of agency that the posthumous divorce cat-

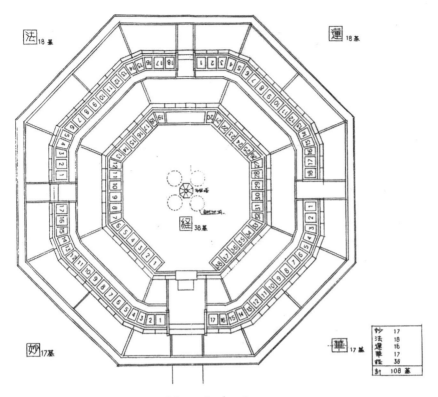

Fig. 8. Schematic of an Annon grave

egory misses when it focuses only on the exertion of control in this life. Buying a spot in an eternal memorial grave is also very much about controlling death.

One of the most frequent comments I received from interviewees— often as an aside after they had told me their wishes for the care of their remains after they die—is that in the end you will be dead so there is no real way you can know or control what will happen. If that is how they actually feel, though, why bother? How are we to interpret this type of statement? Is this disavowal, much like the not uncommon insistence that buying a spot in an eternal memorial grave has nothing to do with religion, a reaction to the scholar, uttered in an attempt to prove the speaker is acting rationally and not out of superstition? Or, is it rather an identification of the very anxiety they are trying to confront in the purchase of these graves? Is it, in a word, religious?

The Endōs—Finding Buddhism

I would like to now turn to a narrative by Annon members who are more explicitly and consciously looking not only for a burial site but also for a deeper understanding of Buddhism.

The Endōs are a wealthy Tokyo couple in their sixties. He is a former engineer who consults for technology firms, and she used to do volunteer work reading books to the blind but is no longer working. They have one son who is married but whom they do not expect to have any children. Although Mr. Endō is the eldest of five siblings, his younger brother is taking over the family grave because he has grandchildren. This explains in part why they had been looking for some time for a grave that does not require descendants. In fact, Mrs. Endō had even started a scrapbook of articles and advertisements relating to potential burial sites for the two of them. Though they did not visit too many sites, they did do a tour of the forest burial site in Iwate prefecture and also researched municipal communal graves in Tokyo.[34] In the former case, Mrs. Endō felt that the system at the forest grave lacked any spirituality (精神性 seishinsei), and in the latter, Mr. Endō thought that the municipal grave was nothing more than a "garbage dump for bones." When I asked them if they had considered scattering, they replied that, while they were not against it per se, they did not feel it was right for them. They decided that they wanted something in between the traditional family grave and simply discarding the remains. Mr. Endō, in particular, was concerned with having some kind of marker or monument and a place where a priest would perform memorial services. It was also essential that they find a spot that would not burden their son. They read about Annon in a national newspaper in 2001 and traveled to Myōkōji the very next day. After meeting Ogawa they decided almost immediately to take a spot in the Mori no Annon grave. For Mrs. Endō, it was the environment and the architecture of the temple that moved her; for Mr. Endō, it was the contrast between Ogawa and the priests at his own home temple. The current abbot of the Shingon temple that houses Mr. Endō's family grave is the fourth in succession whom Mr. Endō has known and is apparently no different from any of his predecessors in his sole focus on funerary Buddhism and his complete inability to offer meaningful sermons. Ogawa, on the other hand, is seen by Mr. Endō as someone who not only thinks deeply about things but also compels others to do so.

34. For a discussion of the forest burial site, see chapter 5.

Much of my conversations with the Endōs involved a series of contrasts, often involving a comparison between Japan and other countries:

> Mr. Endō: Today, Japanese Buddhism is just funerary Buddhism. It's something for when people die or for memorial services, but I think this is wrong. I think religion is something that is really important when we are alive. For example, I don't know about America right now, but last year when we visited Romania, we went to Easter celebrations at midnight and saw young people there praying and doing confession. This was really great, not like Japanese funerary Buddhism at all.

Mrs. Endō added that she thought it was just so wonderful that these people had a religion like this. Her husband agreed, but then noted, "We went as tourists, right? And when these people were praying, we just marched on in there. I thought this was quite rude. I really felt resistance to this." She countered that it is a question of what is in your heart, and that, if you go in there with the right feeling, it is fine. Mr. Endō concurred, "If you go in there with the right awareness, it's okay. If you go in stomping about, it's just tourism."

The intersection of tourism and religion came up at another point in that conversation when they recounted a visit they had made to Varanasi, India. Along with a group of other tourists, they went out on the Ganges River as the sun came up to take in the incredible explosion of activity and color that takes place on the riverbank every morning. Mrs. Endō recounted the experience in the following way:

> Just watching it all, I was embarrassed. I don't care if it's just a tour. It's troubling. If you were just walking along behind all the people performing their morning ablutions and observing, that would be fine. But for sightseers to ride on a boat in between the morning sun and those people—I'm not really the type that is easily embarrassed, but riding on the boat that day, I was.

There is, in these contrasts and in the Endōs' feelings of embarrassment, an intriguing possibility for thinking about the question of religious authenticity. With their upper-middle-class wealth and the frequency and breadth of their travel abroad, the Endōs cannot be taken as an "average" Japanese couple, and yet in their desire to develop a deeper understanding of Buddhism, to achieve the same level of faith that they perceive in religious adherents in other countries, they represent a significant, if small,

group of burial society members. These are members who are joining Annon not simply because of the scenic location or the open policy but also
because they are looking to find something genuine and they think that
Ogawa is the real thing. In Mrs. Endō's words before taking part in an
overnight training session at the temple, "I am not doing this so that my
funeral will be at Myōkōji. I am doing it for myself now. I want to believe
in Abbot Ogawa's religious awakening."

The Endōs took part in the first training session in March 2005, and
it was during this practice that Mr. Endō had what he called an extraordinary experience (非日常的体験 hinichijōteki taiken) while chanting the
daimoku at the famous cave behind Myōkōji. He insisted that he could
not explain it with words, but he said that he had not been so moved since
the first time he entered Eiheiji 永平寺, the famous head temple of the
Sōtō sect of Japanese Zen.[35] He also admitted that initially he felt a strong
resistance (抵抗 teikō) to chanting the daimoku because as a child he had
lived near a Tenrikyō 天理教 church and had had to listen to chanting every morning growing up.[36] Unlike his previous experiences abroad, where
his negative images of Japanese religious practices were formed in contrast
to the "genuine" expressions of religion he was seeing as a tourist, this
time his previously negative view of the daimoku came into contrast with
his own authentic experience of chanting. Although his wife did not have
the same kind of transformative experience, she was deeply moved by the
training. Both say they are committed to participating in the next level of
training. They are also sure that at some point they are going to take part
in a Buddhist initiation ceremony (授戒式 jukaishiki) in order to receive
Buddhist ordination names while still alive.[37]

Ogawa's Narrative—Contemporary Temple Buddhism

To this point I have discussed how the Annon grave offers new choices
for members. It is now necessary to consider how it, as well as other similar eternal memorial graves, represents new possibilities for temples. The
Endōs, in particular, represent a new type of temple membership that is
distinct from that of traditional danka. To further flesh out the potential

---

35. The Sōtō sect has two head temples: Eiheiji in Fukui prefecture and Sōjiji 總持寺 in
Yokohama.

36. Tenrikyō is a Shinto-based new religion. Regular services, involving music, chanting,
and hand dancing (手踊り teodori), are carried out at small churches (教会 kyōkai) in people's
homes across the country.

37. Taking Buddhist names will be discussed in the following chapter.

for change that new graves like Annon offer to temples, I would like to include one final narrative: that of Ogawa's views on contemporary Japanese temple Buddhism.

Ogawa's telling of the modern history of Japanese Buddhism starts, as do so many narratives concerning the so-called malaise of modern Buddhism, with the beginning of the parishioner system in the Tokugawa period. Although the formalization and solidification of relations between temples and their parishioners at that time became the cornerstone for the growth of institutional Buddhism into the modern period, that growth was not without cost. As noted earlier, for many commentators and Buddhists alike, the Tokugawa period marked the spiritual death of Japanese Buddhism as temples became tools of state control.

Ogawa's story then jumps directly to the land reform of the postwar period. He is convinced that this policy most directly affected temples, particularly rural ones, because it led, in large part, to a shift in temple income from being supplemented by offerings (*fuse*) for memorial and funerary services, to being almost entirely dependent on them. According to Ogawa, this switch to a *fuse*-based economy led to both a formalization and commercialization of temple donation and simultaneously meant that temple income was far less consistent. Since there was no way to accurately predict how many funerals would be performed in a given year, priests had no way of knowing what their income would be from month to month. The reliance on variable income from funerary services for *danka* started becoming a real liability with the massive urbanization that began in the 1960s. Ogawa's work on temples and depopulation at the Nichiren Contemporary Religion Research Center clearly informs the way he views postwar Japanese Buddhist history, but he also sees a deeper problem below the demographic shifts:

> The idea that depopulation is destroying temples only scratches the surface. At the spiritual and substantive level, the real cause is that people were no longer allowed any freedom with graves and ancestor worship. And this is why it is not just a matter of depopulation because the same thing is happening to temples in cities. If you want proof, look at the people from those depopulated areas who are going to the cities. When they get to the city, they are not joining a temple in the same sect as their home temple, they are joining New Religions.[38]

38. Ogawa could not cite a specific survey, but offered as proof the fact that despite massive urbanization, temple membership in cities was not increasing.

You may then wonder how city temples are surviving—it is not with income from parishioners, but from real estate agents.[39] And when the [economic] bubble burst, both of these types of income disappeared. Temples need a new system, but this is not easy to establish.

No matter how much Ogawa may believe in the need for a new type of relationship between temples and the general populace, he acknowledges that it is extremely difficult to change the way people think: "I can't just turn around and say, 'Okay, let's forget all this ancestor worship stuff; from now on please gather at temples for a new reason!'" He maintains that while the shift is occurring there needs to be a way to support the temple and a way to get it through the dangerous period of transition. Ogawa frequently evokes an analogy of Annon as a bridge from the traditional obligations of the parishioner system to a new type of temple relationship based on individual choice. On the practical side as well, Annon generates the funds necessary to weather this transition; the grave thus acts as both bridge and safety net. The question then becomes: What is this new type of temple relationship that Ogawa envisions? He insists that this new Buddhism is "not new at all" but rather a reworking of the best elements of traditional Buddhism. When I pressed him on what these elements were, he suggested something between the parishioner system and what came before. His ideal elements include a temple that is not dependent solely on donations, but also one that is not in a coercive relationship with its members.

Despite the fact that the *danka* system has provided the main support for Myōkōji for several centuries, Ogawa opposes it because of its dependence on an outmoded ideal of the extended family (*ie*). He hopes that temple membership will become more fluid, but fears that the family grave, which binds people to a single temple, will continue to impede any real change. In his view, graves should be based on individual choice and membership. People should be allowed to change temples freely and choose the place where they would like to be laid to rest. If their children choose to be elsewhere, that should be fine. Evident here is Ogawa's conviction that temple priests have no one to help them except themselves. He insists that if temples were no longer able to count on a captive parishioner base, they would be forced to improve and compete. He is aware of the parallels with

39. This is a reference to the large number of temples that were selling or renting out part of their landholdings during the economic bubble of the late 1980s in order to build parking lots or rental properties.

market principles but believes that there are far too many temples in Japan already. Taking the Nichiren sect as an example, if, as his research group concluded, only three thousand of the roughly five thousand temples currently counted as belonging to the Nichiren sect are actually worth saving, this would have startling implications for the nearly seventy-six thousand Buddhist temples across the country (Bunkachō 2008, 36). Interestingly, one of the clearest expressions of Ogawa's view on temple Buddhism came in a discussion we had about the current state of Japanese farming:

> Japanese agriculture is extremely important, but Japanese farmers are really spoiled by the government and thus are not making the appropriate effort. I don't necessarily think that market principles are a good thing, but with even a little competition, farmers will work harder and the average citizen will endorse protecting them. If they get government subsidies without making any effort, the populace will not accept it. Today's farmers have forgotten what it is to struggle. Who is going to take over from the current generation of farmers? Since they feel there is no future for Japanese farming, in the end it is the son who doesn't care one way or the other, the one without any drive, who takes over. And as Japanese agriculture gets steadily worse, the quality of the food we eat declines. That's why it is said that Japanese farms will be no good in the future. But there are in fact children of regular salarymen who want to become farmers. There are lots of people who are very worried about the current state of Japanese food. The thing is that there is no way for them to get into the farming world. That's why you need some kind of middleman.

Of all our discussions, I think these comments provided the clearest statement of Ogawa's thoughts on, and condemnation of, Japanese Buddhism today. Though temples, unlike farms, do not receive government subsidies, they do enjoy tax benefits and are thus seen by the public as receiving some kind of special status from the government. Yet temple priests, free from competition, have forgotten what it is like to struggle and can no longer provide the necessary sustenance to their parishioners. Furthermore, successive generations of priests, aware that their profession is in decline, lose the drive to make positive changes. Ogawa's thoughts explain, I think, the rather surprising decisions he made regarding the future of Myōkōji.

Ogawa's farm analogy included the need for someone to mediate between the farm/temple and the general public. In the case of Myōkōji, Ogawa's middleman was Sakaguchi Yasuhiko 坂口靖彦, a Keiō University graduate with experience in venture capital and corporate headhunting. Sakaguchi signed a three-year contract with Myōkōji in early 2005 to run the temple office, train an office manager, and find someone to succeed Ogawa as abbot. Having secular office staff at a temple is not particularly rare, but Sakaguchi's training and background gave him a viewpoint on temple management that was quite different from Ogawa's. In our conversations, Sakaguchi naturally spoke of business models and brands, as well as his frustrations with how the temple "product" is unlike any other. As he explained to me more than once, though graves and memorial services are something that everyone wants, they cannot be marketed and advertised like other products.[40]

By hiring Sakaguchi to help him find a successor, Ogawa made clear his belief that the current crisis in Buddhist circles over temple succession is not simply a demographic or hereditary problem, but rather a result of priests today having given up. His decision to run an open search for his own successor was in no small part due to his low opinion of the current generation of priests. As noted, Ogawa has no son to take over the temple when he dies. His assistant priest, Kamata, has no intention of becoming the next abbot, and none of his daughters, all in college now, wants to be a temple wife, let alone bring in a priest through an arranged marriage. While Ogawa says that he would not be opposed, in theory, to passing Myōkōji on to a Nichiren priest from another temple, he is doubtful that someone of any caliber would agree to take over a rural temple. Most priests, he insists, are hungry for a spot in the big city, which leaves bringing in a lay person, and it is here that the story gets interesting. A year after hiring him, Ogawa had Sakaguchi run an open invitation for applicants in media outlets throughout the country. These advertisements included Buddhist publications, but were primarily disseminated in newspapers and recruitment magazines. The plan was to choose three candidates from all the applicants. The chosen three, who could include women or foreigners, would be brought in to live and train at the temple for up to three years. At the end of that time, one person would be chosen to take

---

40. One measure of how far Myōkōji has succeeded in developing a new model for temples is its inclusion (the first time for a temple) in the business magazine, *Bing*, published by Recruit, one of the top business publishers in Japan. In a special section titled, "Cutting-edge enterprises of the business world—What's the next move?," Myōkōji was included along with profiles of the fastest growing broadband provider in Japan, a securities company, and an internet startup. The temple profile focused on the success of the Annon grave system in meeting contemporary needs as well as Ogawa's bold policy of making all temple finances open to the public (*Bing*, September 8, 18–19).

over Myōkōji. When I told Ogawa about the popularity of Donald Trump's reality television program, *The Apprentice*, he became excited, but he was quick to point out that "[his] methods would be a little different." Ogawa's main condition was that the person he brought in would have extensive experience in the real world, particularly in business. He assured me that life experience was far more important to him than religious background or Nichiren affiliation. Indeed, his plan was to train someone for three years at Myōkōji before he or she would be allowed to go through "official" training with the sect. The search produced some viable applicants, but it proved ultimately unsuccessful. Though he was able to train two candidates, one for three years, Ogawa felt that the young men simply did not have the qualities necessary to take over Myōkōji.[41] Since that time, Ogawa has taken on a young priest from a Nichiren temple in Kyūshū who looks very likely to succeed him.

When I asked Ogawa directly what it means to be a temple priest he told me that the answer depends on who is asking. For someone who knows something about priestly life, Ogawa would admit that he is still looking for the answer, but he asserted that he could never give such a response to someone who is still lost. For such people he must be a source of support and not doubt. When I pressed him on what job he thinks is closest to that of a temple priest, he answered, after some thought, that it must be high school principals: "They are managers. They have to consider the management of the school, they have to have connections outside of the school, and they have to be strong leaders. They also have to understand education. Of course it's not education, but religion that is being passed on in temples. So the focus of what we are doing is different, but the position is the same as a high school principal."

EPILOGUE: ONE DAY AT MYŌKŌJI

To better contextualize this chapter's themes within the quotidian rhythms of life at Myōkōji, we will now turn to a brief description of a day I spent at the temple in the summer of 2005.

Mornings at Myōkōji start before 7:00 a.m., when Ogawa's wife, Nagisa, is up preparing breakfast. Ogawa's assistant, Kamata, arrives after 7:00 a.m. and opens up the main hall where he and Ogawa perform the morning services around 7:40 a.m. On this day, however, Nagisa was down with a cold,

41. One of the young men has decided to continue his Nichiren training elsewhere with the hope of eventually taking over another temple.

and Ogawa was barely able to walk after spending the previous two days
hiking up Hakusan mountain with a group of friends and colleagues who
visit religious sites once a year. Ogawa decided to spend the morning in
bed, leaving the morning services to Kamata and the office to Sakaguchi.

Unfortunately, there are certain tasks that have to be handled by the head
priest. On this day it was an elderly parishioner who arrived at 10:00 a.m.
with a bag of fresh corn and an important question about his family grave.
The gentleman, who was in his eighties and whose wife had recently
passed away, was concerned because he had no children to take over his
grave after his death, and he wanted to know whether it would be acceptable for him to hire a lawyer to be a guardian over the grave. Myōkōji rules
prohibit ownership of parishioner graves to be held by anyone who is not a
parishioner, so Ogawa refused this request and instead suggested that the
man buy a spot in Annon and transfer all the remains there.[42] The man rejected this idea, saying that he liked his grave and did not want to be buried with a bunch of strangers. Although they both decided to think some
more on the matter, Ogawa later told me he could only see two possible
outcomes in this, not uncommon, situation: either the man would enter
Annon, or he would work out an arrangement whereby a certain amount
of money would be paid in advance for the temple to maintain the grave
for a set period of time. The problem with the latter choice, aside from
setting what Ogawa saw as an open-ended, and therefore dangerous, prec-
edent, was the question of deciding how many years and at what cost. It
would also place undue burden on the temple in the future, since succeeding abbots would have to continue attending to the graves probably long
after the initial payments had been spent.

Ogawa went back to bed but was again woken up by a phone call from a
female parishioner with mental problems, saying she was going to die and
asking him to come right over. Ogawa, who is long used to such calls from
the woman, sent Kamata in his place.

Meanwhile, Sakaguchi was busy with two tour groups that showed up
at the temple unannounced. The second group, consisting of about ten elderly people, poked around the Main Hall and Abbots' Hall as though they
were in a local curiosity shop, even flipping through Ogawa's sutra books
at the altar. Later, Sakaguchi and I watched them nervously as they tried

42. Myōkōji rules also state that a grave that is abandoned for three years reverts to the
temple. The remains are placed in the communal ossuary. Until recently this was a separate
grave, but Ogawa now plans to put all remains into the shared ossuary in the center of the
Annon graves.

to peek into the private spaces in the back. They then spent a long time commenting on the sliding screens in the visitors' hall. One asked if he could smoke inside, and two more asked for *shūin* 集印 (also 朱印 *shuin*), a small, paper amulet imprinted with the *daimoku* and the seal of the temple in red that visitors purchase to commemorate their visit. Sakaguchi, who had anticipated a rush of requests and had me help him hastily prepare six of them, was clearly chagrined.

A short time later, a woman in her early fifties came up to the reception window and asked about the Annon graves. She had read about them in the paper and was worried that there were none left. Sakaguchi assured her that there were still plenty of spots left in the Annon Forest, but she made it clear that she wanted a spot in the "big one." She then asked if the temple would take reservations for a grave. She explained that she wanted an Annon plot but first had to pay off her car loan. She was worried that by the time she would be able to pay for Annon, there would be no spots left. Sakaguchi told her about the available payment plan and provided her with an information packet. When I asked why he did not call Ogawa to speak with her, he noted that she would be back when she was ready. As he put it, "We are not trying to sell something here. They are not customers in that sense, who need to be fawned over and pitched to. When they are ready to buy the grave, then they can speak with Ogawa. When he speaks to them, they almost always decide to enter Annon."

Things quieted down in the afternoon, and Ogawa worked in the back office catching up on all the office work that had piled up in the two days he was away. Before dinner we assembled a giant candleholder that was going to be placed in the pond by the three-story pagoda for the upcoming Annon festival. With only a month to go, preparations for the one-day event and the anticipated five hundred visitors were in high gear. The candle stand, made by a parishioner who works at a local steel factory, had to be positioned in the middle of the pond. With Ogawa unable to walk, it was left to Sakaguchi and the visiting researcher to strip down to our underwear, wade into the water, and set it up so that everyone could see how it looked. These preparations were taken care of just in time, as a young man from the light company showed up with a new type of halogen balloon light that would be used to illuminate the area in front of the main hall where the party was to take place. After a discussion of generator capacity and what to do when the breakers inevitably failed, we all headed in for dinner. It was past 8:00 p.m., and the rest of the family had already eaten, but Nagisa's mother, who had come in to take care of the family while her daughter was sick, made sure we were met with a feast of fresh vegetables, pork cutlets, and tempura. We decided to start without Ogawa, who was negotiating the rental price with the person from the light company. It turned out that the young man had some family issues he wanted to discuss with the abbot. We later learned that the man's family situation was complicated by divorce and remarriage and that he was interested in buying a spot in Annon. After speaking with him for more than an hour, Ogawa finally joined us, and we ate, drank, and talked about the logistics of the festival until past midnight.

CONCLUSION

Ogawa's creation of Annon in response to the demographic and social changes in postwar Japan afforded people an alternative to the restrictions of traditional temple graves. Now anyone could join, regardless of whether they were parishioners, had children, or were married. Beyond offering people like Naoko and Tome a suitable burial spot, the Annon grave also furnished them with an arena in which to confront long-standing social norms. Intriguingly, their stories demonstrate that, while for many this could be accomplished by creating new types of bonds between people outside one's traditional cohort, for some, it was done by cutting off connections with those inside it.

In addition to the insight the narratives of these two women provide into the societal changes occurring in contemporary Japan, there is also something to be learned here about the complex ways in which graves connect with, for lack of better terms, the religious and the secular. Indeed, the Annon grave at Myōkōji offers exciting possibilities for the study of religion precisely because it forces us to question frameworks that would presume to separate economic factors from religious concerns, faith from practicality, or religious consumption from other forms of consumerism.

The Endōs' story illustrates how eternal memorial graves like Annon may also offer important possibilities for temples. Although the overall percentage of Annon members who join with the idea of gaining deeper religious insight may be small, they are still significant. By offering an alternative to multigenerational, temple parishioner membership, the Annon grave opens up the temple in a way that the *danka* system never could. Whether eternal memorial graves of this kind will radically transform temple Buddhism is impossible to say now. What is evident, however, is that in the activities of this rural Nichiren temple, we are witnessing a highly provocative and successful response to the obstacles facing contemporary temples.

The factors that have shaped Ogawa's view of the current state of Japanese Buddhism also encourage scholars to reconsider the conceptual frameworks we use to examine Buddhist practices and institutions. I have suggested elsewhere that we need a category of analysis that takes into account the different kinds of Buddhism that occur even within a single sect (Rowe 2004, 383–86). Ogawa's history, both before and after becoming the head priest of Myōkōji, demonstrates the myriad forms that Nichiren Buddhism might take. Doctrinal differences between the major sects are far less determinative of temple identity than the regions in which temples are located, the degree of urbanization or depopulation that has occurred, and the individual views (not necessarily religious) of the person running the temple. To speak of "Ogawa's Buddhism" is to speak of a focus on the local temple as a center of religious activity and as a locus of community. This community must not be one bound by mutual obligation, forced onto children, but must be based on choice and flexibility. It should be joined not simply out of need for graves but from a willingness to participate. Ogawa's is a practical view of Buddhism and temple management, one that is quick to move outside the Buddhist world to incorporate the expertise of sociologists, lawyers, business managers, activists, and artists. It is a view that includes a nostalgia for an idealized past, but with an awareness of the dangers and limits of the coercive and finite nature of the existing parishioner system. Ogawa's view of Buddhism also carries a conviction, born of conflicts with other priests, *danka*, and his own family, that in order to change people's ideas of things—be they graves or temple Buddhism itself—one must move beyond mere words and change the structure of those things. And because of this conviction, his view contains an inner conflict that arises out of the belief that the very mechanism of Buddhism's success in Japan, the extended, multigenerational family, has now become its greatest liability.

CHAPTER FOUR

Limitless Connections—Tōchōji

To have no bonds (無縁 *muen*) does not mean loneliness, but rather that
one can connect to people without any limits.
—Tōchōji Pamphlet

In this chapter we turn from rural Niigata to downtown Tokyo and arguably the most successful eternal memorial grave in Japan. Tōchōji was
already considered quite prosperous when it first created its eternal memorial grave and burial society, En no Kai 縁の会, in 1996. With some seven
hundred parishioner families (檀家 *danka*) supporting it, Tōchōji was doing considerably better than the Sōtō Zen sect's national average of less
than one hundred fifty *danka* per temple.[1] Within eight years, however,
En no Kai was approaching six thousand new members, and by 2008 it
had sold out all of its ten thousand spots. Needless to say, such staggering
numbers would have been impossible with traditional graves, particularly
in central Tokyo, where any land, let alone that designated for graves, is
at a premium. Looking down on the Tōchōji precincts from a neighboring
skyscraper, there is no indication that this temple will potentially host
over ten thousand dead. The temple is surrounded on all sides by busy
streets, high-rise apartments, and graveyards. Indeed, after selling the land
that held part of its own graveyard to raise the money needed to rebuild
the temple in 1989, Tōchōji could only accommodate the displaced parish-

Portions of this chapter appeared as "Where the Action Is: Sites of Contemporary Sōtō
Buddhism," *Japanese Journal of Religious Studies* 31, no. 2 (2004):357–88.
  1. The sectwide survey conducted in 1995 found an average of 146 *danka* households per
temple nationwide (Sōtōshū Shūmuchō 1998, 149–57). Tokyo and Osaka priests whom I interviewed from all sects consistently cited 250–300 as the number of households needed to support a temple in a big city.

ioner graves by moving them to an indoor space in the basement, three floors below the new main hall.

Located on three-quarters of an acre (900 坪 *tsubo*) near the heart of Shinjuku, Tōchōji is hardly representative of the nearly fifteen thousand Sōtō Zen temples spread across Japan.[2] Established early in the Tokugawa period (1600–1868) and last rebuilt in 1989, this wealthy urban temple displays a fascinating mixture of traditional and modern imagery. The large main hall is sparsely decorated and is constructed of concrete and cypress, not yet stained by decades of incense smoke. The central image of a 160 cm, plain, unfinished wooden carving of Śākyamuni is attended by the Bodhisattvas of Wisdom, Mañjuśrī (文殊 *Monju*), and of Practice and Meditation, Samantabhadra (普賢 *Fugen*). Less than half the wooden floor is covered with tatami mats, and the walls are lined with one hundred twenty small stools—a concession to the comfort of elderly visitors and a clear indication of the large number of people who attend the monthly memorial and other services.

Throughout the precincts one is struck by a series of juxtapositions not often encountered in Japanese Buddhist temples. The bell tower by the front gate houses one of the temple's two elevators. The immaculate modern French toilets, which can compete with those of a luxury hotel, are guarded over by a statue of Ususama Myōō 烏枢沙摩明王, one of the bright kings who purifies defilements.[3] The temple also contains a small, elegant coffee shop in the basement under the main gate (山門 *sanmon*) with a piano, art exhibits, and regular music performances. Throughout the temple buildings one also finds modern and abstract ceramics left over from the days when the room underneath the main hall was taken up by P3, a well-known Tokyo pottery gallery that hosted regular exhibits and events until 1996.

There are several reasons why I chose this temple as a research site. Though clearly not an "average" Sōtō Zen temple, Tōchōji is highly influential both within and without the Sōtō sect. The temple abbot, Takizawa Kazuo 瀧澤和夫, was a high-ranking priest within the Sōtō sect hierarchy

2. The Sōtō sectwide survey of 2005 was sent out to 14,637 temples nationwide (Sōtōshū Shūmuchō 2008, 10).

3. The sign outside the toilet identifies it as a traditional monastic *tōsu* 東司. Tōchōji pamphlets emphasize the temple's adherence to the seven structure (七堂伽藍 *shichidō garan*) layout of Zen monasteries in China during the Song period (960–1279). Visitors are told that the toilet, or *tōsu*, is one of these seven structures, that it must be located in the eastern part of the precincts, and that it houses the deity Ususama Myōō, who holds the power to purify. We are also informed that, along with the monks' hall (僧堂 *sōdō*) and the bath house (浴室 *yokushitsu*), the *tōsu* is one of the three areas of silent practice in a monastery. These rules are not enforced at Tōchōji.

who had created, at least in terms of membership, the most successful eternal memorial grave in the country. Tōchōji thus represents both the Sōtō establishment and the cutting edge of approaches to the burial problem. It affords a view of Buddhism that is attempting to negotiate normative doctrinal positions with the social, economic, and emotional realities of trying to secure grave space in contemporary Japan. In its mingling of business and Buddhism, Tōchōji encourages scholars to rethink approaches to religious affiliation in Japan that would attempt to distinguish the commercial from the spiritual. Finally, like the Annon grave at Myōkōji, the success of Tōchōji's En no Kai burial society derives from radical adaptations of the temple/parishioner relationship.

In the previous chapter I outlined the different ways in which people see the Annon grave as a potential alternative to various traditions, and I argued for eternal memorial graves as a place to challenge such societal norms as dutiful wives (Naoko), dutiful daughters (Tome), and dutiful parishioners (the Endōs). This chapter will take up similar themes, but here I would like to focus more specifically on Tōchōji's emphasis on bonds (縁 *en*). From the regular communal and ritual events, to the image in temple literature of *en* spreading out across the world like ripples on the surface of a pond, to the very name of the burial society itself, the eternal memorial grave at Tōchōji is allowing people to rethink what bonds, or lack of such, might mean. Beyond the social implications, the attempt by Tōchōji to recast the sphere and potential of *en* clearly demonstrates how fundamental bonds, as opposed to nonattachment, are to temple Buddhism.

THE EN NO KAI BURIAL SOCIETY

As with other eternal memorial graves, Tōchōji's new grave is open to anyone, regardless of nationality, sectarian affiliation, or whether one has descendants.[4] Rather than becoming a temple parishioner, applicants become members (会員 *kaiin*) of what I call "burial societies," groups of people who either already have friends or relatives in the eternal memorial graves, or who have reserved a spot for themselves. En no Kai members pay

---

4. There are a small number of first- and second-generation Koreans and Chinese in En no Kai. Since identifying one's nationality is not part of the contract, however, it is impossible to accurately determine the number of members who are not Japanese. Judging from the increasing percentage of temple-run eternal memorial graves that include clauses about nationality in their advertising, this is a growing market. Tōchōji's head abbot, Takizawa, insists that Tōchōji was the first site to include the idea of nondiscrimination and feels that this has been a significant factor in En no Kai's success.

a one-time fee of eight hundred thousand yen, or roughly one-fifth the cost of a regular grave. Unlike traditional grave costs, this price includes the interment ceremony, yearly memorial rites, and space for one's cremated remains for up to thirty-three years, the length of time for which individuals are traditionally memorialized before becoming anonymous ancestors. At the end of this period, the remains are moved to a communal ossuary in the two-story pagoda (多宝塔 *tahōtō*) near the main gate.

Like many other eternal memorial graves, Tōchōji's new site bears little outward resemblance to traditional extended-family graves. Entering the front gate of the temple, a visitor encounters a large reflecting pond that stretches all the way to the main hall (fig. 9). This water garden (水の苑 *mizu no niwa*) contains forty-two "islands" each made up of eighty-one granite grave markers. The tops of these stones are inscribed with the living name (俗名 *zokumyō*) of the departed and have a small space inside to place some favorite item of the deceased.[5] The significance of the pond is emphasized by the fact that one cannot approach the main hall directly, but must walk around the water on either side. The site is extremely striking visually in the way that it reflects the main hall, and it is even more impressive on the first evening of every month, when a memorial service for En no Kai members is held and the one hundred or more attendees float small votive candles in the water during the memorial service of ten thousand lights (万灯供養 *mantō kuyō*). Temple literature emphasizes the physical, spiritual, and propagative elements of the site: "Constructed as a forecourt to the main hall, the *mizu no niwa* contains earth (stone), fire, wind, and space, and represents the teachings of Śākyamuni and the bonds (*en*) of the members spreading out across the world like a ripple in water."

In place of a spot in the water garden, members can choose to have a stone in the moss garden (苔庭の苑 *taitei no niwa*). Located to the side of the main gate beside the bell tower, the garden holds the same stone islands, but these are interspersed with thick green moss rather than water. A third possibility is to have one's name engraved on a small, ten-centimeter-square, gold-lacquer plaque located on the walls along the side of the water garden. These walls are lined with brightly colored, lacquered pictures depicting a Chinese artist's interpretation of the intersection of Buddhism and modernity. One double panel shows the Bodhisattva Kan-

5. This practice resonates with the custom of placing some of the deceased's favorite possessions into the coffin before cremation. In the case of Tōchōji, however, these items are not cremated along with the body and thus, one could argue, do not accompany the deceased to the other world.

Fig. 9. Tōchōji's water garden

non sitting in contemplation near lotus blossoms with what appears to be a mushroom cloud blooming in the background. On the accompanying panel the lotus blossoms continue, along with a self-immolating priest in full conflagration and an all-too-familiar Tokyo scene of a busy subway station, presumably Shinjuku, with station attendants straining to cram passengers into a packed rush-hour train. In many ways, the images epitomize the eclectic blend of urban, traditional, modern, and Chinese influences that make up Tōchōji.

No matter which of the these three memorial spots a member chooses, the actual remains and memorial tablet (位牌 *ihai*) reside two floors below the main hall in the Hall of Arhats (羅漢堂 Rakandō; fig. 10). The Rakandō is a large, open room with three of the four walls taken up by sixteen-tiered, red-lacquered shelves holding the small gold memorial tablets of members. One does not really have a sense of what ten thousand members actually means until one encounters the overwhelming number of tablets, lined up side by side and stretching the length of the room on three sides.[6] The

6. Once the shelves filled completely, an additional room down the hall had to be converted to hold the overflow.

Fig. 10. The Rakandō

urns (骨壺 *kotsu tsubo*) of the individual members are stored out of sight beneath the shelves. At one end of the room, evoking the traditional Buddhist altar (仏壇 *butsudan*) that one still finds in many Japanese homes, stands a six-sided altar. A painting of Śākyamuni, his two bodhisattva attendants, and the sixteen arhats adorns the inside.[7] In front of the altar stands a small shelf with a single memorial tablet that reads, "The site of the spirits of departed En no Kai members" (縁の会物故者諸精霊位 *En no kai bukkosha shoseireii*). At the behest of the temple, those who come to visit friends and family are asked first to offer incense before the main altar for the benefit of those deceased who may not have any other visitors. The Rakandō, secluded below the main hall, offers members a more private space to pray for the dead, while also providing a sense of community, if not family, for those mourners who come before the society's group altar. Members know that even after they are gone, people will continue to offer incense, flowers, prayers, and thoughts for them. As must be the case with all graves, memorial offerings are carried out by others. Unlike the

7. Arhat, often glossed as "Buddhist saint," is a Sanskrit term referring to someone who has attained enlightenment. For more details on arhats, see Bond 2004 and Joo 2007.

traditional grave, which relies on relatives, however, the eternal memorial graves at Myōkōji and Tōchōji enable a different set of relationships to take part in the memorial cycle.

En no Kai literature describes its dual-grave system in the following way:

> The first site is the "*En* Stones" (縁の碑 *En no ishibumi*) in the water garden. These memorial monuments to the lives of the members offer a place to pray for the well-being of their spirits. The other site is the ossuary for the remains of the departed and is meant as a quiet resting place. Here in the Hall of Arhats, one prays to the images of Śākyamuni, his two attendants, and the sixteen arhats. All members are provided with these two graves.

The En no Kai grave system thus offers an intriguing take on the double-burial system discussed in ethnographic studies of Japanese burial practices. In certain areas of Japan, graves are divided into two sites: a burial grave (埋墓 *umebaka*) that contains the actual remains and is to be avoided and a worshiping grave (詣墓 *mairibaka*) that is visited and where memorial services are held.[8] Conversely, Tōchōji's grave system, though dual, is not premised on a pure/impure distinction but rather on one of rest (眠る墓 *nemurubaka*) and remembrance (追憶の墓 *tsuioku no haka*).

In addition to the avoidance of death impurity, mortuary ritual in Japan traditionally includes processes to protect all those involved from malevolent spirits, while ensuring the pacification of the spirit.[9] Again, there are no such references in Tōchōji literature, which instead contrasts the bright and public space of memory of the deceased in the pond with the quiet repose of the transformed remains below the main hall in the presence of the Buddha and his attendants.

The question of memory and memorializing here is informative not only for the possible shift it indicates in conceptions of death impurity but also for what it reflects about Japanese responses to the dead. For exam-

8. For an English summary of the debates over the origins of the double-grave system, see Smith 1974, 75–78; and Suzuki 2000, 33–35. For an overview in Japanese, see Haga 1996, 151–55.

9. Evidence of fear of angry spirits includes rural practices of binding the corpse, but also arming it with a ceremonial knife (Aoki 1996); Buddhist rites at the deathbed and posthumous ordination (Williams 2008, 210–19); and folk customs that continue today, such as returning home from the crematorium via a different route.

ple, Japanese-English dictionaries regularly translate the term *irei* 慰霊 as "memorial," as in "memorial service" (慰霊祭 *ireisai*) or "memorial tower" (慰霊塔 *ireitō*),[10] but in Japanese dictionaries the word maintains the distinctiveness (and caution) of its two components: "to soothe or comfort" (慰める *nagusameru*) the "spirit" (霊 *rei*) of the deceased. In English, the emphasis is on the living (memory), while the Japanese term is attentive to the potential agency of dead spirits. Tōchōji literature, in contrast, centers on a more passive and positive view of the deceased. It is important to note the use in the pamphlet of the term peace (安寧 *annei*) in regards to the stones in the water garden, whereas enshrine (安置 *anchi*) is used to refer to the memorial tablets (位牌 *ihai*) in the Hall of the Arhats. Although the latter is traditionally used in references to the remains and spirit of the deceased, the former refers to peace or well-being on either a personal or societal level. It appears, then, that the division Tōchōji simultaneously makes and bridges may also be characterized as one existing between a traditional idea of memorializing—the *ihai* and remains kept in their secluded place alongside the Buddha and his attendants—and a contemporary representation of memory—the stones in the gardens, inscribed with the living names of the deceased and holding, in suspended animation, objects of recollection.

The dual grave system at Tōchōji also parallels the multilocality of ancestors more generally. The apparent contradiction of praying to ancestors before the family altar at home while also visiting them at graves and inviting them home from the other world (あの世 *ano yo*) for summer *o-bon* お盆 festivities, has long puzzled anthropologists, but, in fact, rarely seems to trouble their informants.[11] Within En no Kai, as well, the two main sites evoke a variety of reactions. Although the pamphlet informs us that the water garden is the site for family and friends to visit the deceased (and I have often encountered members praying there), one En no Kai staff member assured me that the pond was "just for show." For others, however, it may depend on whether there is anything of the deceased placed inside the stone. One member, whose mother is interred at Tōchōji, told me that since there was no memorial item inside the stone that she had no feeling toward it. She then confided that she had been talked out of putting in her mother's glasses by an elderly acquaintance, who assured her that, "in the next world you don't need glasses, or a cane, or anything."

10. For example, see Kenkyūsha 1974, 549.
11. See, for example, Smith 1974, 66–67.

BONDS AND PRECEPTS

In addition to refiguring how members deal with memory and memorialization, Tōchōji also offers a space for new forms of social relations. As noted in chapter 2, societal bonds in Japan are most commonly based either on blood relations (血縁 *ketsuen*) or regional ties (地縁 *chien*). Significantly, in the name of Tōchōji's burial society, En no Kai, or "Society of En," the term *en*, or "bonds," is offered without any modifier. As temple literature and En no Kai members both attest, the group is striving to break free of traditional bonds to allow people to choose where and with whom they will be interred. This transformation requires a new concept of social relations, based on friendship and choice, which can alleviate fears of dying without someone to tend one's grave—of becoming one of the disconnected, wandering, anonymous dead (無縁仏 *muenbotoke* that were discussed in chapter 2. The pamphlet for Tōchōji's En no Kai explains:

> The members of En no Kai create bonds that transcend those of blood and region, and pray for each other's souls. To have no bonds (*muen*) does not mean loneliness, but rather that one can connect to people without any limits. As this temple moves into the future, we will pray for the souls of all those resting here.

This positive refiguring of dying without connections, traditionally seen as a lonely and frightening possibility, represents a fundamental linchpin in the success of En no Kai. Without this sense of community and the concomitant promise of continuity, the temple's eternal memorial grave would be nowhere near as successful. This "death by association" also represents a radical change in the conception of social relations and reveals, in ways statistics on increased numbers of nuclear households cannot, how far removed many urban Japanese now are from the ideals of the extended household.

In addition to helping members create new connections with each other, En no Kai membership is also premised on helping them create new bonds with the temple and Buddhism more generally. Within two or three months of joining, members are expected to take part in the "First-of-the-Month Service" (一日法要 *tsuitachi hōyō*), an all-day event designed to provide the participants with a medley of traditional monastic experiences culminating in their acceptance of Buddhist precepts. On the first day of every month, roughly thirty to forty new members arrive at noon and are asked to put on priestly work clothes (作務衣 *samue*) and a name tag.

The group is divided in half, and the rest of the afternoon is spent taking turns wiping down the main hall, sitting *zazen* 坐禅 meditation, copying out (写経 *shakyō*) the *Heart Sūtra*, and attending memorial services in the main hall. The events are tailored to the elderly members and are thus not overly taxing—the work (作務 *samu*) of cleaning the hall lasts about ten minutes while the *zazen* session is only fifteen, with several members doing their sitting in chairs. Though it might be easy to discount this brief "tasting" of monastic routines, here presented as ideals, all the members I interviewed spoke positively about the day and felt that it had drawn them closer to each other and to the temple. The priest who designed the program at Tōchōji pointed out that the average Japanese has an image of life at Zen temples as being very severe and thus would not be satisfied unless they had at least done some *zazen* under the watchful eyes of a stick-wielding (警策 *kyōsaku*) monk.

On March 1, 2004, at 4:00 p.m., all the new members who had spent the day at the temple, along with a few, who, for physical reasons, could not participate in the day's events, gathered in the main hall for the precept conferral ceremony (授戒式 *jukaishiki*), a one-hour adaptation based on the traditional seven-day ceremony (授戒会 *jukaie*). This ritual is considered the most important for En no Kai members and is the point where Sōtō propagation (教化 *kyōka*) is most evident.

Before the actual ceremony began, there was a dry run during which the attendees were told what would occur, what they had to do, and the significance of each act. Members received a yellow piece of paper called the record of repentance (懺悔帳 *sangechō*), which advised them to "write down mistakes, second thoughts, or disagreeable events from your past. Taking the precepts is the point when you reflect on your past and, as a disciple of the Buddha (佛の御子 *hotoke no miko*), take the first step of a new life."[12] In large print below there is a passage in Chinese (漢文 *kanbun*) that reads "I take refuge in the buddhas of the ten directions and transfer merit to the great saint Śākyamuni Tathāgata. May the winds and rain be favorable, the people be at ease, and the ten stages of the bodhisattva be instantly transcended, [accomplishing enlightenment] without difficulty."[13] Members were asked to write as many regrets or misdeeds as they liked

---

12. Note the similarity between this phrasing and the discussions of becoming a Buddha (成仏 *jōbutsu*) in chapter 6.

13. 南無帰依十方佛、回向大聖釈迦如来、風調雨順民安楽、十地頓超無難事. These phrases were pieced together from different Chinese Buddhist texts by the assistant abbot, Okamoto Wakō 岡本和幸. He told me he was doubtful that more than a handful of En no Kai members would understand the meaning and that he was sure none would doubt its authenticity.

on the paper, which would be burned during the *jukaishiki*. When the young priest explained this to the participants, he took pains to contrast the Buddhist *"sange"* 懺悔 with the Christian *"zange"* (both written using the same characters). Although the Christian version was interpreted as an apology (謝りayamari), the Buddhist repentance was said to focus on self-reflection (反省 hansei). To help the participants during the ceremony, large posters displaying key texts for the ritual were hung on the front wall beside the altar.[14] Included among these was the Repentance Verse (懺悔文 sangemon), which reads: "All my past and harmful karma, born from beginningless greed, hate, and delusion, through body, speech, and mind, I now fully avow."[15]

After offering incense before the main altar, the members then received their *wagesa* 輪袈裟 (a sort of abbreviated cloth robe that is worn around the neck), took refuge in the three treasures of the Buddha, the Dharma, and the Sangha, and then promised to uphold the three ideals of a bodhisattva (三聚浄戒 sanju jōkai) and to observe the ten grave precepts (十重戒 jūjūkai).[16] After each prohibition was named, those in attendance all responded, "I will uphold it well" (よく保つ yoku tamotsu). During the explanation for the ceremony, the priest informed the participants that there were more prohibitions in India, but in Japan only ten were recognized. Another important distinction was that, while in India the prohibition was against any drinking of alcohol, in Japan, it simply warns against drinking too much. This is a good thing, he confided, because he too is fond of a cold beer now and then.

After swearing to uphold the prohibitions, the new disciples circled around the front again to receive the small card that held their posthumous name and connected them in a direct line of descent through the head priest back to the historical Buddha (血脈 kechimyaku). A priest then sang the names (唱名 shōmyō) of the ten buddhas and bodhisattvas, to which, after the recitation of each name, all gathered responded with "I

14. I was told these were put up to mimic the atmosphere of Chinese temples. It was also clear from the constant sideways glances that they provide helpful guidance to those participating in the ceremony.

15. This passage is taken directly from chapter two of the *Shushōgi* 修証義, a compilation of sayings from Dōgen's 道元 writings compiled in the Meiji period by lay Buddhist Ōuchi Seiran 大内青巒. The *Shushōgi* is the core text of modern Sōtō sect liturgy. I will return to this text in chapter 6.

16. The three sets of ideal precepts are as follows: keeping all precepts, practicing all virtuous deeds, and granting mercy to all sentient beings. The ten grave precepts prohibit killing, stealing, sexual excess, lying, selling liquor, various types of slander, and anger. For details, see Mochizuki 1954–1963, vol. 3, 2218–21.

take refuge in the buddhas of the past, present, and future" (南無三世諸佛 *namu sanze shobutsu*).[17] The priest explains *namu* 南無 to the group as an extremely polite form of address that means something similar to the honorific Japanese term *sama* 様, used after someone's name.

Next, the head priest Takizawa set all the repentance registers on fire in a metal pot and mounted the main altar, which had been cleared for the event. The members passed before him in turn as he tapped them lightly on the head with a small brush that had been dipped in water and first touched to his own forehead. This was explained to the group either as grateful water (有り難い水 *arigatai mizu*) or wisdom water (智恵の水 *chie no mizu*) and was meant to signify the bond between the members and the head priest, as well as to indicate that they were all equal.[18] After all the members had been anointed, they mounted the platform in three groups of about thirteen people. The eight junior priests and Takizawa then performed nine full prostrations before the new, rather nervous-looking disciples. Finally, the members took the four bodhisattva vows, which were also written out at the front of the hall.[19] The ceremony ended with all the priests circling the room ringing bells and chanting. The group of initiates then moved downstairs, where they shared an evening monastic meal (薬石 *yakuseki*) and asked the junior priest to explain their Buddhist ordination names.

It is difficult to determine exactly how the new members perceive the *jukai* ceremony. Although a cynical reading of the ceremony might see it as just so much smoke and vows, the finale, when the new members stand atop the dais with the priests and other members bowing before them, is an undeniably powerful moment that none of them have ever experienced in a temple before. To stand atop the main altar in front of a hall full of people while nine or more priests are prostrating themselves before you is not an average temple experience in Japan. In fact, I would wager that very few Japanese have ever conceived of, let alone experienced, such an event (see fig. 11).[20] It is also vital to note here that for almost all lay Japanese, including the *danka* of Tōchōji, the Buddhist ordination name

17. *Namu* is often seen in liturgical formulas and means "to pay homage to" or "to submit oneself to."

18. This ceremony also brings to mind esoteric consecration rites (skt. *abhiṣeka*).

19. The vows can be translated as follows: "Sentient beings are innumerable, I vow to enlighten them. Delusions are inexhaustible, I vow to eradicate them. The dharmas are limitless, I vow to master them. The Buddha way is unsurpassed, I vow to attain it."

20. A typical Buddhist ceremony is much more likely to involve briefly offering incense before the central image while priests chant sutras.

Fig. 11. The precept ceremony at Tōchōji

(戒名 *kaimyō*) and precepts are given posthumously.[21] For laity to take the precepts while alive is extremely rare, even when performed in a short-ened ceremony such as that offered by Tōchōji.

THE BUSINESS OF RELIGION

The En no Kai counter in the downstairs lobby of the temple provides a recognizable and approachable access point for guests. There are five regu-lar staff members who interact with En no Kai members, potential mem-bers, and temple priests. None of the staff is a priest, however, and all work for Annex, the business consulting company that manages En no Kai in partnership with Tōchōji. Despite the fact that the rebuilding of the tem-ple in 1989 was accomplished without any additional monetary support from parishioners, money was still needed to maintain the temple. These

21. According to one of the priests at Tōchōji, since the beginning of En no Kai, roughly one parishioner a year has decided to take the precepts while alive.

funds could have been raised by selling more temple land or erecting more buildings to generate rental income, but according to one of the En no Kai staff, Takizawa wanted to make the money through religious activities (宗教活動 shūkyō katsudō).[22] It was at this point that he met the president of Annex, who, along with his staff, came up with the idea for En no Kai. Annex had already been involved in joint ventures with temples, building a large Buddhist statue in Ibaragi prefecture, for example, and thus was willing to go beyond planning stages to actually selling membership in the new grave. The initial arrangement was for Annex simply to sell the graves and then dissolve the partnership, but as the Annex staff members became more involved in the lives of their En no Kai "clients," it became harder for them to leave.

When potential members inquire at the temple about joining En no Kai, it is one of the Annex staff who outlines the process, takes them on a tour of the grounds, and will later become their liaison with the group and the temple. Each of the En no Kai staffers is in charge of anywhere from five hundred to fifteen hundred members. They dress in regular clothes but do not volunteer the fact that they are employed by an outside company. Though one senior staffer always wears Buddhist work clothes while at the temple, I did not initially think that he would ever be mistaken for a priest. However, during one interview with a couple that had joined En no Kai together, I was barely able to hide my surprise when they referred to the staffer who had signed them up as a priest. Other conversations with members indicated that this assumption was not uncommon.

Staff members explained to me that their role at the temple was to deal with the office work and consultation, while the priests took care of the religious rites. However, this distinction is not always so clear in practice, as is demonstrated by the staff members' role in helping new members choose their posthumous names. With roughly forty people joining every month, I was told that the head priest is unable to meet with all the new members personally. The job of helping new members choose their posthumous names and explaining their significance then falls to the En no Kai staff. Teshima Jirō 手島二郎, a young staff member, admitted to me that when he discusses the kaimyō with new members he does not really understand the religious meaning and simply explains the process as a way to reflect on one's life. He feels that, through their job of talk-

22. It is worth noting here the tax status of temple income generated from religious versus nonreligious activities. The former are not taxable. On temples and taxes, see, for example, Nakajima 2005, 137–56.

ing to new members about their lives, the staff operate as new counselors (新しいカウンセラー *atarashii kaunserā*). He also added that, at thirty-five, he was just the right age to be a son to most of the members, who are in their sixties. Other, older staff members are closer to the age of the average member and are thus able to interact as equals. He pointed out that in both cases Annex staff reached a level of intimacy with the members of En no Kai that the priests of the temple could not attain. Teshima also felt that the staff members, with a wide variety of real-life experiences among them, were better able to interact well with people of different backgrounds and to speak before crowds.[23] Intriguingly, though, he told me that his experiences at Tōchōji have led him seriously to consider taking the tonsure.

This, then, is the paradox that En no Kai and Tōchōji pose, both to scholars of religion and to other Buddhist temples, for it is at this point that the business interests of En no Kai and the role sought by many Buddhist temples as centers of emotional and spiritual support coincide so successfully. Regardless of how one interprets the role of a business company co-operating a large-scale enterprise on temple grounds, the effects of this particular partnership clearly benefit both the temple and its new members. In speaking to several female members who have had their spouses interred at Tōchōji, what most struck me about their stories was the glowing terms in which they speak of how the various En no Kai staff members took care of all the funeral and burial arrangements for their respective husbands. The women often related how, with one phone call, everything was arranged for them. While this may not seem particularly striking, it is in fact quite rare, particularly in urban areas, for people to call a Buddhist temple first when there is a death in the family. As noted in chapter 1, there has been a conspicuous shift from temples to professional funeral companies (葬儀社 *sōgisha*) in the shouldering of mortuary rites since the 1960s. It was therefore surprising to hear of a metropolitan temple being called to make all the mortuary arrangements, and my initial reaction after hearing this was one of cynicism. "Evidently," I thought, "Tōchōji has simply bypassed the middle man and added the role of the funeral company to its long list of services." In fact, I was later able to confirm with the head priest Takizawa that this was precisely one of the factors that he had considered when creating the burial society.

23. Teshima's assessment of the younger generation of priests is validated in part by recent studies by Sōtō sect researchers on the training and education of priests (Sōtōshū Sōgō Kenkyū Sentā 2008, 335–62).

Takizawa once complained to me that because of their complete control over the funerary industry, the funeral companies treated priests as mere chess pieces (駒 *koma*). He confided that part of his goal in starting En no Kai was to reclaim some of the social and practical authority of mortuary services. Unfortunately, in Takizawa's view, this has meant that En no Kai has come to look much like a funeral company. By having the En no Kai staff coordinate all aspects of burial and, for most members, funerals as well, they appear almost indistinguishable from the *sōgisha*.

For Takizawa, the extreme (or perhaps merely most pedestrian) example of this commodification of services was demonstrated when people began asking if they could make donations (布施 *fuse*) to the temple through bank transfer (振り込み *furikomi*). Although this is a very common form of payment in Japan, it is usually reserved for paying gas and cable bills and not making offerings to temples. The requests initially came when En no Kai members, paying their entry fees by bank transfer, then asked if it might be acceptable to make other payments in the same way. Though he has not banned the practice, Takizawa is concerned that allowing offerings, which for him are a fundamental element of Buddhism, to be electronically automated will set the tone for all future interaction with the temple.

Like nearly every Japanese priest with whom I have ever spoken, Takizawa laments the perceived loss of local community life, within which priests were part of the social fabric and were consulted on a wide variety of subjects. So while his ideal situation would allow Tōchōji priests to speak directly to members about costs, how to run the funeral, and what everyone should eat after the service, Takizawa admits that with such a large organization this would give the impression that they only cared about profit—something that came up several times in our conversations and something that he wants to avoid at all costs. For Takizawa, then, one of the primary functions of the En no Kai staff is to act as a "cushion" between the priests and the financial dimensions of funeral arrangements.

Takizawa also likes to speak of the En no Kai community as part of the Buddhist community (*sangha*) with the members and staff taking the role of committed lay followers of the Buddha (優婆塞 *ubasoku*; skt. *upāsaka*).[24] He explained his expectations for his staff in the following way:

I am not talking about following specific sects like Nichiren or Jōdo. I mean as a follower of Buddhism, as people who live a life based on

---

24. This term applies only to males. Female followers are called *ubai* 優婆夷 (skt. *upāsikā*).

the Buddha, they must be believers (仏教徒じゃなきゃだめ *Bukkyōto ja nakya dame*). Otherwise it is just business. I don't tell them to become priests. I tell them that they have to become a member of the *sangha* who supports the broad teachings of Buddhism.

As an example, he points to the fact that all members of the staff have taken the En no Kai version of the precepts, described above. Takizawa is fully aware that these staff members are in many ways the public face of the temple: "Putting aside whether what I say is right or wrong, the way to transmit the principles of this temple, the course of this temple, to the members is through the office staff. In a word, they are the atmosphere of the temple. That's why I think they are so important."

One metaphor for conceptualizing the place of the En no Kai staff within the temple that came to my mind several months into my research was of a computer operating system that provides an interface between the confusing and often indecipherable code which makes the computer run, and the casual user who needs access. The staff provides a middle ground within the temple precincts, between Buddhist rituals and teachings that most Japanese know little about and a public that is still very much dependent on their performance. Furthermore, they are able to speak the language of customer service, but years of intimate conversations with members about life and death have also turned them into more than just salespeople. As Takizawa himself noted, the staff also provide a space within the temple to articulate the language of the consumer—a language that Buddhist priests are often unable or unwilling to speak.

BETTER LIVING THROUGH GRAVES

Marketing constitutes another key facet of temple activity that lies firmly within the purview of the Annex staff. Tōchōji's eye-catching advertisements have run in national papers since the start of the new burial society and are a key component in the success of the temple's eternal memorial grave. In addition to striking graphics, the simple and sometimes controversial ad copy suggests numerous insights into the perceived target audience. These ads register and, one could argue, reinforce changing perceptions of family, gender roles, and traditional burial.

In February 1997, not long after En no Kai first opened, the following advertisement ran in the Tokyo section of the *Asahi* newspaper. Running a full third of a page, it included large, bold fonts and an abstract, black and white sketch of water rippling out from one of the stones in the temple's water garden.

> For a life of effort, choosing your own personal grave now is just the
> thing.
> As for how others will view it,
> I would respond that I arranged my own personal grave as testimony to
> a life well lived.
> This isn't at all strange.
> If you think about it, I've lived a life that's just right.
> So I want the perfect grave—where I can be alone.
> It's as simple as that.
> But really, that's how I've always enjoyed doing things.

Many of Tōchōji's advertisements carry similar messages about choosing one's own grave while still alive. They are never couched in terms of Buddhist soteriological benefits but are presented rather as a lifestyle choice. Although such statements clearly represent an attempt to tap into an emerging national trend toward individualism (attributed by its critics to Western influence), this advertisement also contains a gendered aspect that must be considered. Though lost in translation, the language in the original Japanese copy has some feminine speech markers. The "but" in the final line, for example, is *"datte"* in Japanese, which would not normally be used by a man. Furthermore, the first line, addressing how such an act would be viewed by society, speaks to social pressures on a woman both to marry and to enter her husband's graves. Although this copy, along with all of those for En no Kai, was written by the only full-time female member of the Annex staff, this one in particular is clearly aimed at a target audience of single, divorced, or widowed women. The phrasing matched almost exactly that of several women whom I interviewed at Tōchōji. They all spoke of how they had lived a life of their own choosing and therefore wanted to decide for themselves where and how they would spend the next life as well. For many of them, the idea that they might end up in an anonymous ossuary or, even worse, in their ex-husbands' family graves was a real concern. Although the advertisement does not specifically target them, there is another small group of married women who, like Naoko at Annon, are joining such burial societies so as to avoid having to enter their husbands' family graves.

Advertisements with main lines like "Can't those of us without children have a grave?" are not surprising given the initial impulse for eternal memorial graves as a response to the growing number of Japanese without male descendants to maintain the family line. But, as mentioned previously, new technologies always carry unexpected consequences. For example, the following advertisement speaks to one of the most significant ways in which people have adapted new burial possibilities to their own needs: "I was looking for a grave for myself that wouldn't be a burden on anyone." This ad represents a trend that surprised Tōchōji's staff in that a majority of those couples who join the temple actually have children (and sons, specifically) but do not want to burden them with the chore of maintaining a family grave. According to En no Kai staff, roughly 60 percent of all members have children. Furthermore, an internal survey showed that the number-one reason for seeking out an eternal memorial grave was to "avoid burdening family members" (58 percent), whereas only 17 percent were choosing such a grave because they had no descendants to care for a traditional grave.[25] Moreover, while the En no Kai staff actively promotes the advantages of a grave that does not burden descendants, Takizawa and other Sōtō Zen priests who help out at Tōchōji continue to voice concerns about what they perceive as the loss of traditional family values. The first time I took part in one of the yearly discussion meetings (法座 hōza) at Tōchōji, it quickly became apparent that nearly everyone present had joined En no Kai in order not to burden his or her children with a traditional grave.[26] This revelation came as quite a surprise to me since, to that point, I had been working under the impression that most Japanese were entering eternal memorial graves precisely because they had no children (or at least no sons). It turned out that this phenomenon of protecting one's children from the burden of a family grave had also produced a strong response from the priest, an abbot from another Sōtō temple in Tokyo who often helped out at Tōchōji. He told the group that before the advent of funeral companies, it was a lot of trouble to organize and carry out a funeral; therefore, people appreciated the importance and gravity of death. As the funeral and care of the dead have become easier, however, the importance of death has become "lighter" and every successive generation of young people hold life in lower regard. He therefore urged all the mem-

25. Conversation with En no Kai staff, July 2004.
26. An important event for integrating En no Kai members into the Tōchōji community is the yearly hōza. The ninety-minute gatherings of up to twenty people are taken up primarily by self-introductions that turn into long narratives about how each person came to join the group. Outside of the jukai services and yearly temple trips, the hōza provides the longest and most intimate space available for members to meet and share their reasons for joining.

bers to fight this trend by consciously choosing to trouble their children (迷惑をかけて *meiwaku o kakete*) and cause them worry (心配をさせるべき *shinpai o saseru beki*) so as to teach them the significance of life and death.[27] Although the priest's lecture was meant to urge a return to a simple era of "spare the rod" parenting and thus was pitched to appeal to the older members present, it also seemed to contradict the primary reason that most choose En no Kai.[28] And while Confucian ideals of filial piety have long influenced mortuary practice in Japan, the popularity of eternal memorial graves among those trying not to burden their children has led some commentators to speak of a growing social trend toward descendant worship (子孫崇拝 *shison sūhai*) (personal communication, August 2004).

Another example of how En no Kai membership has signaled a changing vision of the traditional family came in 1999, when the temple ran the following advertisement in the *Asahi* newspaper: "My wife and I don't really want to be buried in the ancestral grave way out in the sticks." This copy caused a flood of complaints to the headquarters of the Sōtō sect about the betrayal of fundamental Japanese family values, which was here symbolized by the rural family grave that most urban families are expected to visit during the summer festival of the dead. Perhaps not surprisingly, it also generated the biggest surge in new En no Kai members at Tōchōji since the site had opened. As Takizawa admitted:

> When that ad came out I got really angry with the staff, but they said that since it produced the highest response rate of anything so far, they had no choice but to keep running it. They told me, "If we don't do this, we won't sell spots. This ad will sell spots." So they used it a lot. You can check with the staff, but I think we used this ad the longest. But this is advertising—the toxic ads are the most popular, the dangerous ones produce the biggest response. And of course, by response, I mean both good and bad. We received a postcard accusing us of making light of that person's ancestors and telling us that "this was not Buddhism and that this was not what a temple was supposed to do."

Although the temple got a call from Sōtō headquarters complaining about the advertisement, Takizawa maintains that the sect was merely respond-

---

27. These expressions represent the polar opposite of what most Japanese would hope for in regards to their children.

28. Takizawa told me on more than one occasion that he views this desire not to burden children as selfish and haughty.

ing to numerous complaints from the laity. They only got involved, he told me, because there was outside pressure.

PARISHIONER REACTION

Of the range of effects on a temple brought about by the influx of new burial society members, the most difficult to investigate was the reaction of temple parishioners. Most priests who offer eternal memorial graves, Ogawa and Takizawa included, will insist that the *danka* fully support the burial system and the influx of new faces to the temple. Any dissent is placed in the distant past. The most common response I got to these queries was always along the lines of: "There were some complaints at the beginning, but once they understood what was going on, everyone supported it." Television specials, news reports, and temple-produced, promotional videos always include at least one temple parishioner assuring viewers how happy all the *danka* are with their new friends. Unfortunately, gaining direct access to *danka* without going through the temple abbot or office staff is often next to impossible, and so one is unlikely to find a parishioner introduced by the temple who is willing to openly criticize the temple's activities. This is not to say that there is a widespread secretive opposition to eternal memorial graves by temple *danka*. However, when one considers the rapid influx of all these new people, not to mention the fact that En no Kai members gain the same advantages immediately that many *danka* members may feel to be their privilege, which was gained from supporting the temple for generations, there is bound to be a certain level of resentment.

One very public display of *danka* displeasure came in the form of a highly caustic letter sent to Takizawa that was then published in its entirety in the temple's newsletter.[29] Written by "A single *danka*," the short letter is at times bitingly sarcastic, and, judging from the use of katakana

29. En no Kai members and parishioners are kept up-to-date on temple happenings through *Banki* 萬亀, a glossy, forty-page quarterly magazine. In addition to a message from Takizawa and regular contributions from members about the meaning of En no Kai, the magazine also includes information on the Dharma Talk and Vegetarian Meal Club, the monthly Buddhist Culture lecture, the *zazen* club, the origami and flower arranging circles, the chorus, and the yearly trips, both local and abroad, sponsored by the temple. *Banki* also features regular articles by priests, scholars, and En no Kai staff on a wide variety of subjects ranging from the *Shushōgi* to Alzheimer's disease. The letter from the parishioner was carried in the March 1997 edition of the newsletter.

and older character forms, written by an elderly male, who likely came of age before World War II. While the letter cannot be taken as representative of all parishioner opinion on En no Kai, it does point to a specific type of concern that I encountered in casual conversations with *danka* both at Tōchōji and at other temples that run eternal memorial graves. Furthermore, Takizawa's detailed response, published alongside the letter, offers crucial insights into how he wants to represent En no Kai to his *danka*, which is at times different from how he wants to present it to the media, potential En no Kai members, and meddlesome scholars. At one point in his reply, for example, Takizawa refers to a *Yomiuri Shinbun* 読売新聞 article from the previous year in which he was quoted as saying that the lack of objections from his *danka* made him question whether they supported En no Kai or simply did not care ("Obōsan ganbaru," *Yomiuri Shinbun,* August 15, 1996). He apologizes for this callousness, putting it down to nerves over the start of En no Kai. I have included the full letter below along with excerpts from Takizawa's response.

To Head Abbot Takizawa Kazuo:
With the fall equinox approaching, I know that you must be very busy. Our cultural bureau seems to specialize in reporting on the so-called En no Kai, announcing that it has been in the paper nine times and is creating big waves. Reading this, I can imagine the abbot elated with his success. I will admit that there was no special response from *danka* who seemed to accept En no Kai, but the fact is that secretly we are not pleased. It is one thing to make a lot of money, but you should know the feelings of the *danka* who are currently supporting the temple.
    It was explicitly announced that En no Kai members pay 600,000 yen, but I do not remember ever hearing a single word about the cost of [funeral or memorial] services for parishioners.[30] Is it not now the time to make a clear announcement about this cost as well? The other day, after hearing the news [about En no Kai costs], I met with two or three people I know and we discussed the matter, but no clear answers were forthcoming. In the end, someone decided it was clearly just about business. It was resolved that we've got a pretty shrewd (*subashikoi*) abbot.
    This is an unrelated point, but there is next to no one who knows

30. This price represents the cost of joining En no Kai when it first began. The price was subsequently raised to eight hundred thousand yen.

the story of the head of the parishioner representatives who is running
the temple support group.³¹ If there is enough space to allow it, I would
like the next issue to include an article on this. It would really make
me happy if you could run this in the next issue.

Next, we should be able to find some means to lower the high cost of
sending this magazine to under 100 yen. Also, by using a little plainer
printing (but with solid content), should we not be able to save something on costs? Perhaps this will lighten the load that the parishioners
are shouldering.

As a single *danka* I have included the thoughts of other people and
presented you with this bitter pill of candid advice. I look forward to
your response in the next issue.

Signed,
A Single *Danka*

Taking each of the letter's original paragraphs in turn, Takizawa wrote
a detailed, two-and-a-half-page response. Throughout this letter and in
his greetings, which appeared on the first page of the temple newsletter,
Takizawa took pains to point out that both the temple and En no Kai are
entirely dependent on and would never have existed without the long-
standing support of the *danka*. Takizawa presented En no Kai as a way for
the temple to both acknowledge its dependence on parishioners and, more
importantly, to lighten the financial load they had been carrying:

> Steeped in a tradition that has long been supported through everyone's
> efforts, En no Kai should be thought of as an enterprise (事業 *jigyō*) for
> preserving Tōchōji, which is caught up in problems of a lack of graves
> and descendants. While its finances are bound to become a topic of
> gossip, the real value of En no Kai lies in its intrinsic spirituality
> (本来の精神性 *honrai no seishinsei*).

Takizawa pointed out that, despite the fact that the temple had been consistently short on funds, he had not raised the dues for the temple support
society (護寺会 *gojikai*) in the seven years since it was formed. Temple upkeep requires a lot of money, he warned:

31. For details on the function of the *danka* representative (総代 *sōdai*) within a temple,
see Covell 2005, 34–38; and Borup 2008, 68–70.

"For example, if we were going to raise five hundred million yen for renovations, we would need close to one million yen from every family. I think that it is the economic function of En no Kai to prevent us from running a deficit each year as well as to provide the money we need for the future." He also pointed out that ten years earlier, when they rebuilt the temple, he did not ask for any extra donations whatsoever. Later in the response, after explicitly evoking the role of En no Kai in "stabilizing temple finances," Takizawa finally touched on other possible benefits:

> Putting aside the distinction between parishioners and burial society members, En no Kai is a way to have many people experience Buddhist teachings, not only after death but also by using the temple while they are alive. I am convinced that as an open temple we can retrieve the true essence of temples.

In response to the parishioner's call for more transparency in regards to costs for funeral and memorial services, Takizawa turned the discussion to offerings, which he admitted might seem unclear to the younger generation, but are nevertheless essential to the temple and "fundamental to Buddhism." *Fuse* are part of the parishioner system, however, and do not fit with the completely new type of relationship evinced between the temple and En no Kai members. The six hundred thousand yen was thus explained as a sort of sign-up fee, not unlike the initial donation people make when they become *danka* (入檀料 *nyūdanryō*), or when they purchase rights to a new grave. Takizawa was quick to clarify, however, that this fee does not include memorial services or a funeral. More significantly, to parishioners, he added that "no matter what the En no Kai members want, they will all get the same *kaimyō* suffix of either *shinshi* 信士 (for men) or *shinnyō* 信女 (for women)." In other words, they will all receive the same basic, undistinguished ordination names.[32] He then listed the more prestigious *kaimyō* endings, including the highly regarded *ingō* 院號, which, traditionally, was bestowed on those who donated a building to the temple. This name still signifies high status that is generally accompanied by more elaborate funeral and memorial services. Takizawa's point was unmistakable. En no Kai members are ranked below Tōchōji's parishioners and will never, either in this life or the next, supplant them.

32. For more information on *kaimyō*, see Smith 1974, 82–84; Shimada 1991; Swarts 2001; and Covell 2005, chapter 8.

Indeed, he made it clear that, in contrast to temple parishioners who are all called temple supporters (檀徒 *danto*), En no Kai members should be called followers (信徒 *shinto*).[33]

Finally, Takizawa thanks the parishioner for his valuable opinions and acknowledges that this is the first time he has ever been surprised by a letter:

> As I said at the beginning of this response, it should not be expected that parishioners and members think the same way, and this is even more true in regards to the long-standing and recurring problems of funerals, graves, Buddhism, and the temple. I think it is only natural that this [new type of temple membership] is difficult to grasp. I myself am proceeding by trial-and-error. Knowing it is best to bear in mind that there are such opinions [as yours], I would like to continue to work hard for the preservation of this temple.

The relationship between parishioners and En no Kai members clearly needs to be considered from a number of different viewpoints. Here we have seen that for the parishioners, the creation of Tōchōji's eternal memorial grave has brought both contentment, due to the resulting growth of the temple, and resentment at the relatively small commitment (economic, temporal, and generational) of the En no Kai members. For Takizawa, the potential tension between parishioners and burial society members needs to be handled with extreme care. Though the success of his temple to this point has been entirely due to parishioners, it is clear that he feels the future success of Myōkōji rests with En no Kai. In the following section, I will turn to how burial society members view their relationship with the temple.

MICHIKO'S STORY

There are some ten thousand different personal stories of En no Kai. To pick one as representative is like choosing Tōchōji to stand for all Sōtō temples or Sōtō to characterize all of Japanese Buddhism. However, rather than trying to present a pastiche of different stories, combined into a sin-

---

33. Though it is also possible to translate *shinto* as "believer," the term is most frequently used by priests to refer to members of a temple who do not have a temple grave. The implication is that the latter group does not have the same kind of stake in the temple and thus has lower status. It is also worth noting that sectarian surveys also treat *danto/shinto* as distinct categories.

gle narrative, I have decided to offer one individual case study. The point is not to essentialize En no Kai members but rather to personalize their stories and hint at the diversity and complexity that exists at the individual level of burial society membership.

"Michiko" was born in Nagoya in 1942 as an only child. Her mother divorced when Michiko was very young, and, for various personal reasons, the two of them moved to Tokyo in the early 1960s. Having broken their ties with Nagoya, they decided to find a new grave for just the two of them in Tokyo. They soon realized, however, that it would be nearly impossible to do so without proof of descendants who would take care of the plot after they were both dead. As Michiko told me, "Even if you go in and lie about having descendants, after you die there will be no one to keep up the grave and you will end up abandoned (*muen*)." After searching in vain for several months, around 1997 she and her mother began noticing ads for new graves that did not require descendants, including one for En no Kai.

Taking the tour of Tōchōji, Michiko was impressed by the temple architecture: "I really liked the main hall. It was so simple. Sōtō temples are usually so garish!" The other deciding factor was the professionalism of the En no Kai staff member whom she met: "I never spoke to a priest, but the contract was solid and the staff member was thorough and professional." Michiko and her mother had seen other advertisements, but what got their attention and what cemented their decision to have Michiko's mother join was the fact that En no Kai was backed by an actual temple.[34] "It was very important to me that the name of the temple was included in the ads. Otherwise you don't know what will happen. If there isn't a temple behind it, the place might go under at some point." When I pressed her on whether her desire for a temple backing the grave was only out of fear that a commercial site might fold, she agreed that this was part of it but insisted that she was also concerned about memorial services (供養 *kuyō*) for her mother: "I didn't really have any religious feeling myself, but I wanted *kuyō* for my mother." Michiko knew that even if she lived a long life she would not be alive to perform services for another thirty-three years:

> I worried that if I didn't find an alternative, then I would have no choice but to ask that my mother be accepted back into the family grave in Nagoya. And they probably wouldn't even take her. This is why *muen*

---

34. See chapter 2 for a discussion of grave management. For a related example, see Hardacre 1997, 212–16.

is so frightening. I don't care if I am abandoned, but I could not let that happen to my mother.

By this time, her mother was physically unable to take part in the precept ceremony, so Michiko did it in her place. She jokes that this makes her one of the only members who has performed the ceremony twice. After she participated in the initiation ceremony (授戒式 *jukaishiki*) in her mother's place, Michiko did not return to Tōchōji again until her mother died in 2003, some six years later.

Michiko decided to join En no Kai herself on the hundredth day after her mother's death: "After my mother died, I couldn't help but enter. I think she decided for both of us." When I asked about her experience of receiving the precepts, she admitted that she did not really understand the explanation of the ceremony:

> I was very nervous at that time. I didn't really know what was going on. Most of us were just worried about falling off the platform, but what can you do? When I stood on the platform and they said we had become disciples of the Buddha—those words are the only ones that stuck with me. Later when I thought back on it, I decided that they do that because it's a ceremony. Of course, how you take it really depends on your age. I guess you could say that it brought out some religious feelings in me.

She then clarified this remark by pointing out that this was how she felt when she did the ceremony on her mother's behalf while she was not yet a member herself. As she told me, "When I did it again recently, I did not think about these things. I just went about it like a ritual event."

Since her mother died, Michiko visits the temple twice a month, on the first and on the day of her mother's death. Rather than taking part in the evening ceremonies that occur on the first of each month, she always goes in the early afternoon, before the crowds arrive. She also attends temple services during the two equinox services, the summer festival of the dead, and to ring the temple bell on New Year's Eve (除夜の鐘 *joya no kane*). When she visits, she first bows before the gate in front of the main hall but does not go to the water garden. Instead she goes straight downstairs to the Hall of the Arhats. There, she bows and offers incense before the En no Kai memorial tablet and altar before attending to her mother's memorial tablet. She has the position memorized—"xx shelf xx from the left." Like many En no Kai members, however, she also has a Buddhist altar in her home, where she speaks to her mother every day. When I asked where her mother is now, she answered without hesitation: "At home."

Michiko does not feel that she is a *danka* because she is not obligated to support the temple economically. In fact, she told me, it is almost the opposite—she feels that the temple supports her and the other En no Kai members. When I asked her if she thought of Tōchōji as her home temple (菩提寺 *bodaiji*), she replied,

At some point I might feel that way, but not now. I know I am contra-dicting myself. Even though I want the temple to do my *kuyō*, I don't yet feel like this is my *bodaiji*. As I get older, I think the feeling will slowly come. I haven't been involved for that long. When I am older it will be more fun to come to the temple.

Unlike the narratives that were presented in the last chapter, Michiko's story does not contain the strong independence shown by Naoko or any inkling of the revenge carried out by Tome. Nor does her experience at Tōchōji include anything like Mr. Endō's apparent spiritual breakthrough at the cave. Instead, she presents us with a very practical view of burial society membership, and, in so doing, she reminds us of how entirely or-dinary a relationship to a temple can be. The ambiguity of her reaction to the precept ceremony provides a strong sense of how the majority of En no Kai members experience Tōchōji. The ceremony might have evoked some vague religious feeling, but it did not last. There is also no sense, in talking to her, that she cares whether Tōchōji is a Sōtō Zen temple (as op-posed to some other sect), and, though she admits that her feelings might change, she does not think of Tōchōji as her home temple. In many ways, it is hard to distinguish Michiko's relationship with Tōchōji from that of many parishioners and their home temples. All of this is not to suggest that Michiko's story is not revolutionary—it is. We cannot forget that if her mother had died even fifteen years earlier, Michiko would have had little choice but to ask her relatives in Nagoya to accept her into the fam-ily grave. And if, by some chance, they had been able to secure a grave elsewhere, there still would have been no one to attend it after she died. Though Michiko's particular story is unique, shifting demographics, in-crease in divorce, and decrease in the birth rate are making her circum-stances all too common.

O-BON SERVICE AT TŌCHŌJI, 2005

Turning now to an *o-bon* service I attended in summer 2005, I would again like to give a sense of what life is like on the ground at Tōchōji. Of particular interest is the short talk that Takizawa gave at the end of the service and what I believe it reveals about new forms of temple membership such as that represented by En no Kai.

On a hazy, muggy afternoon in mid-July, I attend the last of the day's three *o-bon* services.[35] Like most Tokyo temples, Tōchōji conducts its rites for departed spirits in July, since most Tokyoites travel to hometowns for *o-bon* festivities in mid-August. I stop at the reception desk on my way in and am called to the back door where Takizawa is putting on his robes for the service. It is not often that I see him without an appointment, so I jump at the chance to chat for a few minutes while he gets ready. Takizawa quickly turns to one of the most common themes in our conversations—his dissatisfaction with what he sees as the negative elements accompanying En no Kai's remarkable success. He tells me that the day before, a family had wanted to drop off ashes for interment with En no Kai but insisted that no sutras be recited. In the end, the family was convinced to at least have one of the younger temple priests visit the crematorium to perform a short service, but Takizawa sees this as indicative of a larger trend. Like many temple priests, he is concerned with the ongoing simplification (簡略化 *kanryakuka*) of mortuary services.[36] He fears that even as more people join En no Kai, for most urban Japanese, Buddhist ritual and teachings are losing significance both within the mortuary process and within Japanese culture as a whole. He then turns and points to the Annex staff members at their desks and says, "Because of these guys, it's all business." The three staffers within earshot look up and smile. They have heard this complaint many times before, but the success of En no Kai seems to overrule other considerations.

Takizawa returns to his preparations, and I head upstairs to the main hall. With the massive influx of En no Kai members, Tōchōji offers most of its yearly services three times throughout the day to accommodate all the

35. Though this passage describes a specific event in the past, I have chosen to use the present tense in order to better emphasize the immediacy of the experience. It is not my intention to portray these events as timeless and universal, which is a common side effect of using the present tense to describe the past.

36. In the past, Takizawa had specifically mentioned to me what he considered rather disturbing results from a survey of urban parishioners' views on funerals and knowledge of Sōtō sect doctrine (Sōtōshū Shūmuchō 1993).

visitors. The first service of the day, held in the morning, is reserved for *danka* only, so the afternoon crowd of about one hundred fifty people consists mostly of En no Kai members, many immediately identifiable by the green *wagesa* they wear around their necks. The short conversation with Takizawa on my way in causes me to arrive in the main hall a few minutes late. As usual, the crowd is being warmed up by the popular priest Okamoto Wakō 岡本和幸, who has his own Sōtō temple in rural Chiba and who most members and *danka* assume will eventually succeed Takizawa as abbot of Tōchōji. Okamoto offers an outline of the day's ceremony as a sort of warm-up act, not unlike what one would see before the main performance in a nightclub. The tall, heavyset, forty-year-old priest is totally on his game today, and by the time I come in, he already has the crowd eating from his hand. His delivery is rough and fast—there is no flowery phrasing or dramatic pausing, only short, staccato sentences repeated for emphasis with a heavy dose of sarcasm. He details how and when they are to stand up and walk before the temporary altar for wandering spirits arranged at the front of the hall (opposite the main altar). With this many people in attendance, the visitors must be divided into smaller groups that stand up in turn and walk in a specific direction so that they all come to the altar from the same side. As Okamoto explains all of this, he tells the story of a previous year where everything was going fine until one elderly gentleman decided that he needed to perform an additional bow at the main altar on his way around. Once this happened, everyone who followed started imitating him. The excessive bowing created a log jam at one end of the hall and disrupted the timing of the ceremony. While Okamoto tells the story, many in the hall are nodding, and the woman next to me whispers to her friend, "Yes, it's so true. I never know what I'm supposed to do!"

The ceremony goes smoothly, with Okamoto and the younger priests telling people when to get up, what sutras to chant, and when to clasp their hands together (合掌 *gasshō*). All the people in the hall have been given a small sutra book so that they can chant along. As the sutras are all written in *kanbun*, most Japanese can only get a very general sense of the content and must be informed, via phonetic markers along the sides of the text, how to pronounce the words. Everyone is happy to participate, and with the five priests leading the way, all the voices resonate in a powerful way.[37]

37. I have noticed several times at Sōtō temples that there is one text that does not lend itself to chanting. Though a central text for contemporary Sōtō temples and regularly recited

Immediately after the *o-bon* ceremony, Takizawa addresses the crowd. In contrast to Okamoto, Takizawa's style is more polite, his speech more lilting. This talk is longer and serves as a short lecture relating to the day's services. Takizawa begins with a rather dry, meandering history lesson about Japanese Buddhism in the modern era in which he identifies three recent periods of "danger" to Buddhism. The first, he tells us, was the Meiji reformation (1868), which brought with it the forced (and unnatural) separation of temples and shrines (神仏分離 *shinbutsu bunri*) as well as the persecution of Buddhism (廃仏毀釈 *haibutsu kishaku*). The second was the postwar period, which brought the land reforms that stripped rural temples of much of their agricultural base. The third, which he called the contemporary period, began with the decades of high economic growth in the 1950s and 1960s.[38] Addressing the crowd of people mostly in their fifties and sixties, Takizawa attributes this most recent period of danger to changing ideas and values, and nostalgically laments the loss of traditional knowledge and ways of doing things. He then speaks of the role of temples in performing memorial rites and of debts to ancestors. While it seems that he is providing a fairly stock narrative about the negative social effects of modernization, he suddenly switches the conversation to the temple, acknowledging that the Tōchōji of today is not the Tōchōji of the Meiji or the immediate postwar period. This distinction refers not only to the new buildings but also to how things are done. "However," he assures us, "our search for truth and our feelings about the ancestors have not changed at all." Some things must change, he admits, but his challenge is to think about how to carry on those feelings from the past.

Takizawa then shifts gears again to talk about the training of Sōtō monks and their constant questioning of meaning (意義を質す *igi o tadasu*). For Takizawa, this "meaning" is identified not with doctrine but with Buddhist ritual and proper etiquette (作法 *sahō*). He then provides exam-

---

at Sōtō ceremonies, the *Shushōgi* always produces a certain dissonance, and, I would even say, discomfort for temple visitors. Because of its modern provenance, the phrases do not read like the short stanzas that make up most sutras; instead it is composed of complete sentences. These phrases simply do not lend themselves to the sort of rhythmic chanting that constitutes most sutra recitation and are thus very difficult to chant well. Every time that I have observed the *Shushōgi* being chanted, it has gone badly—people stumble over the rhythm and timing and eventually just give up and let the priests do it. Even then it is so noticeably different from the rest of the ritual experience as to be jarring.

38. Note the ways in which Takizawa's historical account parallels that of Ogawa. In fact, almost all the priests with whom I spoke recounted postwar temple history in similar fashion.

ples of the proper way to offer incense and clasp hands together in *gasshō*. He warns us, however, that abstract discussions of etiquette are not effective and quotes another priest who once told him, "If we do not bring *sahō* to the level of everyday life, if we do not apply it to real problems, then Buddhism will not come to life." "*Sahō*," Takizawa emphasizes, "*is* the very principal; *sahō is* the very bosom of the Sōtō sect."[39] For Sōtō monks, this teaching is encountered in the strict training of the monastery, where every aspect of their daily lives is strictly regulated, right down to how they use the toilet.[40] Takizawa jokes that when he was training he wanted a written list of everything they had to do but that he was repeatedly reminded that these were actions to learn with the body and not to be memorized. Takizawa then shifts the conversation to the laity, specifically those in front of him (whom he now has completely in his narrative grasp). He tells us that he realized that *sahō* is not about "do this and don't do that." Quoting from the Precept Verse of the Seven Buddhas (七仏通戒偈 Shichibutsu tsūkaige), he recites the first two rules: "Shun all evils, perform every good" (諸悪莫作、衆善奉行 *shoaku makusa, shūzen bugyō*), and then tell us that this real meaning is not simply "do good," but rather "*try* to do good things and *try* not to do bad things" *(ii koto o suru yō ni shiyō, warui koto o shinai yō ni shiyō)*. "Do not think of it in terms of commandments (戒律的 *kairitsuteki*)—'this is bad, this is good.' It is about that feeling growing naturally within yourself. It is not about being told to do these things but about doing them naturally—this is the true teaching of Śākyamuni." There are heads nodding all over the hall and whispers of agreement. Though it started rather poorly, Takizawa's talk has now hit home with the crowd.

What, then, is one to make of this *o-bon* sermon that starts with the historical dangers facing Japanese Buddhism, touches only briefly on ancestors and memorial rites, revels in how difficult monastic training is, and ends with a morally relativistic reading of the Buddhist precepts? Typically, in temple sermons during *o-bon*, the focus is on the ancestors with some attempt to connect memorial rites to fundamental Buddhist tenets. Takizawa's sermon, however, seemed almost autobiographical. On the one hand, the talk was aimed not only at the current En no Kai mem-

39. This quotation echoes a passage from Dōgen's *Shōbōgenzō*: "Etiquette is itself the teachings" (作法コレ宗旨ナリ *sahō kore shūshi nari*).

40. For an English translation of Dōgen's monastic rules, see Leighton and Okumura 1996.

bers but also at potential members, in effect saying, "We may be a Sōtō
Zen temple, known for our strict monastic discipline, but we understand
the needs of our members and parishioners and do not expect too much of
you." As with the instructions during the *jukai* ceremony, all that matters
is that people "try" to uphold the precepts. On the other hand, Takizawa
appeared to be justifying the direction in which he has taken the temple.
Note his talk of change and the clear implication that this is "not your
father's Tōchōji." In this context, the idea that the truth is not in the letter of the precepts but in how one internalizes the lessons inherent in
the rules and adapts them to one's own circumstances, makes particular
sense. Takizawa's statements represented more than a vague nod to Buddhist tenets of innate Buddhahood; they also offered an explicit message
about his management of Tōchōji in a specific historical period. The question, then, given Takizawa's repeated concerns over the loss of Buddhist
meaning, is how his "Do what you think is best" interpretation of the precepts is going to renew Buddhist thought and teachings in contemporary
Japanese society.[41]

Taken along with Okamoto's earlier explanation to the group on when
and how to bow, the day's sermon brought something into clear focus for
me. Most of the visitors at Tōchōji, and at many temples (particularly urban) I have observed, simply do not know what to do. They do not know
the proper way to clasp their hands in veneration (*gasshō*), they do not
know when to bow during services, they do not know to whom (or what)
they should bow, and they often do not know how many times to offer incense. This is not to say that they do not care. They want to know and des-
perately want someone to tell them. There is a feeling, perhaps akin to the
one felt by all of the people who mimicked that one man who bowed inap-
propriately, that they might be doing something wrong and that someone
else knows more than they do. Without descending into essentialist pronouncements on supposed Japanese uniqueness, one can say that proper
behavior in formal occasions is a valued aspect of Japanese culture. Buddhism often presents a dilemma for many Japanese today in that it has
been so thoroughly connected to definitions of Japanese cultural identity
that it seems like a club to which they all belong. And yet, in nearly every

41. I am not arguing that Takizawa is misinterpreting the precepts for lay Buddhist followers. On the contrary, his reading is fairly standard. Rather, I am trying to place his explication within the broader context of how he contextualizes recent developments at Tōchōji to an
audience of both En no Kai members and *danka*.

facet of temple interaction—from what to do during rituals, to what the rituals mean, to how much to pay for them—most Japanese have no idea what to do. They are, then, members in a club whose rules they do not know and are generally afraid to ask. As I mentioned above, surveys of the general public consistently reveal that the most common worry when arranging a funeral is the amount to donate to the temple. Viewing this solely as a budgetary concern misses the more deep-seated apprehension of (ritual) exchange gone wrong.

BREATHING EASIER

I have written extensively in this chapter about the business side of En no Kai and the multifaceted role of the staff as temple intermediaries. By talking to members of En no Kai, however, it became obvious that they had not joined simply for the sake of expediency. Those whom I interviewed or spoke to casually never used terms such as convenience (便利さ *benrisa*) or simplicity (簡単さ *kantansa*), which one usually hears in reference to business services. Instead, the two most common expressions I heard both at Tōchōji and at other eternal memorial graves were "I was able to put my mind at ease" (安心出来た *anshin dekita*) and "I was so relieved," (ほっとした *hotto shita*). Time and time again, when asking people how they felt about joining En no Kai, I received these same two answers. This latter response, "*hotto shita*," represents an onomatopoeic expression for breathing a sigh of relief and reminds us how significant these new graves are to the people who enter them. For it is in these exhalations that one understands that in contemporary Japan much of the apprehension over death centers on the anxiety of arranging one's grave and ensuring that it will be looked after. I would also argue that these sighs of relief may tell us a lot about why people are joining these burial societies and the kind of religious affiliation they represent.

Part of the answer to the question of why people choose eternal memorial graves is straightforward: they chose them either because they have no choice, such as those who lack descendants; or because this offers them a choice, such as those women who choose not to enter their husbands' family graves; or simply because, as consumers in a fantastically consumptive society, they expect choices in all facets of their lives. There is another aspect of the "why" question, however, that must address the reason these people choose to join eternal memorial graves at temples over municipal or explicitly commercial alternatives. I have addressed this question to some extent by arguing that there is a pervasive belief that temple graves are free from the market fluctuations that might wipe out a commercial cemetery. In speaking to members—both those who joined temple burial societies in order to find a place for a loved one and those who were looking to find such a place for themselves—I believe there is something more in their sense of relief that deserves further attention.

When I first began interviewing members of En no Kai and hearing about how relieved they were to find Tōchōji, I always tried to get "behind" their relief to what I imagined were "deeper" feelings about religion and what having a grave at a temple meant to them. I spent a good deal of time and energy during the early part of my fieldwork trying to identify the degree to which this new form of temple affiliation could meaningfully be called "Buddhist." I took part in En no Kai rituals and services; I spoke to members both formally and informally; and I questioned the temple staff and priests on how En no Kai members were different from temple parishioners. Much of the framework for my investigation was based on trying to determine precisely how Buddhist these members were interested in becoming. Ironically, in my attempt to investigate Buddhism on the ground at an urban temple, I was still very much imposing a top down, elite/popular framework for my questions. How much doctrine did they understand or even want to learn? Did they know any Sōtō sect history? Were they taking part in *zazen* sessions? In trying to locate what I felt was identifiably Buddhist in their posture, I may have been missing what was actually drawing them to the temple. By privileging a normative view of Buddhist salvation based in doctrinal texts I had failed to give due weight to this-worldly forms of daily succor.

It is interesting to note that Takizawa may be taking a similarly normative stance. In many of our conversations, he brought up his goal of ten thousand En no Kai members. Indeed, the number seemed to have an almost magical hold on his imagination.

> Without ten thousand you cannot do any genuine teaching (*kyōka*). For example, if you get one thousand people and only 5 percent really develop some faith, that's only fifty people, right? That's a great thing, but fifty people cannot take the temple to the next level. With ten thousand people, though, you would get five hundred believers. This is another type of power altogether. And I don't mean just economic power but also in terms of faith. As for those people who are just in it for the relief [of having a grave], nothing can be done.

Takizawa came up with the figure of 5 percent after I asked him if burial society members were more enthusiastic about temple activities and services than parishioners. It was not that En no Kai members were more enthusiastic—Takizawa was quick to point out that the same percentage held for regular parishioners—but rather that there were simply more of them. For Takizawa, like Annon for Ogawa, En no Kai represents a way to spread Buddhist faith. In both cases there is an effort to reach out beyond temple parishioners to instill in burial society members (many of whom have no formal connection to a temple) a belief in Buddhism and a sense of temples as more than just storage facilities for the family dead. Ogawa accomplishes his propagation by inviting a small number of Annon members and temple parishioners to take part in religious training sessions. Takizawa's philosophy is to cast as wide a net as possible in the understanding that 5 percent will develop what he considers true faith. As he put it:

> When I talk to other priests and abbots, I ask them if there really is such a thing as propagation and teaching (布教教化 fukyō kyōka). What exactly is kyōka? Is it about trying to form connections with people who have had no bonds with temples or Buddhism before? No, [for those other priests] it's about having a danka membership—people who have been connected to the temple for generations. It's about telling these people that Sōtō is this sort of religion, that the teachings of Sōtō are such. In other words, fukyō kyōka is only about raising the level of danka faith.[42] There are lots of people who say this. I was totally shocked. Of course, I think that educating parishioners is important, but within the thinking of the extended-family system there is no awareness of bringing in those who have no previous connection to Sōtō or of spreading the teachings. From where I stand, this kind of raising the level [of danka faith] involves too much heavy lifting and creates a kind of bottleneck at the entrance. I guess I am saying that we need to focus on the entrance.

This idea of parishioners as a burden and En no Kai members as offering the real potential for temple and sectwide growth, expressed seven years

---

42. As Covell has convincingly shown in the case of the Tendai sect's Light Up Your Corner Movement, the propagation movements that each of the major sects developed in the 1960s and 70s were not aimed at new members so much as at raising the faith of existing members (Covell 2005, 45–61).

after his placatory response to parishioner complaints, appears to represent a remarkable change in Takizawa's thinking. In the undeniable success of the En no Kai staff, in Takizawa's concerns over commercialization and his excitement at the possibility and power of ten thousand members, in a certain parishioner's complaints about all-inclusive graves, and in the relieved sighs of a woman who has found a peaceful resting place for herself and her mother, we can see why eternal memorial graves are gaining so much popularity among temple priests and the public. We can also see their potential for drastically altering the makeup of temple management and affiliation.

EPILOGUE—THE POWER OF TEN THOUSAND

In summer 2007, I phoned Tōchōji to catch up on recent events and arrange a time to drop in and see everyone. One of the senior Annex staffers who, despite his unvarying dour appearance, had always been incredibly supportive of my work, answered the phone. "Have you heard the news?" When I told him that I had only just arrived back in Tokyo, he simply stated, "Abbot Takizawa is dead. He passed away last month at only fifty five. It was cancer. The public funeral (本葬儀 honsōgi) is tomorrow and the wake is tonight. You're coming, right?" I borrowed a jacket from a friend, bought a black tie and a special envelope for condolence money (香典 kōden) at the local convenience store, and rushed to the wake. When I arrived, the actual ceremony had ended and everyone was eating. I had been warned that there would be a few hundred priests, but I was not prepared for the sheer number, many of them representing the Sōtō sect elite. The gathering itself was lavish: champagne, sushi chefs, and female hosts, or "companion ladies," in evening gowns making sure that glasses were never empty. I went immediately to the main hall to pay my respects and was then called over by Okamoto to say hello to Takizawa's wife and son. Okamoto, smiling broadly, wasted no time in telling me I had gotten fat and wondering if I might have grown shorter since we had last met. Though I had spoken with Takizawa's wife several times, I had never actually met his son. My first impression was of a young man completely out of his element. The plan, as per Takizawa's last request, is for Okamoto to run the temple for a few years until the son finishes his training and is ready to take over. Looking at this young man in his middle twenties, who until recently had been studying in Europe, it was hard to imagine him running Tōchōji. At the same time, remembering Ogawa's account of his first steps as abbot, I realized that I had probably never met a priest who was *ready* to take over a temple.

The funeral ceremony the next day was enormous. There were several hundred priests present and over one thousand guests. There were so many priests in attendance that they completely filled the main hall, and everyone else had to stand or sit outside. A huge wooden stage had been constructed over the pond to allow invited guests to sit and others to walk up and offer incense. The service was carried out in accordance with Sōtō rules for the funeral of an eminent monk (尊宿喪儀法 *sonshuku sōgihō*) and thus included an elaborate series of distinct rites, each conducted by high-ranking Sōtō priests.[43] As Okamoto led Takizawa's son through his role at the funeral, I was again struck by how bizarre this must seem to him. Though occurring all the time at temples throughout the country, succeeding one's father as abbot was rarely carried out on such a scale and in front of so many people. Looking at Okamoto almost manhandle the young Takizawa through the ritual—turning his body in the right direction, pushing him in the back when needed—I was immediately reminded of a conversation with his father from the year before. Having observed Ogawa's crucial role in the ongoing success of the Annon grave, I once asked Takizawa whether he thought En no Kai could continue without him. He granted that it could, though he thought it needed to reach ten thousand members before it would have the power to continue on its own. It should have come as no surprise, then, that this number would come up again at his funeral.

Hanging from the roof in the main hall, just to the right of the funeral altar, Takizawa's death verse (遺偈 *yuige*) was painted on a large white sheet.[44]

[After] fifty-five years of comings and goings in this world,
[with] barely a glimpse of doctrinal essence,
I take respite from the ten thousand bonds.

Here again Takizawa provides a glimpse into his ongoing and evolving relationship with En no Kai. The first three phrases (two lines of translation)

43. For a description of funeral services for eminent monks, see Yifa 2002, 217–19; and Matsu'ura 1985. For pictures and further details on Takizawa's funeral and those in attendance, see *SOGI*, September 2007, 6–7.
44. 江湖往來, 五十五年, 毫窺宗要, 休息萬緣.

would seem, in their self-deprecation and reference to Buddhist teaching, entirely appropriate to a Sōtō abbot. The ending, however, offers some fascinating possibilities. The word for ten thousand in Japanese, 萬 *man*, can also mean "countless" or "myriad." If we took it as such, the final line would read, "I take respite from the myriad bonds." In other words, a fairly straightforward: "I take leave of this world." Given the significance of the specific number for Takizawa (not to mention his caustic wit), however, it is worth considering alternative interpretations. Is Takizawa offering a last barb, telling the world that he is finally free of En no Kai? Or is he telling the world that he has accomplished his goal of getting the group to ten thousand and can now pass the torch? Whether ten thousand or myriad, Takizawa's final, public, and possibly most enduring words are replete with bonds.

CONCLUSION

It should come as little surprise that the discourses emerging from Tō-chōji's burial society focus on connections between people—on the ties that bind across communities and across generations. The multigenerational grave and the memorial services that it hosts represent the core of temple Buddhism. Even as that grave changes to host new types of families and independently minded individuals, it is still dependent on connections; it is still, and must always be, based upon a matrix of relations. Temple Buddhism stands on these bonds. The reactions of both the priest in the *hōza* and Takizawa to those parents who do not wish to burden their children with memorial responsibilities emphasize how strongly temple priests rely on generational ties, even as they develop burial technologies that potentially allow people to severe those bonds.[45] Of course, as Michiko's valiant attempts to find a place for her mother and herself show, this technology can also be used to maintain family bonds, even when the traditional burial system cannot, or will not. Tōchōji teaches us that even as the *danka* system fades, relationships must continue.

Takizawa, like Ogawa with Annon, maintained an ambivalent relationship to En no Kai. If these new burial sites are indeed a bridge, then they are traversing a chasm. Both priests have had to be very careful in how they embrace this new type of temple membership while maintain-

45. Consider the strong reactions from sect headquarters to the advertisement campaign belittling rural family graves.

ing traditional parishioner ties. What does transcend this gap is *en*. It is worth noting, then, that it is far more simple to integrate these new burial society members doctrinally, through tenets of the interdependence of all things, than it is socially. The ideas of deeper connections are easy to handle doctrinally, but, as separate seatings for ritual services and the letter from that single *danka* demonstrate, not always logistically.

CHAPTER FIVE

Scattering Ashes

> The true grave lies in the heart.
> —Yasuda Mutsuhiko

A lthough demographic, household, and economic shifts have weakened the hold that temples have on Japanese deathways, as the previous four chapters have argued, Buddhist identity in Japan is still intimately connected to the central role of temple priests in mortuary rites. What happens, then, when that monopoly is challenged by other, non-Buddhist possibilities? This chapter moves outside the idiom of Buddhist graves and memorials to consider the scattering of ashes, an innovative burial practice that began around the same time as eternal memorial graves. Despite that fact that more than 99 percent of all Japanese are cremated today, scattering is still a very recent and controversial practice.[1] After tracing the modern development of scattering and the civic group that has been instrumental in its promotion, this chapter will explore a wide range of responses and consider what further insights they may offer into the relationship among Buddhist doctrine, families, and burial.

In an editorial to the *Asahi Shinbun* on September 24, 1990, Yasuda Mutsuhiko 安田睦彦, former *Asahi* editor and soon-to-be founder of the Grave-Free Promotion Society (葬送の自由をすすめる会 Sōsō no Jiyū o Susumeru Kai; hereafter, GFPS), wrote an essay titled "Is Scattering Ashes in the Ocean or in Mountains Really Illegal? We Are Losing the Freedom of

This chapter was originally published in 2003 as "Grave Changes: Scattering Ashes in Contemporary Japan" in the *Japanese Journal of Religious Studies* 30, no. 1:185–218. A modified version also appeared in Cuevas and Stone 2007.

1. Bracketing regional variations, cremation overtook burial nationwide in the 1930s. For a detailed history of the modern spread of cremation in Japan, see Bernstein 2006.

Mortuary Practices, Not Because of Regulations, but Through Preconceptions."[2] Yasuda argued that, despite popular belief, the scattering of ashes was in fact not covered under any of the laws then in effect and was therefore not illegal. He then went on to urge people to consider "scattering" as both an environmentally friendly and much more traditional style of burial than the overpriced, family-centered form of ancestral graves that had emerged, along with mandatory temple registration, during the Tokugawa period.

Less than five months later, on February 2, 1991, the first meeting of the GFPS attracted more than three hundred people in Tokyo; within that same year, the GFPS had completed its first official scattering ceremony.[3] By its twelfth year the society had over eleven thousand members and thirteen branch offices nationwide and, as of December 2002, had conducted 719 natural funerals (自然葬 shizensō) for the remains of 1,258 people.[4] In 2010, almost twenty years after the founding of the GFPS, less than 1 percent of Japanese chose scattering. Although these numbers remain relatively insignificant on a national scale, the group has generated nationwide attention and debate completely out of proportion to its size.[5] Owing in part to its media savvy and timely emergence after the economic bubble of the late 1980s, the society has had a dramatic impact on the public conception of mortuary practice. A government survey showed national acceptance of scattering ashes jumped from less than 20 percent in 1990 to almost 75 percent by 1998, with one in eight people saying they would choose a natural funeral for themselves (Mori 2000, appendix: 1–38). In 1997, largely in reaction to the society's success, the Welfare Ministry began investigations into the need for the first change in the grave laws in more than fifty years, and in 1998, the term shizensō officially entered the Japanese language with the publishing of the fifth edition of the Kōjien 広辞苑 dictionary.

As one would expect, however, in a country still dominated by a patrilineal family-grave ideal, ancestral rites, and Buddhist deathways, support for the society and its objectives has been far from universal. By transgressing the boundaries of graveyards and tradition, natural funerals pose

2. This is the same Yasuda who appeared at the first Annon festival. See chapter 3.

3. The Sōsō no Jiyū o Susumeru Kai officially translates its name into English as the Grave-Free Promotion Society. A direct translation of the name would be the Society for Promotion of Funerary Freedom. For a book-length treatment of the GFPS, see Kawano 2010.

4. A single scattering ceremony often involves the scattering of more than one person's remains.

5. In 1999 alone there were almost one million deaths nationwide (Sōmushō Tōkeikyoku, 2002).

a direct challenge to more than three centuries of Buddhist funerals and memorial rites. Despite Yasuda's claims of historical precedents for scattering in the ancient and medieval periods, the near-universal Buddhist mortuary rites and graves for people of all classes—practices dating from the Tokugawa period—are considered by most to constitute proper mortuary tradition in Japan. Furthermore, Yasuda's attempts to connect the society's version of scattering to wider environmental concerns and issues of personal and religious freedom have provoked opposition from various Buddhist organizations, local civic groups, scholars, and even former GFPS members. The society's success has also spurred imitation by professional funeral companies, splinter groups, and some Buddhist temples, leading to calls for new regulations for scattering if not a complete revision of current laws governing burial.

Scattering sits at the intersection of legal battles over the ambiguous status of remains, historical debates over what constitutes "traditional" funerary practices, Buddhist arguments for the necessity of posthumous ordination and memorial rites, as well as social and medical concerns over locating the dead. Despite its limited scale, the GFPS and the debates surrounding it provide valuable insights into changing conceptions of family, religious freedom, self-determination, and the long-standing Buddhist monopoly over death.

THE BEGINNINGS OF THE GFPS

On October 5, 1991, in Sagami Bay near Tokyo, the GFPS quietly held its first official natural funeral. A portion of the cremated remains of a young woman who had killed herself over lost love some thirty years earlier was scattered in the sea during a short, simple, nonreligious ceremony. Present along with Yasuda, the head of the society, and three other members were former Welfare Ministry official Saitō Nanako 斎藤奈々子, two boat operators, and three private photographers.

Ten days after the ceremony, the society made an official announcement about the event, and the following day, all the major papers and television networks carried the story. By performing the ceremony before making it public, the society both avoided a protracted legal battle and revealed its media savvy. Note that there were as many photographers at the ceremony as there were society members, and having a former Welfare Ministry member present no doubt projected to the public an essential element of credibility if not outright government acceptance. Furthermore, by scattering only a small portion of the remains of a woman who had already been interred for thirty years, the society eased public concerns over macabre practices. Finally, the love-suicide narrative gave the event a certain romantic appeal.

Yasuda's gamble paid off when the media carried the reaction of the related ministries the day after the society's announcement. As Yasuda had predicted in his editorial a year earlier, neither the Justice Ministry nor the Welfare Ministry was ready to declare scattering illegal. The Justice Ministry, commenting on article 190 of the criminal code (遺骸遺棄罪 igai ikizai), which prohibits the discarding of corpses, responded, "Since the aim of this regulation is to protect the religious sentiments of societal customs, as long as this [shizensō] is for the purpose of a funeral and takes place with moderation, there is no problem" (Yasuda 1992, 122–23). In addition, the ministry conceded that scattering did not constitute discarding (遺棄 iki) of, and cremation was not equivalent to destruction (損壊 sonkai) of, the corpse. Scattering, therefore, did not break any existing laws.[6]

For the society, the ruling was an "epoch-making" event that was taken as total approbation for the practice of scattering remains. Within the year, it had put out numerous articles and published two books. The first, You Don't Need a Grave: It's Precisely Because You Love Them That You Should Have a Natural Funeral (actually published before the first shizensō), included a reprint of Yasuda's Asahi editorial and reiterated his main arguments on the legality and history of scattering and its relationship to the environment. The most striking aspect of the book is its surreal cover, which shows an old, decrepit, overgrown cemetery with cracked gravestones in complete disarray. The earth hovers in the sky above, forcing the reader to reconsider what planet he or she is actually on. On the back cover, we see only the blue-green earth ordering us to "Bury the dead in the hearts of the living."

The second book, Freedom from "Graves": Natural Funerals That Return Us to the Earth, was published a mere two weeks after the announcement of the first shizensō and offers the first complete manifesto of the GFPS, as well as details on the logistics of scattering and legal advice on all necessary paperwork. The six-part manifesto of the society's basic rules includes respect for the wishes of the individual and for religious

---

6. Article 190 states the following: Anyone who damages, discards, or removes the corpse, remains, or hair of the deceased, or an item placed in a coffin, shall be imprisoned for no more than three years (Cited in H. Inoue 1990, 247).

beliefs, the promise of no discrimination, harmony with nature, and a not-for-profit pledge. Most notable for what it reveals about the society's historical views, is the following definition of *shizensō*:

> The natural funeral, as the final rite for the deceased, returns the remains (ashes) to nature and moreover pays tribute to his or her memory. This is a new creation that takes scattering, a funerary method established in our country since before the Nara period (710–94), and revives it in a form that is appropriate to contemporary custom. (Sōsō no Jiyū o Susumeru Kai 1991, 176)

We shall return to the question of what exactly constituted pre-Nara scattering below, but it is worth considering here how the society intended to adapt this putatively honored and ancient tradition to modern sensibilities.

As material objects, human remains require physical treatment and necessitate action. Although it is easy to forget when discussions focus on "returning to nature" and "funerary freedom," natural funerals involve the basic act of disposing of human remains. In the case of the GFPS, the physicality of burial is most evident in the need to prepare the cremated remains for scattering. Japanese crematoria are designed to burn bodies at a specific temperature that leaves the bones fairly intact in order to facilitate the tradition of picking up the bones (骨揚げ *kotsuage* or 収骨 *shukotsu*) and placing them into a funerary urn for interment.[7] In response to public fears, the GFPS advises that these bones must then be crushed into powder so that there are no pieces larger than five millimeters.[8] The society offers several methods for crushing the bones, including a wooden stick, a vase, a golf club, or, if available, an electric grinder. One measure of both the success of the society and the difficulty posed to family members when faced with having to crush the bones of a loved one is indicated

---

7. For details in English on *kotsuage*, see Kenney 1996/97, 423; Suzuki 2000, 117–18; and Rowe 2000, 369.

8. Despite the government's apparent acquiescence on the legality of scattering, there was still much debate in the national press over the actual degree of acceptance given the "within moderation" phrase in the Justice Ministry's opinion. Articles, editorials, and letters to the editor all voiced concerns that ranged from the pollution of oceans and mountains to "indiscriminate scattering of remains." Notwithstanding the society's assurances that human bones are made of calcium phosphate and therefore environmentally beneficial, there remained a fear that someone would now be able to throw away large, recognizable pieces of human bone in public spaces (Yasuda 1992, 123).

by the emergence of funerary companies that, for a nominal fee, will grind the remains for you.[9] Once the remains are prepared, they are generally scattered in the mountains or at sea. In *Freedom from "Graves,"* the reader is given general instructions about choosing the space for scattering, transportation to that spot, the method of scattering, and suitable containers for the ashes. For ocean services, the society recommends international waters, which begin roughly twenty-two kilometers from land, and for mountain scattering, a remote spot, ideally a place the deceased had visited. In either case, if the ashes are to be placed in any type of container, it must be completely biodegradable. The book also reminds readers that ashes do not settle in any one spot: some are taken by the wind, some are washed away, and some enter the earth. Because the natural funerals advocated by the society have no fixed religious elements, mourners are told there is no need to have Buddhist rites or Christian hymns (Sōsō no Jiyū o Susumeru Kai 1991, 182).

While the society was working hard on the promotional front, it also continued to perform funerals. In 1992 it held three more *shizensō*, including the first one on land, and in 1993 there were nine more natural funerals for thirteen people. In spite of these early successes, the legal and social ambiguity of scattering has yet to be clarified. While the society continues to grow and to arrange natural funerals all over the country, it is still fighting an ongoing battle to gain acceptance for what, despite its claims of tradition, is a revolutionary form of burial.

FROM LEGALITY TO REGULATION

Yasuda made clear in the early days of the GFPS that he felt the two main hurdles that had to be cleared were (mis)perceptions of the law and of history. Three years before the first *shizensō*, then Diet Member Ishihara Shintarō 石原慎太郎 focused national attention on the question of the legality of scattering human remains. Asked by his brother, the famous entertainer Ishihara Yūjirō 石原裕次郎, to scatter his ashes in the ocean, Ishihara consulted various groups and became convinced that scattering was not legal. Ultimately he did not follow his brother's wishes, and the issue of scattering was widely considered to have been settled. It was in reaction to this conclusion that Yasuda wrote his 1990 editorial in the *Asahi*.

---

9. For examples of reactions by society members when faced with this process, see Yamaori and Yasuda 2000, 96–214.

Yasuda's position, justified by the ministries, was that the grave laws, written in 1948 in response to sanitation concerns in the immediate postwar period, had no provision for the scattering of remains. As for criminal code prohibition against discarding corpses, Yasuda, employing one of his favorite hyperboles, noted, "If the scattering of ashes in mountains and oceans were covered under this law, then the family that leaves some amount of the remains behind at the crematorium, as well as those workers at the crematorium who dispose of the remains as industrial waste or garbage, are all criminals" (Yasuda 1997, 116).[10]

As the GFPS's success grew and government surveys showed a marked increase in national acceptance of scattering, the debate shifted from arguments over legality to questions of regulation. A spate of articles by Buddhism scholar Fujii Masao 藤井正雄 and engineer/graveyard specialist Yokota Mutsumi 横田睦 calling for some form of scattering regulation helped bring about a Welfare Ministry roundtable inquiry into contemporary grave practices.[11] Composed of scholars, priests and professionals, the roundtable, called "An Open Discussion on the Future of Grave Practices," held twelve sessions over seventeen months from February 1997 to June 1998. The committee focused on two concerns: first, the crisis over insufficient grave space and abandoned graves; and second, a clarification of the position of the current grave laws in regard to scattering and a determination on whether some form of regulation was in order. At issue was not only the uncertain status of cremated remains in a country with a 99 percent cremation rate but also fundamental questions of religious freedom. As the committee report makes clear, the postwar grave laws were only intended to protect public health and thus to apply a broader interpretation of them in order to regulate what constitutes "acceptable customs" would be highly problematic.

Not surprisingly, when Yasuda and other representatives from the GFPS were invited to speak before the committee, it was on precisely this point that they mounted their defense. Switching tactics from the society's staple argument that ashes were not covered under the grave law as

10. There are inevitably some remains left over after the process of picking up the bones and placing them in the urn. Generally, in western Japan a large percentage of the remains is left over, whereas in eastern Japan most of the remains are entombed with only a small amount left behind at the crematorium. However, it is not the case that the remains are simply treated as industrial waste. Some crematoria put the remains in a single memorial grave, and others actually scatter them in the mountains (Suzuki 2000, 164–7).

11. See Fujii 1995, 211–32, and 1996, 30–52; and Yokota 1996, 56–63, and 1997, 60–3.

outlined in article 4, Yasuda instead focused on article 1, which, along with the protection of public health and welfare, ensures burial practices that will conform to the "religious sentiments" of the people.[12] As Yasuda put it:

> What exactly is the religious sentiment of the people that is listed in the first article of the grave law? If this is not carefully debated, then this sentiment could be bound up with control by the State. Among all the different religions, is there a single religious sentiment? This is not something that should be regulated by the State, and we would like to discuss this matter carefully. We believe that what we are doing in the society is a manifestation of our religious sentiments. . . . Natural funerals are a new religious practice and are protected under freedom of expression and belief. . . . In order to debate problems that would arise if scattering became more common, we must pin down what is meant by religious sentiments. The idea that new practices are strange and therefore must be regulated is a dangerous one.[13]

This bold assertion marked an important shift in the status and policy of the GFPS. Yasuda's arguments were no longer based on establishing the legality of his fledgling civic group, but rather on fighting for its rights to the same kind of freedom that religious groups are guaranteed under the Japanese Constitution. Although Yasuda had always argued for freedom of choice, these statements represented a new focus. As we shall see, the claim that scattering represents proper Japanese burial tradition is premised on a vision of family graves as tools of state ideology in the Tokugawa and Meiji periods. In transposing this argument to the present day and questioning the very essence of religious freedom, Yasuda placed the GFPS in a highly political position vis-à-vis the state by making funerary freedom a battle against state oppression and scattering the most fundamental of human rights. The potential consequences of these statements regarding freedom of religion and state control are particularly significant in the

---

12. Article 4 of the laws covering graves and burial states, "Burial or interment of ashes shall not occur in an area outside of a graveyard." Article 1 states, "The intent of this law is to ensure that the management of graveyards, ossuaries, and crematoriums, as well as burial and the like, shall, in conformity with the religious sentiments of the people and in accordance with public sanitation and communal welfare, occur without hindrance."

13. See http://www1.mhlw.go.jp/shingi/s1023-1.html. Last accessed May 14, 2009.

wake of the Aum affair and subsequent changes in the Religious Corporations Law.[14]

While shying away from strictly defining "religious sentiments," the committee made clear that it was more concerned with the reactions of the people living in areas where scattering was taking place than with the religious feelings of those doing the scattering. As the committee chairman, Waseda University Law Professor Urakawa Michitarō 浦川道太郎, stated, "We are aware of the idea that people 'want daily life and the spirits of the dead to be separate' and that we should consider the religious sentiment of those people who live in areas where ashes are scattered" (*Mainichi Shinbun* 毎日新聞, August 17, 1998). Along with the need for a clear definition of scattering, some system of authorization, and punishment for breaking the laws, the biggest concern of the committee was with the location of scattering. Specific fears included people shying away from seafood caught in places like Sagami Bay, where scattering often takes place, as well as reports of individuals simply digging holes and dropping in ashes in clear violation of the law. Another potential problem stemmed from the practice of scattering ashes on private land or in gardens and then reselling that property. The grave specialist Yokota, one of the society's most vocal critics, produced the following imaginary advertisement to illustrate his opposition: "House for Sale. 165 square meters, southeast facing corner lot. Ten years old. Fifteen minute walk from train station. Human remains included" (Yokota 2000, 113). In the end, the committee recommended to the Welfare Ministry that scattering be regulated at the prefectural level and that there be unified administration of locations, methods of scattering, and records of each case (*Mainichi Shinbun*, August 17, 1998). The committee meetings did not result in changes to the grave laws in regards to scattering ashes.

THE "TRADITION" OF SCATTERING

In addition to legal issues, the GFPS also faced an established tradition of funerary rites and burial practices dating back to the Tokugawa period. It was essential for the society both to show that contemporary practices,

14. As part of its response to Aum's sarin gas attack on the Tokyo subway in 1995, the government revised the Religious Corporations Law in December of the same year, representing the first amendment to the law in more than forty years. For a meticulous and nuanced analysis of the changes in the laws governing religious groups after Aum, see LoBreglio 1997, 38–59. For details on the Aum affair, see Shimazono 1995, 381–415; and Reader 2000.

viewed as "traditional," were in fact the products of Tokugawa *bakufu* 幕府 and Meiji government policies, and, at the same time, to establish a link between scattering and the older practice of abandoning corpses. This two-pronged attack of deconstructing family graves and tradition-alizing *shizensō*, though overlapping, required different arguments and justifications.

To elevate the historical status of scattering, Yasuda frequently cites a variety of precedents, including references to scattering in elegies (挽歌 *banka*) from the eighth-century poetry anthology, the *Man'yōshū* 万葉集; the early Heian emperor Junna 淳和 (786–840) who wrote in his will, "Scatter me in forests and fields and do not build a grave"; and the famous request of the Shinshū founder Shinran 親鸞 that his remains be used to feed the fish in the Kamo river (*Asahi Shinbun*, September 24, 1990).[15] By invoking these well-known markers of "Japaneseness" in almost every GFPS publication or interview, Yasuda is trying to connect natural funerals to some deeper Japanese essence. Although Yasuda is on solid histori-cal ground as regards the treatment of the dead up to the medieval period, important distinctions must be made between the abandonment or dis-carding of complete corpses in mountains owing to fear of death impu-rity and hiring a boat or helicopter to fly out over the ocean to scatter the carefully prepared, cremated remains of a loved one who has specifically asked for such treatment.[16] Aside from the physical differences between scattering ashes and dumping corpses, these two responses originate in very different motivations. Despite references to romantic tropes uttered by famous historical figures, natural funerals are not a glorious return to a golden mortuary age so much as a modern response to the specific eco-nomic, political and social forces at the end of the twentieth century.

Perhaps not surprisingly, critics of Yasuda's claims focus on this fun-damental interpretive question of what constitutes "traditional" burial practices. Shima Tōru 島亨, a researcher on Japan's Jōmon period (10,000–400 BCE) and former director of the Japanese Buddhist Statuary Soci-ety, has written several critiques of the GFPS and of Yasuda's historical claims in particular. Shima accepts Yasuda's basic (and not at all contro-versial) argument that most Japanese did not build graves until the state-

---

15. Another consistent, though not so ancient, example that the GFPS uses is former United States Ambassador to Japan Edwin Reischauer, who requested that his ashes be scat-tered in the Pacific to create a bridge between the two countries.

16. For details on early treatment of corpses in Japan, see Haga 1996.

mandated temple certification system of the Tokugawa period.[17] He does not, however, understand why the GFPS's objective of achieving funerary freedom from state control must involve a return to discarding the corpse. Shima's response is right to the point: "Why must the making of graves by common people from the medieval period be rejected as a transgression against some original practice?" (Shima 1994, 115). Shingon priest Miyasaka Yūkō 宮坂宥洪 makes a similar argument by applying the logic of Yasuda's argument to rice cultivation: "In the Jōmon period we mainly ate acorns. Therefore there is no rule that says we must eat rice simply because we are Japanese. Furthermore acorns don't require the destruction of nature to create cultivated fields nor is the environment poisoned by pesticides."[18] As these debates show, while the history of burial in Japan is not particularly contentious, interpretations, particularly those that lay claim to "true" or "original" Japanese practices certainly are.

ENVIRONMENT

Although Yasuda bases his historical arguments on constructing a connection between natural funerals and earlier practices of discarding corpses, his defense of the GFPS hinges on differentiating between simple scattering (散骨 sankotsu) and the shizensō advocated by the GFPS. Integral to this distinction is the environmental platform of the society, which Yasuda based on his idea for a Forest of Rebirth (再生の森 Saisei no Mori). Yasuda initially came up with the concept in response to a debate in 1990 over the destruction of a riverhead in Tamagawa 多摩川, Yamanashi prefecture. Locals wanted to build a resort and golf course to revitalize the area, but opposition arose in Tokyo, which was dependent on the river for water. Yasuda later proposed that privately owned groves at the head of rivers be designated Saisei no Mori. Those who wished would pay a basic fee of one hundred thousand yen to have their ashes scattered in the woods. The money collected would be used to protect the woods and revitalize

17. See, for example, Shintani 1997. It is worth noting that though the family-grave system was tied to state control in the Tokugawa period, graves were not simply imposed from above. Commoners also aspired to the more extravagant rites, graves, distinguished posthumous names, and promises of salvation afforded to the elite classes. Indeed, as temple cemeteries began to spread in urban areas from the sixteenth century, more and more people wanted their tombs as close to the main hall as possible to ensure the "guarantee of continual prayer for their spirits after death" (Hashizume 1996, 25).

18. See http://www.mikkyo21f.gr.jp/father_shukyo002.html. Last accessed February 2004. This Web site is no longer available.

the local area, while at the same time ensuring clean water for major cities. In this way, people from the city would have their ashes "returned" (還す *kaesu*) to nature, helping to preserve the area and guarantee clean water for future generations. According to Yasuda, the *Saisei no Mori* was aimed at "having humans and the environment live and be reborn together in the great cycle (循環 *junkan*) of nature" (Yasuda 1997, 114).

In 1994, in response to the GFPS's announcement that they had conducted a *shizensō* for two people in a public grove in Tamagawa earlier that year, the local village applied to ban all future natural funerals. There were three main objections: (1) the land also belonged to the locals; (2) scattering would hurt the image of the area, which was trying to attract tourism; and (3) entering mountains littered with human remains would feel strange (*Mainichi Shinbun*, June 19, 1994). The local protest showed that the GFPS had to battle not only what it perceived as some mistaken notion of funeral tradition in Japan but also more fundamental taboos and fears of death in general—the same fears that continue to fuel protests against the construction of new funeral parlors, graveyards, and crematoria in local neighborhoods all over the country. One also has to wonder whether Tokyoites would have been happy with a solution that meant their drinking water was being filtered through human remains. The society now has seven of these forests around the country, but all of them are privately owned by either the society itself or individual members.

A second critique of the Forests of Rebirth comes from Yokota Mutsumi (mentioned above), who questions the entire environmental premise of the GFPS. In addition to his work as an engineer and city planner, Yokota is also a former member and outspoken critic of the GFPS. For Yokota, the society's problems stem from a lack of understanding of the dual position of human remains in Japanese society as an object of both veneration and taboo. He also strongly criticizes the society's attempts to justify scattering by constantly emphasizing the supposed environmental benefits (Yokota 1994, 256). As someone who was drawn to the society because of interest in the problem of insufficient grave space, Yokota felt that the environmental issue was simply "bait" to draw more interest to the cause.

Shima Tōru flatly denies the GFPS's claims as an environmental movement. In the article mentioned above, titled "Some Doubts about the 'Scattering' Movement: Somewhere between a Community and an Illusory Family," Shima argues that scattering ashes is a personal choice that should not be tied to larger issues. Shima believes that by equating scattering with environmentalism, the society is creating a false sense of community centered on environmental issues (rather than treatment of the dead) and projecting a self-righteousness that is ill deserved (Shima 1994, 112–3).

The question then is, what exactly is the concept of nature that the GFPS is putting forward? One could argue, as critics of the society have, that there is nothing particularly natural about cremating a human body in an oven, crushing those remains into powder with a golf club, and then hiring a motor-driven boat or helicopter to go twenty-two kilometers out to sea to dump the ashes into the ocean. Nor is turning private forests into scattering grounds in order to maintain clean water for cities and income for rural areas particularly "natural." The GFPS's use of "nature" or "natural" for their rites is, like its use of tradition, a construct set in opposition to all other forms of mortuary rites. In GFPS rhetoric, returning the ashes to the great blue sea is contrasted with dark, dank, claustrophobic tombs that inevitably fall into ruin.[19] Environmentally beneficial scattering forests are opposed to the growing environmental menace of grave parks, which devour the natural countryside, much as golf courses did in the 1980s. Nature is something that must be protected and nurtured, as well as something that sets the society apart from other groups. Indeed, one could argue that the society's "natural" funerals might more accurately be described as "environmental" funerals. But solely to focus on the merits or lack of merits of the society's platform is to miss the more fundamental challenge that scattering poses to the extended-family grave and the Buddhist rites that surround it.

BUDDHIST RESPONSES

Soon after the announcement of the first natural funeral, the Buddhist press ran articles headlined, "The Pros and Cons of Scattering Remains: Is the Government's Sanction of Scattering a Threat to Buddhist-Style Graves?" (*Gekkan Jūshoku* 月刊住職, December 1991, 2); "A Warning Alarm to Japanese Buddhism" (*Bukkyō Times* 仏教タイムス, October 25, 1991, 4); and "Arguing for the Centrality of the Spirit of Mourning and Memorial Services . . . An Object of Veneration is Essential" (ibid.). Although such concerns are to be expected, given this perceived threat to their monopoly over mortuary rites and the steady stream of income it generates for temples, Buddhist reactions on the whole have been anything but consistent.

19. In GFPS literature, the verb used to refer to scattering the ashes is almost always "to return" (*kaesu*) rather than "to bury" (埋葬する *maisō suru*).

Ranging from damning criticism to approbation, from ambivalence to doctrinal support, the variety of responses reveals less about the GFPS than
it does the contentious state of Japanese Buddhist positions on burial at a
time when the Buddhist monopoly is under siege.

Given the fact that the natural funerals advocated by the GFPS include
no Buddhist service, posthumous name, merit transfers (追善供養 *tsuizen
kuyō*), or subsequent memorial rites, it is no surprise that Buddhist critiques of the society often emphasize the need to make continual offerings
on behalf of the dead.[20] One fairly standard line of attack on the GFPS by
Buddhists depicts scattering as a highly unfilial act that shows disrespect
both in the initial act of "discarding" the remains and in failing to secure
a place for regular memorial services. For some Buddhists, such as the
Tendai priest quoted below, natural funerals are seen not merely as severing family and social bonds, but as "a threat to the very moral foundations
of Japanese culture" (Covell, 2005, 186).

> If we recognize the majesty of human life, it should be clear that the
> body cannot just be thrown out. Whatever excuse one uses for scatter-
> ing remains, it comes down to throwing them out. Usually one visits
> the grave thinking of the parents. What do people who throw out the
> remains do? Visit the mountains or forest? . . . The extended family
> has already collapsed. But I don't think it is all right to destroy parent-
> child relations as well. Even in a nuclear family, parent-child relations
> are authoritative. They are tied to good neighborly relations. We should
> reaffirm the fact that the family line is extended through the grave . . .
> The lack of an ethical view is a major problem. Ethical views begin in
> the family . . . Set the mind straight, train the body, support your fam-
> ily, govern the country, make all equal under heaven. Are these just
> too old-fashioned? I think reaffirming the importance of the family
> and the importance of community relations will shed light on the anti-
> social nature of scattering remains." (*Kōhō Tendai* 1998, 12–13. Quoted
> in Covell 2005, 186–87)

Here, the grave is painted as an essential site of family continuity that
serves as the very basis of morals and ethics, both for the individual and
the entire nation. Scattering remains no longer simply reflects larger so-

20. In her survey of GFPS members, Kawano notes that sixty-three of seventy-one respondents either never revisited the site of the scattering or did so only once or twice. Additionally,
less than 40 percent received posthumous names (Kawano 2004, 244–47).

cial problems but also actively contributes to the final disintegration of what remains of the traditional Japanese family.

On a similar track, Tendai priest and scholar, Katō Eiji 加藤栄司, in an article titled "Funerals after Funerary Freedom," allows that since individual freedom, which includes funerals, is protected under the constitution, people should be allowed to choose their last rites. With this acceptance, however, comes an important caveat: "The funerary process is not limited to the rite alone. There is a 'form' (型 kata) that determines everything from the participants' clothes to words of condolence." Kato argues that rather than "philosophical Buddhism" or Buddhist discourses on the meaning of life, what people really want is the conventional Buddhist funerary form. This form requires Buddhist priests who are able to take the soul of the deceased ("wild spirit," 荒御魂 aramitama), decisively return it to the other world, destroy its sins, transform it into a Buddha ("peaceful spirit," 和御魂 nigimitama), and perform memorial services" (Katō 1993, 61). According to Katō, the funerary rite is but one type of cultural "form" which, like an organic entity, does not like sudden changes or discontinuity. By consistently following an unchanging funerary pattern, the form handles the "rupture" of an individual's death and preserves the "continuity" of the social body:

> As long as the communal body continues to exist, it will seek to preserve the continuity of cultural "forms." Today, only Buddhism can provide people with a funeral "form." We really should stop placing so much importance on the debate going on in temples over "funerary freedom" (sōsō no jiyū). Isn't it just "freedom from funerals" (葬送からの自由 sōsō kara no jiyū) that is being debated? (Ibid.)

Katō's functionalist reading of mortuary rites aside, it is worth noting that he explicitly downplays the importance of Buddhist philosophy so as better to emphasize the cultural necessity of Buddhist ritual. However, in detailing the priest's role in transforming the deceased into a Buddha, Katō actually provides a fairly standard expression of Buddhist doctrine.[21] His claim to Buddhist culture, a concept that I shall discuss in more detail

---

21. I will discuss tensions among doctrinal ideals, cultural norms, and temple realities in the following chapter, but it bears noting the ways in which the priests discussed here see Buddhist doctrine as integral to (as opposed to being contradicted by) Japanese mortuary practices. For more on this "orthodox heresy," see Tanabe 2008.

in the following chapter, allows him to expand his critique and chastise the GFPS both for shirking its duties to the departed ancestors and for its inability to pacify and transform the spirits of the dead—something only a Buddhist priest can do.

Rinzai priest Ishizaki Yasumune 石崎靖宗 is one of several commentators who place ancestor worship in binary opposition to funerary freedom and then attempt to trace the change from the former to the latter.[22] Furthermore, like Katō, his critique is based on the assumption that doctrinal principles and cultural practices are not distinct. In a dharma talk on ancestor rites, Ishizaki emphasizes Buddhism's role in explaining causality (因果 inga) and the impossibility of an independent condition. He sets up this position to counter what he perceives as the society's imported Western notions of individuality and self-determination. Ishizaki transposes Buddhism's core tenet of codependent origination onto ancestral rites, arguing that memorial rites benefit not only the deceased but also the descendant, who, through previous generations, remains tied to and in some way dependent on, all the life in the universe. For Ishizaki, the GFPS's abandonment of ancestral rites ignores some fifteen hundred years of Japanese ancestor worship and appears self-centered and selfish: "When you look from the standpoint of this [long history], the trend toward 'funerary freedom' over the last few decades seems like just a flash in the pan."[23]

Shingon priest Komine Michihiko 小峰彌彦 also focuses on what ancestor worship—and, more specifically, Buddhist forms of memorializing the dead—can teach the living. His consideration of natural funerals begins with an extended history of the treatment of human remains in early Mahayana Buddhism and then proceeds to the importance of Buddhist stupas and five-tiered grave markers (五輪塔 gorintō). According to Komine, "The meaning of building a five-tiered stone monument above the remains is to pray that the deceased will be embraced by Dainichi Nyorai and become one with his eternal dharma body" (Komine 1995, 119). For Komine, the grave, while primarily a site for memorializing the dead, also provides an opportunity for guiding the living toward enlightenment. This is contrasted with scattering, which leaves nothing behind: "Scattering cuts off this important site that leads us to something of value. This is why I have misgivings" (ibid.).

22. This shift is a central theme in Mori 2000, chapter 5.
23. See http://www.geocities.co.jp/Bookend-Soseki /5166/senzo.htm. Last accessed January 24, 2003. This Web site is no longer available.

Komine also focuses on the beneficial lessons of causality as part of his critique, though in a different way than Ishizaki. He argues that while both direct cause (因 *in*), which he interprets as "the power of one's volition," and contributory cause (縁 *en*), "which is the power that surrounds and fosters direct cause," are both essential, it is the latter that provides the source of everything we experience. According to Komine, "This reckless scattering, which destroys the opportunity to direct a person's spirit, must be thought of as severing *en*, which for us Buddhists is the most important thing" (ibid.). There is a significant conflation here between very different uses of the term *en*. As noted in chapter 2, on the one hand, it is a technical Buddhist term that is usually translated as "indirect cause" (or condition/circumstance) and placed in opposition to "direct cause" (*in*) in explaining how phenomena arise in mutual dependence. In other words, it forms the basis of the Buddhist understanding of existence, it explains causation, and it provides the possible means to salvation. On the other hand, in common usage, *en* refers to a "relationship" or "bond" and generally takes the form of family or regional ties. Komine's comments provide a clear example of how deeply intertwined doctrinal and social concepts are in the realm of mortuary rites and how crucial that multivalence is to temple priests. As we will see in the next chapter, attempts to connect Buddhist doctrinal concepts to Japanese social norms through the site of the traditional family grave are also at the very center of debates over the current status and future of institutional Buddhism in Japan.

Although these types of critique of the GFPS may come as little surprise, Buddhist support for scattering comes from unexpected directions. In an article on the first *shizensō* performed by the GFPS, the *Bukkyō Times* solicited the opinions of four Buddhist priests and scholars. Despite the "warning bell" headlines noted above, the reactions were not entirely negative, and in fact three of the priests offered at least partial support for the idea of scattering. For Sōtō priest and director of the Buddhist Information Center, Suzuki Eijō 鈴木永城, scattering has lit a helpful fire of critique that, far from undermining Buddhism, may actually "provide the key to how individual temples should react to current [funerary] problems" (*Bukkyō Times*, October 25, 1991, 4). Although he does not specify why, Jōdo Shinshū scholar and priest Ōmura Eishō 大村英昭 considers scattering to be both folk religious and an extreme form of secularism. Echoing the criticisms above, Ōmura sees natural funerals as "severe individualism" but then admits that, as an individual, he too has the desire to have his remains scattered. He then allows, in a surprising but doctrinally consistent statement, that "the leaving behind of bones is of course a type of attachment" (ibid.).

For some priests such as Shinbo Yoshimichi 新保義道, former head of the Jōdo sect's efforts in Hawai'i, scattering is the best way to deal with the increase of individuals who die without descendants to take care of their graves, both in Hawai'i and in Japan. Echoing Ōmura Eishō's return to the doctrine of nonattachment, Shinbo argues, "Surely, the best method for protecting against the crude handling of ashes is to return them to nature at a suitable time. . . . Buddhism originally preached emptiness and discarding attachments to all things. Is it not important that we now discard our attachments to bodily remains? If we are going to cling to our bones, then there is no way we should throw away even one fragment of remains after cremation" (ibid.). Shinbo's last statement is of particular interest because it parallels doctrinally the oft-invoked legal defense of scattering made by GFPS founder Yasuda regarding the potential criminality of everyone who leaves behind even a small portion of remains at the crematorium.

Another voice that must be included in this debate comes from Buddhists who are also members of the GFPS, such as Shingon Buzanha priest, Okada Hirotaka 岡田弘隆. In a special issue of a Buzanha research journal, Okada quotes from a 1748 work entitled *A Compilation of Buddhist Rites for Monks and Laity* (真俗仏事編 *Shinzoku butsuji-hen*), which outlines three ways of dealing with a corpse: earth burial (土葬 *dosō*), cremation (火葬 *kasō*), and water burial (水葬 *suisō*).[24] In a section titled "The Superior and Inferior Merits of the Three Types of Burial" (三葬の功徳の勝劣 *Sansō no kudoku no shōretsu*), the three burials are defined in the following way:

Earth burial is an act that disposes of the whole body as it is. Therefore it is a very lonely practice. Cremation involves taking the bones and dividing them among the relatives. This follows the cremation of Śākyamuni. Water burial is a practice that offers the flesh of the body to other living things. (Okada 2001, 93)

These practices are then ranked so that earth burial is considered a lesser merit (下品の功徳 *gebon no kudoku*) and cremation is a midlevel

24. I discuss this journal in more detail in chapter 6.

merit, whereas water or forest burial (林葬 *rinsō*) offers the highest merit (上品の功徳 *jōbon no kudoku*). Though the above classifications are taken directly from the original, Okada then proceeds to equate the water and forest burials of the text with the natural funerals of the GFPS:

> This Buddhist view of placing the body in the water or in a forest as a superior practice comes from a very different historical background from today, but surely we can also value the act of returning powdered cremated remains to mountains and oceans as a "superior practice." This is because we can assume that eventually the ashes will become an offering (*fuse*) to living creatures. (Ibid., 93–94)

Doctrines of emptiness and nonattachment notwithstanding, the Buddhist fascination with bodily remains—seen, for example, in relic cults—appears across a wide variety of cultures and historical periods.[25] In the case of Japanese Buddhism, since the Tokugawa period a devotion to relics has been gradually replaced by a dependence on graves. With the majority of Japanese Buddhist temples' social authority and economic livelihood based on graves and memorial rites, the various sects and individual priests have naturally sought doctrinal justifications for the significance of these traditions. Despite the fact that some Buddhist priests have recognized that the scattering advocated by the GFPS appears to exemplify the ideal of nonattachment, most Buddhist criticisms of *shizensō* can be seen as attempts to maintain a multigenerational attachment to the grave through a focus on continuity, social bonds, and the importance of family. Though such family oriented arguments may appear to contradict established doctrine, they are in fact a defining characteristic of Japanese Buddhism, now and in the past.

FOREST BURIAL AT A RINZAI ZEN TEMPLE

One of the more fascinating Buddhist responses to the growing influence of natural funerals has come from a small Rinzai temple in Iwate Prefecture. Located in the town of Ichinoseki 一関 (pop. 61,000), Shōunji 祥雲寺 has been attracting both Buddhist and secular media attention since it began offering forest funerals (樹木葬 *jumokusō*) in November 1999. Like GFPS leader Yasuda, head priest Chisaka Genbō 千坂嵯峰 came up with the idea as a way to preserve the environment of the area and deal with

25. See, for example, Faure 1991, chapter 8; Sharf 1999; and Strong 2004.

increased demand for grave space. Located thirty minutes by car from the temple, the twenty-seven thousand square-meter wooded hill holds hundreds of graves and has been expanded several times since 1999.[26]

In a typical *jumokusō*, a spot is chosen in the forest where relatives, using only their hands, dig a hole about thirty centimeters deep and pour in the remains. A favorite flower or tree is planted to mark the spot, and finally Chisaka offers a short Buddhist prayer, the Dhāraṇī of Great Compassion (大悲呪 Daihiju), to end the ceremony.[27] When the forest was first opened, the location of each new grave was carefully recorded using a handheld global positioning system (GPS) that calculates exact longitude, latitude, and altitude via a satellite uplink.[28]

Though the forest funerals practiced at Shōunji offer intriguing parallels to the *shizensō* of the GFPS, there are several essential differences between them. The most important distinction is that a *jumokusō*, though a "natural funeral," consists of earth burial, not scattering, and thus is covered under the current grave law.[29] It is for this reason that the mountain area where the *jumokusō* take place is registered with the prefecture as a licensed graveyard. Thus, despite differences in appearance, the mountain used by Shōunji is technically no different from a regular graveyard except in that it contains no concrete graves. When confronted by comparisons to the GFPS, Chisaka is careful to point out that, because in a *jumokusō* service the remains are buried rather than scattered, there is no need to break them up into tiny pieces, as with scattering. He says, "I oppose scattering because it ignores the religious sentiments of the locals. When ashes are dropped on the ground, they are blown about by the wind, as are the flowers people put there as offerings. . . . [Yet in order to avoid trouble,] the bones must be crushed. This seems inhuman" (*Jimon Kōryū* 寺門興隆, February 2000, 46–47). The final distinction from GFPS scattering practices is that Chisaka offers a Buddhist ceremony at the burial.[30]

26. See http://dm18.cside.jp/~s18067-1/description/index.html. Last accessed May 2009.

27. This dhāraṇī is primarily used by the Rinzai and Sōtō sects. For a list of funerary prayers for each of the Buddhist schools, see Fujii 1980. For a discussion of dhāraṇī in Japan, see Abé 1999, 5–8. For dhāraṇī in China, see Copp 2008.

28. Subsequently a new system was employed where grave location is recorded in relation to surrounding trees and natural landmarks.

29. At Shōunji, the term *maisō*, "burial/interment" (as opposed to scattering), is used to describe the act of placing the cremated remains in the ground.

30. Official temple policy regarding religious affiliation is as follows: "Regulation #2: The temple does not inquire into the patron's religious affiliation, but at the time of burial the service will be conducted in a Zen sect format" (*Jimon Kōryū*, February 2000, 48). Religious tolerance is demonstrated by the fact that four of the first thirty people buried at Shōunji were

Having specific gravesites means that Shōunji can also offer traditional memorial services, as well as yearly gatherings for a group memorial service. At the 2001 memorial I met several families from Tokyo who
travel to the memorial service every year as part of their summer vaca-
tion. Ironically, one of the biggest complaints against the natural funerals
and the *jumokusō* graveyard at Shōunji is that they are far too natural. As
previously noted, the forest is thirty minutes by car from the temple and,
even with a recently completed building closer to the site, it is roughly
one kilometer to the closest toilet or running water. Due to its location
in the mountains in northern Japan, the area gets a lot of snow, and thus
the graveyard is officially closed from mid-November to mid-April. This
means that only those who die in the spring, summer, or early fall can
have subsequent graveside memorial rites on the actual anniversary of
death. Limited accessibility also precludes a traditional equinox visit in
March (彼岸 *higan*).

One of the biggest problems with the forest graveyard, despite the use
of twenty-first-century technology, is that relatives still have substantial
difficulty finding family graves. Forest growth changes considerably from
season to season, and many of the families only visit the graveyard once
a year. For those who come more regularly, even with a special map from
the temple, it can be very difficult to find a specific grave. While touring
the site with Chisaka at the annual memorial service in 2001, I witnessed
at least three different groups asking him if he had any idea where their
relatives were buried. Uncertainty about where graves are located also
makes for rather ginger stepping as one walks through the forest. While
some families constructed makeshift grave markers by arranging a small
ring around the plant or tree to mark the spot, most of the graves were vir-
tually indistinguishable from their surroundings. It is interesting to note
that in 2004, when I revisited the site, the temple had bowed to pressure
from members and relaxed the restriction on grave markers. At that time
many members had chosen to place small wooden markers at their graves,
reinforcing the notion that a key aspect of a grave, forest or stone, is its
fixed, easily identifiable location.

Shōunji represents one of the most visible early Buddhist responses
to the GFPS, and it is worth noting the similar environmental platforms.

Christians. At the first annual *jumokusō* memorial service held in June 2001, both chanting
of the *Heart Sūtra* and readings from the Bible by a Christian priest were included. See http://
www.jumokuso.or.jp/news/news010617.html for pictures and a description of the ceremony.
Last accessed May 14, 2009.

Not unlike Yasuda and the forests of rebirth, Chisaka began the project as a way to counter the overflowing graveyards in the area and to promote local conservation. Although Shōunji was initially an isolated case, similar sites are appearing throughout the country.[31]

COMMERCIALIZATION

Perhaps the clearest indication of the GFPS's growing success, aside from the amount of social and legal controversy it has produced, is the increasing number of professional funeral companies that have started offering their own versions of the natural funeral. Within two and a half years of the first *shizensō*, the Tokyo-based funeral company Kōeisha 公営社 became the first professional group to offer ocean scattering (海葬 *kaisō*) services. Charging two hundred seventy thousand yen for individual services and one hundred thousand yen per person for group ceremonies, Kōeisha will charter the boat and transport up to eight mourners to a spot twenty kilometers from land in Sagami Bay, where a simple ceremony takes place.[32] Similar in most ways to the ocean-scattering rites of the GFPS, Kōeisha's service is modeled on a burial at sea with ceremonial intervals marked by moments of silence, the fog whistle, or the ship's bell. The ceremony is presided over by a member of the funeral company, though families may have a priest present if they wish, and it is also possible to have some sort of "traditional" funeral ceremony before scattering the remains in the ocean. The company's Web page advertises the service in the following way:

> With changes in the environment and a shift in awareness from the family to the individual, one can see a reform in the form of funerals and thinking about graves. Scattering arises from a desire for recurrence, one that regards returning to the ocean as the principle of nature and sees humans as originally part of a life energy that was born of the sea.[33]

31. For example, Okamoto Wakō 岡本和幸 (the assistant head priest at Tōchōji), with the help of Annex staff, has created a *jumokusō* site at Shinkōji 真光寺, his Sōtō temple in rural Chiba. Inoue Haruyo, the scholar of burial mentioned in chapter 3, founded a cherry blossom burial (桜葬 *sakurasō*) site at a graveyard in Machida city in Tokyo. For more *jumokusō* sites, see Inoue 2008, 96.

32. Costs for a natural funeral through the GFPS are one hundred thousand yen for a group ceremony and one hundred fifty thousand to three hundred thousand for an individual service.

33. See http://www.mps.ne.jp/company/koueisya/sankotu/no5.htm. Last accessed January 10, 2003). This Web site is no longer available.

Though there are obvious parallels to GFPS ideology of a cyclical relation between humans and nature, Kōeisha manager Aoki Mitsuo 青木満男 insists his company is not in competition with the society, nor is it trying to spread the idea of natural funerals or expand the funerary freedom movement in any way. They are merely offering new services to individual consumers (Aoki 1994, 108). A crucial distinction between *shizensō* and rites offered by professional companies is the degree of self-awareness demonstrated in the former. All society funerals include a specific reference to which number it represents in the overall *shizensō* count. There will also be a mention within the ceremony of the funerary freedom movement in general and its growing success. If the scattering takes place in a new location or form, this is also emphasized. In late 1996, Yasuda was on hand in Miyagi Prefecture to supervise the first *shizensō* held on land. The husband of the deceased wanted to put his wife to rest quietly and had initially refused to allow any television coverage but was later convinced that, as a member of the GFPS, he had an obligation to help spread the society's message (Yamaori and Yasuda 2000, 104–15).

The GFPS does not oppose the commercialization of scattering, but it does make every effort to distinguish itself from commercial scattering services. As noted above, GFPS literature consistently attempts to separate natural funerals, or *shizensō*, from scattering. According to Yasuda, the funeral companies offer scattering as merely one more service and often do not take the environmental element seriously. He frequently complains that pictures in the news of flower bouquets, still wrapped in plastic, alongside other environmentally unfriendly memorial items floating in the sea, do little to further the society's efforts.

Ironically, one benefit of going through a funeral company rather than through the GFPS is that the commercial version may offer more freedom for people who want to have their ashes scattered but do not necessarily agree with all the elements of the society's platform. There are also those who do not want to give up on regular memorial visits. Kōeisha, unlike the GFPS, offers return trips to the scattering spot for yearly memorial visits and will also arrange religious ceremonies upon request.

LOCATING THE REMAINS

As noted above, GFPS literature often contrasts dark, dank, claustrophobic family graves with the bright open spaces of nature. This was also a common theme in the stories of the GFPS members with whom I spoke.

One woman repeatedly told me a story of how her mother-in-law decided to put all the individual family graves into one central grave. Since several of the graves dated to the Tokugawa period, before cremation was the norm, many of these plots contained buried bodies. Although this woman was not there to see the process, she received accounts from relatives that many of the remains were immersed in ground water. Since that time, she says that her only image of graves is of damp, clammy (じめじめ *jimejime*) places.

It is worth juxtaposing, for a moment, the contrasting images of family graves presented in this chapter and the desiccated grave introduced at the start of this book. Whether dark and flooded or dried out and abandoned, these stark images demarcate the limitations of the extended-family grave in contemporary Japan. Both instill a similar sense of abandonment and despair. Unlike the response to this fear offered by eternal memorial graves, which maintain the established idiom of fixed, delineated spaces and regular memorials for the dead, the GFPS offers a potentially far more radical response, one that does not rely on regular memorials, fixed location, or bounded spaces.

Though the GFPS does not often address itself directly to the question of memorial rites, both Yasuda and individual members are certainly aware of the many critics who use this as a point of attack. The society's quarterly newsletter *Rebirth* (再生 *Saisei*) includes brief letters by members describing natural funerals in which they have taken part and sharing their opinions on related issues. A particularly poignant response to the question of memorial rites came from a veteran who wrote of the great number of his fellow navy officers in World War II who had died without funerals in the South Pacific. As if responding directly to the Buddhist critics discussed above, he wrote, "The melody of the endless tide pacifies the departed spirit better than one million sutra recitations. I hope that I too will be scattered in the azure sea" (*Saisei* 41, (2001):19). When I specifically asked Yasuda for his position on ancestor worship he answered that, though he agrees with the concept in general, most people have never even met the generation before their grandparents and thus have little connection to them. He also doubted that any ill would come from not continuing to make offerings to the dead, since there was no way a deceased spirit would want to harm his or her own descendants. Despite the apparent logic of this statement, it is a radical departure from traditional Japanese conceptions of the dead. Both the history and physical landscape of Japan are littered with monuments, shrines, and myriad prophylactic rites to ensure the continued appeasement of departed spirits.[34]

The other tradition that scattering overturns is the clear separation between the living and the dead. By slipping through the loophole in current Japanese grave laws, the GFPS has potentially opened up the entire country to death. Despite finding widespread support for scattering, the Welfare Ministry's 1997 survey also revealed that, even among those who accept scattering, 62 percent felt that specific rules should be laid down regarding location. Over 80 percent of all surveyed thought that scattering in places such as towns, parks, roads, river heads, and beaches was inappropriate, and 70 percent felt the same way about fishing and farming areas (Mori 2000, 28–30). With scattering, the boundaries of a graveyard or memorial park are no longer relevant. There is a real fear that somebody's ashes could conceivably be in your backyard, under your picnic basket, or mixed in with the fish you are having for dinner. The fact that people are reacting so much more strongly to the form and location of scattered remains rather than to the potential undermining of ancestral rites and family continuity shows that the location of human remains may be even more important than whether anyone is memorializing them.

Immediately after death, the corpse is in an ambiguous, or to use van Gennep's terms, liminal state (Gennep 1960). Neither fully present nor completely gone, the deceased must be ritually removed from both the social and the physical sphere of the living and transferred to that of the dead. What is particularly intriguing about the idea of scattering in public spaces is the way that it may extend the liminal period indefinitely. Although interest in van Gennep's work tends to focus on liminality, we need also to keep in mind the importance of reincorporation. It is essential that at some time the dead are plainly situated somewhere other than among the living. Note that while for the bereaved family and the GFPS, scattering may end the liminal stage, for those who live and work in the area where the remains are scattered, the lack of a clearly defined space for the dead means that they are never *in their place.*

This ambiguity of location, or lack of fixity, which scattering entails, also carries over into other areas. There is the unclear position of scattering in the eyes of the law, neither legal nor illegal, neither prohibited nor fully accepted. The remains are also ambiguous in terms of tradition. Scattered in the ocean or in a forest they are taken out of the cycle of ancestral worship and family obligation, not abandoned (遺棄 *iki*), but certainly without ties (無縁 *muen*). In a sense scattering solves the problem of *muen*, not simply by reducing the load on overburdened urban graveyards or redefining traditional bonds, but rather by providing the deceased with an alternative to the ancestral cycle, that of nature.

Temples are also providing alternative cycles and spaces, but these are still within the Buddhist idiom and they are still very much fixed in space and tradition. The rhetoric of permanence inherent in the extended-family-grave ideal is maintained in these new sites. The GFPS ends its relation to the dead as soon as they are "returned" to nature, whereas an eternal memorial grave site continues its interactions, potentially for decades. The GFPS does not reject memorial or the idealized permanence promised by the traditional or eternal memorial grave. Rather, it attempts to replace fixity with fluidity, location with unbounded nature, and tradition with independence.

CHAPTER SIX

Sectarian Researchers and the Funeral Problem

The *responses* to questions may be seen as reflecting social problems . . .
but the *fact that particular questions are posed* is not.
—Morris-Suzuki 2000, 520.

So far our exploration of contemporary Japanese Buddhism and the disposition of the dead has been confined to certain temples and sites of
nonstandard burial. By examining innovative grave systems in a variety
of settings, I have tried to provide a clear sense of the critical and very
practical issues facing priests in Japan today and of the tensions created by
temples' long-standing dependence on the traditional, extended patrilineal
family in the face of drastic demographic and social changes in the postwar period. Chapters 2–4, in particular, illustrated the practical aspects
of the funeral problem such as a failing parishioner system, propagation,
and limited temple resources; in other words, issues with immediate and
quantifiable impacts on temples. This chapter situates temple priests in institutional networks and investigates a more conceptual, but equally critical, aspect of the funeral problem: the changing interpretation and unclear
role of doctrine in mortuary practice. Specifically, I examine how "concrete" aspects of funerary Buddhism are transformed from institutional
dilemmas into existential crises by influential sectarian scholars whose
discourse guides the way Buddhist priests think about their vocation.

This chapter analyses differing conceptions of funerary Buddhism
within the activities of certain sectarian intellectuals and researchers[1]

Portions of this chapter appeared previously in Rowe 2004.
1. All the researchers at these centers are ordained priests. Some are abbots of their
own temples, some are graduate students, and some are professors at sectarian universities.

178

in the Jōdo, Sōtō, Shingon Buzanha, and Nichiren sects.[2] Should funerary Buddhism be distinguished from some purer form of the tradition, or
should it be embraced as the ideal opportunity for propagation? What of
the apparent contradiction between Buddhist denials of any unchanging,
metaphysical entity such as a soul and the need to comfort parishioners
who have lost a loved one? Is this "contradiction" even an issue for temple
priests or is it the creation of a modern group of sectarian thinkers steeped
in Western scholarly categories? These dilemmas take a variety of forms:
from debates over the relationship between "true" Buddhism and folk beliefs, to concerns over the dissonance between the training of priests and
the day-to-day work of local temples, and to irritation over institutional
gaps between sectarian elites and local priests.

For sectarian researchers, intellectuals, and a growing number of temple priests, the mortuary problem (葬祭問題 sōsai mondai) extends beyond
the realm of mere funerary concerns; the discourse surrounding burial
is in fact a debate about the very meaning and future of Buddhism in Japan. By approaching the work of sectarian intellectuals and researchers as
not merely reflective of the problems facing contemporary Japanese Buddhism but also constitutive of how a given sect as a whole fashions its
responses, and, in turn, impacts local temple practices, I argue for a view
of these research centers as key sites in the modern production of Japanese
Buddhism.

This chapter thus focuses on how the efforts of these centers to properly understand the problems facing the traditional sects may be in large
part responsible for producing and disseminating tensions between normative Buddhist positions and the practical realities that most temple
priests must confront as part of their daily activities.[3] I am specifically
interested here in two issues that bring the differences between temples

---

Although all of them are "researchers," I also include the term "intellectuals" to highlight
a select few who represent the public face of a given sect's research efforts. Examples of this
group would include Sasaki Kōkan 佐々木宏幹, often referred to as the "brain" of the Sōtō sect,
Ōmura Eishō 大村英昭 of the Shinshū (Honganji) sect, and Itō Yuishin 伊藤唯真 of the Jōdo
sect.

2. I have chosen research centers at these four sects because I believe they provide a broad
enough spectrum to be considered representative of research efforts by all the major sects.

3. This is not to imply, however, that the discourse surrounding funerary Buddhism can
or should be reduced to a mere conflict between doctrine and practice. It is not enough simply
to identify an opposition between idealized visions of a sect located in sutra literature or the
teachings of a founder on the one hand, and the logistics of running a temple on the other. The
mere existence of incongruity between Buddhist ideals and actual practices is, of course, nothing new. Indeed, I would argue that such tensions are both necessary and generative in most, if
not all, religious traditions.

and sectarian researchers into sharp relief: the soteriological benefits of
posthumous ordination and the doctrine of no-self. Although some sectarian scholars depict temple priests agonizing over the fact that the funerary rituals they regularly perform at temples are inconsistent with core
Buddhist teachings, ethnographic, archeological, and textual studies from
numerous traditions have shown that, if such anxiety actually exists, it
is a rarity in the Buddhist world.[4] Indeed, in the case of Japan, one would
have a hard time finding any widespread belief that such a contradiction
even existed, let alone that it was a problem, prior to the Meiji period.[5]
The question, then, is how and why things have changed in the modern
and contemporary periods. While chapter 1 introduced many of the social,
political, and economic changes affecting Buddhist organizations in Meiji,
here I will explore the ways in which less immediately tangible effects of
Japanese Buddhism's modern encounter with the West have led sectarian
researchers to help create and exacerbate this crucial aspect of the mortuary problem.

SECTARIAN RESEARCH CENTERS

Each of the major Buddhist sects in Japan funds research centers, staffed
with graduate students and academics from Buddhist sectarian universities and charged with conducting research on everything from doctrinal studies to brain death to the status of temple families (for a list of
research centers, see table 2). To date, these centers and the texts they
produce have been approached by scholars primarily as places to engage
with issues of sect history and doctrine. Here, however, I look to certain
research centers to explore the ways in which contemporary issues facing
local priests are both understood and shaped by the upper levels of their
organizations.

Scholars of Japanese Buddhism will be familiar with these centers, often located on the grounds of sectarian universities, which promote "Buddhological" scholarship on the founders, doctrinal texts, and historical
developments of their respective sects.[6] Examples include the Institute for
Zen Studies (禅文化研究所 Zen Bunka Kenkyūjo) at Hanazono University,
the Division of Sōtō Zen Studies (曹洞宗宗学研究部門 Sōtōshū Shūgaku
Kenkyū Bumon) at Komazawa University, and the Research Center for

---

4. See, for example, Schopen 1997, 23–55, 114–47, and 204–37.
5. See, for example, Stone and Walter 2008, 18–19; and Tanabe 2008.
6. For a discussion of the Buddhological approach, see Foulk 1993.

TABLE 2. Sectarian research centers

Name	Sect	Location	Web site
Buzanha Kyōka Center	Shingonshū Buzanha	Tokyo	No public website
Chizanha Kyōka Center	Shingonshū Chizanha	Tokyo	www.chisan.or.jp/chisan/ center/index.html
Jōdo Shinshū Studies and Research Center	Jōdo Shinshū Honganjiha	Kyoto	crs.hongwanji.or.jp/kyogaku/
Jōdoshū Research Institute	Jōdoshū	Tokyo	www.jsri.jp/
Myōshinjiha Kyōka Center	Rinzaishū Myōshinjiha	Kyoto	www.myoshinji.or.jp/webhonjo/book/index.html
Nichiren Buddhism Modern Religious Institute	Nichirenshū	Tokyo	www.genshu.gr.jp/index.htm
Shinshū Otaniha Kyōgaku Kenkyūjo	Jōdo Shinshū Otaniha	Kyoto	www.tomo-net.or.jp/sermon/kyoken/kyoken01.html
Sōtō Institute for Buddhist Studies	Sōtōshū	Tokyo	www.sotozen-net.or.jp/gaku/soken/
Tendaishū Sōgō Kenkyū Center	Tendaishū	Otsu, Saga	http://tendai.jp/

Note: All these centers have conducted surveys of their sects. Names in English when provided. Myōshiniha website link is to list of publications only.

Nichiren Doctrinal Studies (日蓮教学研究所 Nichirenshū Kyōgaku Kenkyūjo) at Risshō University. While the creation of these centers in the postwar period and their activities over the past fifty years have not received
much scholarly attention, my focus here is on those research groups that
are charged with the specific task of studying their respective sects in the
context of contemporary society.

The Sōtō Zen sect, for example, currently operates three separate research divisions. Two of these, the aforementioned Division of Sōtō Zen
Studies and the Division for Mission of Sōtō Zen Buddhism (教化研修部門
Kyōka Kenshū Bumon) were established in the 1950s. Four decades later,
sect leaders determined the need for a research group that could respond
to modern societal changes and problems. Specifically mentioned on the
sect's official homepage are "the problems of human rights, bio-ethics,
the environment, and the emphasis on doctrinal explanations of funeral
rites and ancestor worship."[7] In response, the sect created the Division of
Contemporary Sōtō Zen Studies (現代宗学研究部門 Gendai Shūgaku Ken-
kyū Bumon) in 1994.[8] These three research divisions were then brought
together under the auspices of the Research Center for Sōtō Zen Buddhism
(曹洞宗総合研究センター Sōtōshū Sōgō Kenkyū Sentā), which was established in 1998 to produce multidisciplinary research that downplays tex-
tual/doctrinal studies in favor of ethnographic and sociological approaches
to customs, folklore, education, and Buddhism in the modern world.

Similarly, the Jōdoshū Research Institute (浄土宗総合研究所 Jōdoshū
Sōgō Kenkyūjo, or JSRI) was established in 1989 to bring together the
Doctrinal (教学研究部 Kyōgaku Kenkyū Bu), Missionary (布教研究部 Fukyō
Kenkyū Bu), and Ritual (法式研究部 Hōshiki Kenkyū Bu) research divisions. Referred to in official sect literature as the "think tank" of the Jōdo
sect, the institute, like its counterparts in other Buddhist denominations,
is concerned with applying the sect's teachings to contemporary social
issues. Ongoing topics of research at the center include "Jōdo Teachings

7. See http://www.sotozen-net.or.jp/. The sect has updated the Web site so that the three
most prominent "problems of contemporary society" currently are Aum Shinrikyō オウム真理教,
the religious group responsible for the 1995 sarin gas attack on the Tokyo subway; brain death
and organ transplants; and bioethics. Discussions of funerals, human rights, and peace still
appear throughout the Sōtō Zen homepage. Last accessed January 27, 2011.

8. The English names of the respective centers represent official Sōtō translations as of
2005. These names have since been changed to the Zen Studies Department, Zen and Contemporary Studies Department, and Sōtō Education Department. The entire research center is
now referred to as the Sōtō Institute for Buddhist Studies (http://www.sotozen-net.or.jp/gaku/
soken/f_kenkyu.html. Last accessed January 27, 2011).

and the Present," "Buddhist Social Welfare," "Responses to Contemporary Religious and Social Problems," "Propagation," "International Relations," "Bioethics," and "Contemporary Funerary Buddhism."[9]

The Nichiren Buddhism Modern Religious Institute (日蓮宗現代宗教研究所 Nichirenshū Gendai Shūkyō Kenkyūjo, or NMRI) was established in 1964 with the goal of "[i]nvestigating the realities of the various contemporary religions and contributing to the establishment of a contemporary interpretation of Nichiren doctrine and a belief/propagation system that conforms to the current age."[10] Nichiren sect rules, in addition to outlining the staffing and management of the NMRI, provides a list of ten general topics for which the research center is responsible.[11] This list includes the need for surveys of the actual conditions of both the Nichiren sect and other religious organizations, as well as a clear concern with how best to spread Nichiren's teachings in contemporary society (Nichirenshū Shūmuin 2004, 193).

How research centers fit into their particular institutional structures is further suggested by intriguing visual representations in official sect literature. A Jōdo sect pamphlet shows the research institute in the center of a circle interacting independently with the Jōdo sect parliament (宗議会 Shūgikai), Jōdo parishioners, temples, the sect headquarters (宗務庁 Shūmu-chō), educational and welfare divisions within the sect, and society at large. A literal interpretation of the diagram would lead one to conclude that the Institute is *the* collaborative body of the sect and the only conduit through which different groups within the organization communicate, either with each other or society at large. The very first report put out by the research institute includes a diagram of the staff composition and activities of each division. The diagram makes it clear that the institute's primary function is to receive directions from, and then report its findings back to, the secretary general of the sect (宗務総長 Shūmu sōchō) (Jōdoshū Sōgō Kenkyūjo 1990).

As for the Sōtō sect, the official position, or "vision" of the Research

---

9. A complete list of JSRI projects dating from 1999 to the present can be found at http://www.jsri.jp/Project/projects.htm. Last accessed January 27, 2011.

10. See http://www.genshu.gr.jp/home/syoukai.htm. Last accessed January 24, 2010.

11. Details on the organization and objectives of research centers generally can be found in the official rules of each sect. For example, Jōdo sect regulations (浄土宗門法制類纂 Jōdoshū shūmon hōsei ruisan) include four pages (fourteen articles and forty-one subclauses) detailing the mandate, staffing, and administration of the sect's research organs (Jōdoshū Henshū 2005, 921–24).

Center for Sōtō Zen Buddhism is represented on the sect's homepage by a drawing of an apple tree.[12] The sunshine and rain falling on the tree is labeled "the teachings" (教え oshie), while the three research divisions are denoted by apples. The earth below symbolizes the Sōtō faithful (教団 kyōdan) and society at large, with the Research Center standing as the tree trunk, feeding what one must conclude is energy or nutrients (represented by arrows) both down to the believers and up to the research-division apples. Though perhaps doing so in a way unintended by its designers, the image is also potentially revealing in that the teachings, represented as they are by the elements of nature, are entirely beyond the reach and influence of society, the sect, or the sect's researchers. I would point out that the tree diagram is also suggestive in that these centers in many ways, as the Jōdo pamphlet also indicates, act as the central conduit linking the different elements of the sect—although the exchange is neither as tidy nor effective as the diagrams would make it appear.

Despite variations in research topics, size, and scope, research centers maintained by each of the established Buddhist sects fulfill similar roles within their organizations.[13] They represent a crucial, but as yet overlooked, field within which to approach Buddhist sects as self-conscious institutions, made up of diverse voices struggling in different ways to maintain and propagate certain religious ideals across a broad and equally diverse constituency.[14] In other words, these centers constitute central sites of contemporary Buddhist discourse that should receive the same sort of attention more traditionally applied to temples or texts.[15] And like temples and texts, the activities of these centers allow scholars access to the various dynamics at play within Buddhist organizations.

12. This "vision" of the research center has since been taken down and is now "under construction" (http://www.sotozen-net.or.jp/. Last accessed April 10, 2009).

13. Lack of access prevented me from gathering detailed background on the history of the Shingonshū Buzanha 真言宗豊山派 sect's research center.

14. Scholars have written on specific controversies that involve sectarian intellectuals. Two notable cases include the Critical Buddhism (批判仏教 hihan Bukkyō) debate in Sōtō Zen Buddhism (Hubbard and Swanson 1997) and "Shinshū P" (Reader and Tanabe 1998, 94–97). What I am trying to do here, however, is worry less about the extraordinary issues and concentrate more on the day-to-day work of what people at these centers do. Just as ethnographic studies of Buddhism must properly explore quotidian temple life, so too must our accounts of research centers attend to the ordinary activities of these Buddhist researchers and intellectuals.

15. As with effective studies of specific temples or villages, research centers need to be investigated both historically and ethnographically. Such a project would require extensive fieldwork and ideally would consider the training and background of the researchers, the relationship between the center and the political hierarchy of the sect, and various points of contact between researchers and temple priests. While I am currently working on this research, such detail lies outside the scope of the present work.

SURVEYING EMPTINESS

Mandated in the regulations of most Buddhist sects and carried out by a handful of researchers, sectwide surveys (宗勢調査 shūsei chōsa) assessing the organization's vigor (勢い ikioi) are taken every four to ten years and generally began in the 1960s and 1970s.[16] The first Jōdo shūsei survey took place in 1962, whereas the Nichiren sect conducted its first in 1972. The Sōtō sect actually carried out surveys in 1936 and 1955, but later Sōtō publications often refer to the 1965 version as the first of its kind, perhaps because it represented the first use of an "electronic calculating machine."

Although a detailed history of sectarian surveys lies outside the scope of the present chapter, one can identify certain developments at the time of their emergence. These trends include a growing interest in quantitative research from the 1930s, which spiked in the postwar period with the introduction of new quantitative methods by U.S. occupation forces;[17] the perception among the different sects that they needed to improve their ability to understand and respond to the needs of a rapidly changing Japanese society; the "threat" posed by the success of the various New Religions; and the very structure of the Buddhist sects themselves: large, unwieldy organizations made up of centralized and local bureaucracies charged with overseeing thousands of temples spread throughout the country. Sectwide surveys were, and continue to be, seen by sect leadership as an ideal way both to understand the current conditions of the organization as a whole and to plot a course through the often rough seas of a rapidly modernizing nation.

Researchers send these surveys out to all temple priests and, increasingly, to temple families (寺族 jizoku) as well.[18] The data is entered into computers, collated, and analyzed by sectarian researchers who publish summaries and analysis of the results initially in sectarian journals and later in book-length volumes that are distributed to temples via regional

16. For example, section 10 of the Nichiren Sect Rules (日蓮宗宗制 Nichirenshū Shūsei) details the regulations for the Association of Sectarian Surveys. The group is charged with conducting surveys on Nichiren sect activities, finances, and other subjects. The shūsei surveys of temples, churches, priests, and followers are to be conducted every eight years in order to "grasp the true conditions" of the sect (Nichirenshū Shūsei 2004, 82).

17. According to Morris-Suzuki, one of first Japanese books to include detailed discussion of opinion research techniques was Tokyo University professor Koyama Eizō's 小山栄三 (1899–1983) Shinbungaku 新聞学, published in 1935, one year before the first Sōtō sectwide survey. Survey taking became so common in the postwar period that by the middle of 1953 there were twenty different groups involved in nationwide opinion surveys (Morris-Suzuki 2000, 518).

18. The term jizoku, though literally "temple family," refers to the head priest's wife. See Kawahashi 1995.

sect bureaucracies. The questions, numbering from forty to almost one hundred, depending on the sect, cover a consistent set of themes: inventorying the temple's material conditions, cataloging and evaluating the staff (priests, temple wives, etc.), and gauging proselytizing activities.

Although these general surveys include some questions on funerary activities, researchers also conduct mortuary-specific surveys. More so than the standard surveys, these products of sectarian research and bureaucracy trace fissures between idealized forms of Buddhism and the physical and soteriological disposition of parishioner bodies. One can glimpse in these surveys the attempt by the various sects (research centers representing sect leadership) to both comprehend and control the production of Buddhism that is occurring at local temples.

One thing must be made clear at the outset. Although at times I will cite survey data to illustrate certain points, my main goal here is to read these surveys against the grain. I am not particularly interested here with how many Sōtō sect parishioners say they have Buddhist altars or how many hours per week Nichiren priests purportedly spend on proselytizing activities. I am, on the other hand, fascinated by how and why these questions themselves are being asked, why other questions are not asked, how questions change over time, and how the asking itself is accomplished. In other words, I am primarily interested in the question of what *doing* surveys *does* (Jones 2004, 86). Thus, I will not use survey results to attempt to quantify the "actual state" of funerary Buddhism in contemporary Japan, but to examine normative assumptions and organizational gaps implicit in both the questions and the range of possible responses in mortuary surveys. In so doing, I hope to demonstrate what the *sōsai mondai* reveals about the current state of Buddhist institutions as a whole.

A MORTUARY SURVEY OF THE JŌDO SECT

The first full-length, sectarian research volume dedicated to mortuary issues, *Mortuary Buddhism* (葬祭仏教 *Sōsai Bukkyō*), was published by the Jōdo sect in 1997 and included the results of two surveys conducted a few years earlier. The first of these, a survey of Jōdo priests carried out in 1994, is introduced as an attempt to "grasp the current realities" of funerary Buddhism amidst a variety of many of the problems I have addressed in previous chapters: the commercialism brought on by funeral companies; the stultification and pomposity of funerals that has led to a loss of religious sentiment; the steep rise in grave costs; and the difficulties of maintaining temple graves due to a declining birthrate (Satō 1997, 332).

In the short list of thirteen questions,[19] the overriding goal is clearly to identify the extent of a priest's role in funerals and gauge the degree to which the basic rites, timing, and Buddhist message are being compromised by funeral-company interests.[20] Throughout the survey there is a pervasive and almost palpable undercurrent of anxiety over the power of funeral companies. It concludes with an open-ended question asking the priests if they have any thoughts about what should be done to rectify the current state of funerals. Priests are also asked to identify any significant changes they may have noticed in their lifetimes. Since this is the only open-ended question on the survey, the responses cannot be quantified, but this does not stop the researchers from providing a generalized summary that may reveal as much about their own concerns as it does those of the priests surveyed. The "open" responses parallel almost exactly the central issues raised in the main body of the survey. We are told, for example, that many priests see the current funeral situation as dire and that this is due in large part to encroachment by the funeral professionals into what was traditionally the priest's domain. There is also apprehension over the trend toward simplified funerals that may be resulting in a depreciation of the emotional element (心の部分 kokoro no bubun) of these rites.[21]

More specifically, respondents complained that during the funeral it is the photograph of the deceased rather than the central object of worship (本尊 honzon) that is the focus of the rite. For Buddhist priests, the

19. For a complete list of the questions, see appendix.

20. It is worth noting what the survey method itself reveals about the limits acting on researchers (and thus the sect). Since they did not have the funds to carry out a full-scale survey, researchers instead included the survey questions and a postcard-sized answer sheet in the monthly journal Shūhō (宗報), which is sent to all Jōdo temples. Although this allowed maximum distribution, it severely limited what could be asked and in no way freed researchers from dependence on priests actually mailing in the responses. In the end, 820 responses were received, though only 681 were returned in time for the 'first report. At best, the researchers admit, they had a 10 percent response rate and thus were unable to draw any inferences about overall trends.

21. Fears of such shifts and the impulse to quantify them are in no way limited to the Jōdo sect. For example, the 2003 Shingonshū Buzanha sect survey of priestly opinion included several questions relating to funerals and the future of the sect. In one question, priests were asked how they felt about increases in nonreligious funerals. Two-thirds of the 1,254 respondents were either "worried" or felt a "sense of impending crisis" (危機感 kikikan), whereas less than 11 percent felt "secure" or that the future was "bright." In a second question on the general level of respect toward the ancestors, a total of 64 percent fell into the worried or impending crisis categories. A Sōtō sect survey of funerary issues in 2001 found that just over 50 percent of priests think that in the future funerals will be Buddhist and almost 75 percent think it will be difficult to maintain the temple/parishioner relationship (Sōtōshū Sōgō Kenkyū Sentā 2003).

focal point of the funeral altar (祭壇 saidan) is the Buddhist scroll or image that adorns the central position. It is to the Buddha that mourners bow and offer incense during the funeral in order to generate merit for the deceased. Priests responded that they were troubled by the thought that many mourners may be bowing instead to the image of the deceased (also prominently displayed in the center of the altar). These responses are then presented by researchers as part of a concomitant apprehension (on the part of temple priests) that funerals are becoming increasingly oriented toward folk beliefs and practices (習俗化 shūzokuka) rather than Buddhist faith. The researchers thus paint a picture of a general public that mistakenly views the funeral, not as Buddhist ritual, but as deriving its primary force from "custom."

Here, then, is a blueprint for much of the research center discourse on funerary Buddhism: to highlight (and, at times, suggest) causal links between doctrinal compromise and the increased emphasis on folk practices in funerals. This example of a general sect survey demonstrates how researchers disseminate anxieties regarding decline to their local-level representative priests in temples across Japan. The questions asked and the interpretation of responses, quantitative or qualitative, both instill and naturalize the idea that priests need to worry that Buddhism has become merely the window dressing rather than the substance of funerals.

The second Jōdo funeral survey included in *Mortuary Buddhism* focused on Jōdo parishioners rather than priests and was conducted in 1995. Acknowledging significant dissatisfaction among the public regarding Buddhist funerals, the survey begins with the stated premise that it is not priests in general who are being criticized by the public but only the attitude and behavior of temple priests who deal with funerals.[22] In order to obtain a more thorough understanding of public opinion, the researchers divided the

22. The method again deserves attention because of what it says about the limits Buddhist organizations face in being able to actually gauge public opinion. While again acknowledging that a mail survey would provide the most random sample, the researchers admitted that this was beyond their budget and thus had to depend on local priests to hand out the surveys at their own discretion. The response rate was a healthy 61.3 percent (1,806 out of 2,947), but only 1,428 were usable, giving them an actual return rate of just over 48 percent. This high return, along with the better than expected response rate on the open answer questions, led the researchers to conclude that funerary rites were something very close to people's hearts. How they then relate this to the fact that most of the open responses dealt with the high cost of funerals and posthumous names, as well as complaints about the routinization of funerals, is somewhat of a mystery (Hirose 1997, 352). One is left with the distinct impression, despite explanatory attempts by researchers to the contrary, that complaints by the general public over funerary

survey responses into correspondences between views on funerals and four different areas: family background, faith, living environment, and views on traditional folk practices. As with the priestly survey, the main goal seems to be gathering data about what kinds of people request what kinds of services. Reading the questions, one thinks immediately of a marketing survey, of a large corporation gathering consumer data on its main product line: "Tell us about yourself." "Are you the head of the household, parent of head, spouse of head, child, or grandchild?" "How many years have you lived in your current town?" "Were you born there or did you move after marriage or due to work?" "What was the most recent family funeral you attended?"[23] "Where was the funeral held, and who decided the location?" "Why was that location chosen?" "What was the total cost of the funeral and the individual cost for each of the following: funeral company, temple, and other expenses?" "What was your opinion of the funeral? Please tell us below in your own words" (Itō and Fujii 1997, 385–92).

The surveys also include questions that speak directly to the afore-mentioned anxieties over the public perception of priests.

> Do you agree, disagree, or are you unsure about the following state-ments regarding a priest's role in the funeral: (a) Funerals were not originally connected to Buddhism, so there is no reason for the priest to be involved; (b) To have the priest officiate the funeral and deliver the sermon to the deceased (引導 *indō*) is a characteristic of Japanese Buddhism, so I think his participation is a good thing; (c) The priest should be the central focus of the funeral. The participation of the fu-neral company should be limited. (Ibid., 391)

The perceptive reader will question whether most Japanese would conceive of the priest's funerary function in any of these three ways. If this were an open-ended question, the most common, very possibly the *only* response would be that "the priest is there to chant sutras." As with the survey of temple priests, I would argue that this question may tell us less about what parishioners actually think than what sectarian researchers would like them to be thinking about. It is worth noting that the most common

---

Buddhism have less to do with concerns over the purported decline of Buddhist teachings than with the high costs involved, or, as I suggested in chapter 4, the opacity of those costs.

23. This same set of questions is then repeated for respondents who may have attended a funeral for someone outside their family.

response to these three options overall was "I don't know" (Itō and Fujii 1997, 365).[24]

In many surveys, as with the one under discussion here, the priest's role in the funeral is identified with the *indō* rite—this is despite the fact that I have yet to see a question asking whether respondents even know what this term means or when it actually occurs during the funeral. Literally "leading [the deceased]," the *indō* is a sermon aimed at enlightening the deceased. Although common in the Zen sects, the *indō* is also present in Tendai, Jishū 時宗, Shingon, and Nichiren funerals (Fujii 1980). In some cases, the end of the sermon is punctuated by some dramatic gesture on the part of the priest such as a loud and sudden shout. Scholars have written about the historical significance of koan-like pronouncements by priests as they light the funeral pyre, but discussions with Japanese acquaintances and personal experiences provide a different sort of inflection.[25] For example, one friend, whose family are *danka* at a subtemple of Tōfukuji 東福寺 in Kyoto, recalled to me the family's utter confusion during her father's funeral when the Rinzai Zen priests suddenly snapped the tops off of several flowers on the altar and threw them to the ground with a loud shout. Rather than producing any sudden awakening in the audience (or, presumably, the deceased), this story became a running joke in the family. In my own experience, after my mother-in-law's funeral (also Rinzai) in rural Tokushima, family members all spoke of how grateful they were that the retired head priest, though unable to walk unassisted or speak above a whisper, insisted on leading the ceremony and on concluding it with a powerful shout (喝 *katsu*). Everyone was deeply moved and talked of little else directly after the ceremony. No one, however, knew that the shout represented the culmination of bestowing the *indō* and an indication that he had led our relative to the Buddhist path. Rather than seeing this dissonance as further proof of the degradation of Japanese Buddhism, I would argue that it speaks to the multiplicity of public interpretations of Buddhism with which the temple priest must contend. It is worth noting,

24. A related gap in expectations is evident in the 2001 Sōtō sect funerary survey. When priests are asked about the meaning of the funeral, over 85 percent think it is to bring peace of mind (安らぎ *yasuragi*) to parishioners, 80 percent think it is an important site of propagation, and 74 percent think it bolsters the faith (信仰を支えている *shinkō o sasaete iru*) of parishioners. However, parishioners' thoughts reveal a very different orientation. More than 75 percent think the purpose of the funeral is to pay one's respects to the dead (死者への敬意 *shisha e no keii*), 69 percent think it is to part from someone to whom you are indebted (世話になった人と別れ *sewa ni natta hito to wakare*), and over 65 percent think it is the duty (勤め *tstutome*) of those remaining (Sugawara 2003, 390–401).

25. For more on the *indō*, see Bodiford 1992, 158–64; Faure 1991; and Rowe 2000, 358.

then, the apparent disjunction between the various ways that the *indō* rite may be interpreted by temple laity and the idealized way in which it is being presented in sectarian surveys.

Researchers, working on behalf of sect leaders, are preoccupied with not only the physical state of temples but also the psyches of priests, who, perhaps like undercover spies or missionaries too long in the field, are seen as somewhat compromised by local practices and beliefs. Thus the surveys (and the volumes that predigest their findings for a priestly audience) must be viewed not simply as benign snapshots of the current conditions of a given sect but rather as attempts to delineate sectarian distinctiveness and orthodoxy. As was made clear to me at every research center I visited and summarized most succinctly by one senior sectarian researcher, "These surveys are not about scholarship, they are about politics." There is a view of Buddhism in Japan presented in these surveys that is often at odds with the realities of local temples. That dissonance is apparent to priests both when they take the survey and when they read an analysis of the results. Priests are provided with a normative view of their traditions within which they are supposed to interpret their daily activities—activities that inevitably fail to live up to that ideal.

SŌTŌ INTELLECTUAL RESPONSES TO THE FUNERAL PROBLEM

I would now like to extend the current discussion beyond the sectarian surveys and their primary object, temple priests, into the realm of Buddhist intellectual engagement with the issue of funerary Buddhism. Surveys, though informative, are still somewhat formulaic and opaque as regards how researchers conceive of the funeral issue. To better understand how a sect, as represented by its public thinkers, approaches the matter, we will turn to one specific example of how survey results are interpreted and discussed. In this section, I will focus on the writings of sectarian scholars at the Research Center for Sōtō Zen Buddhism and their attempt to combat the funeral problem.[26]

According to Sasaki Kōkan 佐々木宏幹, a leading Sōtō intellectual, former chief (主任 *shunin*) of the Research Center for Sōtō Zen, and professor emeritus at Komazawa University, for most Buddhist sects, the funeral problem refers to the growing popularity of nonreligious funerals (無宗教葬 *mushūkyōsō*). This category includes scattering ashes or the more recent,

26. I haven chosen the Sōtō sect as an example in large part because of the scale and breadth of its textual production. Similar patterns exist in the other major sects.

primarily urban, practice of direct funerals (直葬 *chokusō*), in which the body is cremated and immediately buried without the involvement of a priest (Sasaki 2003a, 50).[27] For Nara Yasuaki 奈良康明, former head of the Research Center and former president of Komazawa University, the issue includes both practical concerns (e.g., how the sect will survive in the future) and ideals, namely how temple priests can connect with their followers and help them through the mourning process (personal communication, March 31, 2004).

In 1999, the newly formed Research Center for Sōtō Zen Buddhism undertook its first major joint project: a comprehensive, four-year study of the mortuary problem. According to Sasaki, social and religious problems connected to funerary rites have been an issue in Japan since the 1970s and have become particularly acute over the last decade. In response, the Research Center brought together the three research divisions of the sect in an all-out effort to develop a unified response. Sasaki admits that the decision to focus on funerals was far from unanimous and that "several of the research staff wondered if it would not be better to chose a more suitable theme such as 'The current meaning of Dōgen's Zen,' or 'International Zen'" (Sasaki 2003a, 50). For these researchers, the mortuary issue was far removed from the doctrinal ideals espoused by Śākyamuni and the sect's founders. Yet Sasaki insists that it would be impossible even for Buddhist scholars or elite monks to accomplish their work with absolutely no contact with mortuary rites: "Even those who fervently pursue Buddhist ideals, if they are Japanese, must to some extent live amidst 'funerary culture' and 'funerary society'" (ibid., 49).

Though Sasaki identifies the 1970s as the start of funeral problems for Buddhists, I would argue that the 1963 publication of *Funerary Buddhism* (葬式仏教 *Sōshiki Bukkyō*) by Tamamuro Taijō 圭室諦成 most visibly brought the issue to public attention.[28] Within the Sōtō sect one could also point to Hattori Shōsai's 服部松斉 1956 essay "Funeral Recommendations" (葬祭提言 *Sōsai teigen*), which appeared in the very first issue of the Sōtō Missionary Research Center journal *Kyōka Kenshū* 教化研修. While advocating a reexamination of funerary methods, Hattori strongly op-

27. In the years since Sasaki's comments, direct funerals have become a major concern to Buddhist organizations. *Jimon Kōryū* 寺門興隆, the monthly journal aimed at temple priests, has begun a multipart series on the trend, with article titles such as "Exactly Whose Fault is it that the Number of Direct Funerals is Increasing?" and "Who Can Keep the Spread of Religionless Direct Funerals in Check?" *Jimon Kōryū* April 2010: 12–21 and May 2010: 12–27.

28. For a summary of antifuneral criticism in Japan over the last century, see Murakami 1997.

posed what he saw as the common perception among priests that funerals and memorial services were not the true work of Buddhists (Hattori 1956, 54–62). Regardless of the specific origins of the funeral issue, it is a central and ongoing concern for the Sōtō sect and one that parallels, in terms of institutional response, but not academic attention, the well-known "Machida Incident" and subsequent attempts by the Sōtō leadership to address issues of social discrimination within the sect.[29]

Although the *sōsai mondai* is not as politically charged as the problem of discrimination, it has been a public issue for a longer period of time and may well be far more crucial to the ongoing survival of the sect. And while it has not warranted the creation of its own central division, the public perception of Buddhist mortuary rites has been a principal concern for certain research divisions of the sect for as long as they have existed and has remained an object of joint studies between the different research divisions since at least 1969, when a three-year joint project aimed at clarifying a unified stance on the issue and surveying parishioner opinions was implemented.[30] Later surveys and publications, such as *Issues for the Future of Religious Groups* (宗教集団の明日への課題 *Shūkyō shūdan no asu e no kadai*) (Sōtōshū Shūsei Chōsaiinkai 1984), *Seeking Distinctive Characteristics of Sōtō Funeral Rites based on the Shushōgi* (宗門葬祭の特質を探る―修証義との関連において *Shūmon sōsai no tokushitsu o saguru: Shushōgi to no kanren ni oite*) (Sōtōshū Shūmuchō 1985), and *The Religious Consciousness of Urban Parishioners* (都市檀信徒の宗教意識 *Toshi danshinto no shūkyō ishiki*) (Sōtōshū Shūmuchō 1993), as well as those relating to this recent four-year project, indicate that if the "problem" itself has not grown more acute, the sect's concern over the significance of mortuary rites certainly has.

Building on the work of previous research projects and spearheaded by

---

29. In response to the public outcry over Sōtō Secretary General Machida Muneo's 町田宗夫 infamous proclamation at the 1979 World Conference on Religion and Peace that "In Japan today an 'outcaste problem' does not exist," the Sōtō sect, in 1982, formed the Central Division for the Protection and Promotion of Human Rights (人権擁護推進本部 Jinken Yōgo Suishin Honbu). Since its formation, the Human Rights Division has held conferences, published its own material, and throughout the 1980s and 1990s, put out numerous book series relating to discrimination, human rights, and doctrine (Bodiford 1996, 6). Bodiford describes two central ways in which the Human Rights Division tries to spread its message. The first involves regional seminars and the second takes the form of academic conferences aimed at reforming the "education and training of Sōtō clerics." These seminars and conferences generally take two different approaches to Sōtō doctrine: historical/social or doctrinal/philological (ibid., 18).

30. See *Kyōka Kenshū* 12, 1969; and *Kyōka Kenshū* 13, 1970.

Sasaki and Nara, the Funerary-Buddhism Project brought together all three research organs of the Sōtō sect in its most concerted effort to date to address the mortuary issue. Inviting Sōtō and outside scholars from a wide array of disciplines, the Research Center began by holding open forums at each of Sōtō's nine regional precincts (管区 *kanku*) across the country. Approaching the issue from cultural, historical, anthropological, and doctrinal standpoints, these conferences were intended both to propagate the ideas of a range of sectarian researchers, nonsectarian scholars, and other specialists and to gather input from local priests. The contents of the forums were then carried in the sect's monthly report, *Sōtōshū-hō* 曹洞宗報, placed on the sect's home page, and republished together in abbreviated form in 2004. Funeral-related articles and special issues of journals by each of the three research divisions were also published during this period, and special sections devoted to their discussion/presentation were included in consecutive years of the sect's annual research conference.[31]

The culmination of the project came with the 2003 publication of *Mortuary Rites: Contemporary Significance and Issues* (葬祭—現代的意義と課題 *Sōsai: Gendaiteki igi to kadai*: hereafter *Sōsai*). In addition to twenty short articles, the book also contained the transcripts of three roundtable discussions among the top researchers of the project, as well as the results of a detailed, nationwide survey of 1,122 temples. Comprised of two distinct surveys (like the Jōdo survey covered in the previous section), one of temple priests and one of parishioners, the questions covered issues such as conceptions of the spirit, knowledge of the doctrinal underpinnings of mortuary services, and concerns over apparent contradictions between the Buddhist tenet of no-self and memorial services for spirits of the deceased. Only small portions of the survey results, along with analysis, were printed in *Sōsai*. A second, soft-cover volume containing all the questions, cross-tabulated data, a bibliography of over three thousand funeral-related sources, and a scant six pages of interpretation, was published in March 2004 (Sōtōshū Sōgō Kenkyū Sentā, 2004).

The first printing of two thousand copies of *Sōsai* was paid for by the Research Center and distributed for free to all 786 Sōtō parishes (教区 *kyōku*). Copies were then passed around between the individual temples in each parish. A second print run of a thousand copies, paid for by the sect's headquarters (Shūmuchō), quickly sold out, and the book is cur-

31. At the Research Center's fifth annual conference in October 2003, an entire section, including eleven papers, was dedicated to the *sōsai mondai*. The keynote address, by cultural anthropologist Namihira Emiko 波平恵美子, was titled "*Sōsai* and the Modern Person."

rently out of print. In addition, the initial four-year research program was extended for at least two more years to allow the Division of Contemporary Sōtō Zen Studies to conduct further field research and to address the voices and opinions of parishioners who have taken part in funerals.[32] As of January 2010, the *Sōsai* issue is still included on the Research Center's list of yearly research projects.[33]

In the article on discrimination mentioned above, William Bodiford contends that the conferences and publications organized by the reform-minded members of the Human Rights Division have had a significant impact on the social policies of the Sōtō sect and on fields of research at Komazawa University. He adds, however, that "the inherent tensions between the social conservatism of Sōtō institutions and the reform of Sōtō social attitudes are not likely to disappear any time soon" (Bodiford 1996, 18). He also indicates that attempts by the division to educate the sect's clergy has tended to alienate local temple priests, who resent being told how to run their temples. In the case of the funeral issue, we see analogous attempts to affect the sect's policies (with equally ambiguous results), as well as similar institutional fractures. In order to move from simply illustrating these tensions to exploring how a discourse of proper/improper use of doctrine develops, I would like to turn to the issue of posthumous ordination.

DYING FOR ENLIGHTENMENT

In most popular and scholarly understandings, ordination signifies that one becomes a monk or nun and therefore rejects the secular world.[34] In Japan, as elsewhere, "receiving the precepts" could also mean simply forming some type of connection to Buddhism that would ensure one's eventual buddhahood. The adaptation of Chinese Chan-style monastic funeral rites for the laity in the late medieval period began the spread of posthumous ordination among the general populace, a trend that has continued to the present (Bodiford 1992). Today, the posthumous bestowal of precepts and a Buddhist ordination name is generally understood by the laity to indicate

---

32. A common complaint from parishioners about the *Sōsai* book was that it focused only on the priests and had nothing from the point of view of the mourning family. As I shall discuss later in the chapter, this complaint has spurred action among some local Sōtō groups.

33. Further details on these projects are provided below.

34. Through his work on Buddhist monastic law codes (*vinaya*), Shayne Clarke has argued very convincingly that, at least in India, "going forth from home to homelessness" in no way necessitated the cutting of family ties (Clarke, forthcoming).

that the deceased has achieved some sort of favorable rebirth, most typically in a Buddhist pure land, or possibly as a Buddha (成仏 *jōbutsu*).[35] This
exemplary status is achieved without any of the arduous effort required of
a Buddhist novice but occurs simply as a result of the priest's actions during the funeral. In my experience, temple priests provide a diverse range of
explanations for *jōbutsu*, but sectarian researchers and intellectuals often
follow more doctrinally orthodox interpretations.[36]

The term for posthumous ordination that appears throughout Sōtō
literature, *motsugo sasō* 没後作僧, has been used almost exclusively by
the Sōtō sect for some time and refers to the ritual process by which
the deceased is symbolically shaven (剃髪 *teihatsu*), given the precepts
and lineage chart (血脈 *kechimyaku*), and transformed into a Buddhist
priest (僧にする *sō ni suru*) (Shiina 2003, 186).[37] For Sōtō researcher Shiina
Kōyū 椎名宏雄, the problem with this process is that it neither reflects the
will of the lay follower nor is properly understood by the participants, including the priests performing it. According to Shiina, "It goes without
saying that neither the priests nor the mourning family understand the inner meaning of posthumous ordination and are content to simply believe
that the deceased is 'transformed into a Buddha' (成仏する *jōbutsu suru*)
(Shiina 2003, 187). Shiina laments that, despite the fact that priests who
truly understand the meaning of posthumous ordination (as a symbolic
entrance into the monastic order and thus the beginning of training rather
than its culmination) are as rare as "stars at sunrise," the ritual is still
single-mindedly performed and thus reveals the disjunction between doctrinal understanding and actual ritual practice (ibid.).

The question of posthumous ordination was addressed in a series of
three roundtable discussions (座談会 *zadankai*) between Sōtō and other
scholars.[38] Sōtō researcher Tsunoda Tairyū 角田泰隆, while accepting post-

---

35. I would argue that the traditional Buddhist view of transmigration through the
six paths (六道 *rokudō*) no longer holds much sway over the Japanese imagination. It is certainly not the dominant episteme it might have been in the medieval period (LaFleur 1986,
chapter 2).

36. Reflecting the range of understandings of the term, Japanese dictionaries define
jōbutsu both as "becoming a Buddha" and "to die."

37. For the most part, Sōtō funerals for lay followers are laid out in the book *Standard
Rites of the Sōtō Zen School* (曹洞宗行持軌範 *Sōtōshū gyōji kihan*). The rules governing
lay funerals were first codified in 1950 with the publication of the *Showa Revised Edition*
(昭和修訂行持軌範 *Shōwa shūtei gyōji kihan*). Prior to 1950, mortuary rites for laity were modeled on those for monks (Shiina 2003, 187).

38. All of the researchers with whom I spoke agreed that the *zadankai* section was the
best part of the book, in that it produced the most lively and honest discussion of the issues.

humous transformation of the deceased through the granting of precepts and the bestowing of the *indō*, expresses fundamental doubt as to whether one can be enlightened so quickly or easily:

> In Buddhism, one cannot achieve enlightenment (*jōbutsu*) simply by receiving the precepts. One achieves enlightenment by training. In Zen, for example, taking part in a question and answer exchange (問答 *mondō*) with one's teacher. In the funeral, however, this is all done in one go. (Sōtōshū Sōgō Kenkyū Sentā 2003, 309)

For Tsunoda, Shiina and the other participants, bestowing the precepts on the deceased makes him or her a priest in name only. Through repeated references to Dōgen's use of terms such as "the endless cycle of birth and death" (生生世世 *shōjōseze*) and "the long Buddhist path (はるかなる仏道 *harukanaru butsudō*), the roundtable scholars agree that the bestowing of the precepts and the *indō* do not signify the enlightenment of the deceased, but rather the first step on a very long journey.

The question of what becoming a Buddha actually means is a thorny one for scholars and priests. Their positions represent more than scholarly debates over doctrinal interpretation. The importance of receiving the precepts is at the heart of both the Sōtō sect's constitution and its most important doctrinal text since the Meiji period, the *Shushōgi* 修証義. Initially written in 1888 by lay Buddhist Ōuchi Seiran 大内青巒, the *Shushōgi*, a broad collection of snippets from Dōgen's writings edited into a short, five-section, thirty-one-paragraph text, was originally an attempt to incorporate practices (specifically the chanting of the *nenbutsu* 念仏 as in the Pure Land sects) that were seen as simpler and more popular among the laity than seated meditation (坐禅 *zazen*). It was hoped that integrating these practices would increase the popularity of the Sōtō sect (Reader 1983, 105–11). Unable to find any justification in Dōgen's writings for adopting the *nenbutsu*, however, Ōuchi instead focused on the Buddhist precepts. By equating the taking of the precepts with practicing *zazen*, as in the expression "meditation and the precepts are identical" (禅戒一如 *zenkai ichinyo*), Ōuchi was able to provide the laity with the redemptive benefits of rigorous ascetic practice without any of the actual rigor.[39] To date, the only extended study of the *Shushōgi* in English has been undertaken by Ian Reader, who argues that the text provides a doctrinal foundation for

---

39. This expression is not found in the *Shushōgi*, but it does appear in the sect's constitution.

the sect that is incorporated into Sōtō's constitution.[40] He summarizes the text's place in Sōtō's history in the following way.

> Article Five, which has its historical origins in the events of the Meiji era, asserts the principles expressed in the *Shushōgi* and in the underlying principles that the practice of *zazen* and the practice of the preceptual path are one and the same. In this view, the precepts are the gate to enlightenment just as much as is the practice of *zazen*. The assertion of this notion was one of the major aims of those who compiled the *Shushōgi*, for it provided an entry to Sōtō that was more accessible than that of *zazen* for the laity. (Reader 1983, 178–79)

This attempt to make Sōtō Zen more accessible to the laity has, for some Sōtō scholars, created a new set of problems. Shiina Kōyū, presenting the sectarian-studies position on the state of the deceased in Sōtō Buddhist funerals, takes umbrage at the ambiguity surrounding what happens to one after receiving the precepts:

> The problem for me is the way in which the meaning of taking the precepts laid out in the *Shushōgi* is premised on an interpretation of the phrase in the *Brahma Net Sūtra* that reads, "When sentient beings receive the Buddhist precepts, they will enter the ranks of the Buddhas, the rank equal to the great awakening, and they will truly become disciples of the Buddhas." But what is the meaning of "the ranks of the Buddhas," "the rank equal to the great awakening," or "disciples of the Buddhas?" I think it is essential that the priests answer this from the standpoint of their individual faith. (Sōtōshū Sōgō Kenkyū Sentā 2003, 280)[41]

Shiina's last comment highlights the central concern and limit acting on sectarian intellectuals, researchers, and leaders—all their doctrinal assertions mean little unless they can reach local priests and parishioners. Indeed, it is precisely the perceived lack of reach that underlies

40. For an article on the role of the *Shushōgi* in modern Sōtō Zen, see Heine 2003. The dearth of Western scholarship on the *Shushōgi* should be rectified in large part by forthcoming work from John LoBreglio.

41. Here I have followed the official English translation of the *Shushōgi* that is included in the *Sōtō School Scriptures for Daily Services and Practice* (Sōtōshū Shūmuchō 2001, 85–96).

SECTARIAN RESEARCHERS AND THE FUNERAL PROBLEM

survey production and much other research center activity. Thus, in addition to their own concerns over the proper interpretation of postmortem status in Dōgen's writings, the scholars involved in the roundtable discussions also focused on the issue of how temple priests can draw on doctrinal teachings in a way that resonates with the needs of parishioners. For research center researcher Matsumoto Kōichi 松本皓一, the problem lies in the actual status of taking the first step toward enlightenment: "Of course, if you do not take the first determination to pursue enlightenment (初発心 shohosshin) as already entering the ranks of the Buddhas, then you will have nothing to say to the average lay person" (Sōtōshū Sōgō Kenkyū Sentā 2003, 312). Sasaki extends the discussion into a question of divergences among the different sects:

> It may be that it is necessary for a renunciant always to engage in ascetic practices, but if you tell a group of lay followers that when you die you are made a monk and must always continue training, there will be those who think 'we don't want to put the dead through such hardship.' In the Jōdo schools they have Amida, or at least people think they want to go to Śākyamuni's side and take a leisurely rest on a lotus pedestal. (Sōtōshū Sōgō Kenkyū Sentā 2003, 314)

This soteriological branding of the different sects comes up often in my discussions with priests and scholars. In one conversation with a group of Jōdo researchers, I was told that not only were Sōtō funerals far too complicated, but also that Sōtō doctrine had no ready solution, such as a Pure Land, to address parishioner fears over the posthumous fate of a loved one.

The lack of a unified, doctrinally consistent response among local priests to fundamental questions over the state of the deceased is troubling to sectarian intellectuals and researchers who feel that these sorts of inquiries provide a unique opportunity to clarify and deepen parishioner understanding of orthodox Sōtō teachings. Generic answers, or, even worse, those that evoke images of other sects, lead to fears of thinning sectarian identity. Articles such as Awaya Ryōdō's 粟谷良道 "From Folk Belief to Doctrine" are part of the *Sōsai* project's larger goal to promote a deeper sectarian awareness among parishioners and temple priests through instruction in doctrine and in the uniquely Sōtō elements of funerary practices (Awaya 2003). This response is in part a reaction to the successful entrance of New Religions into the ancestor worship market, as well as an attempt to provide local priests with a stronger sense of identity and the doctrinal ammunition they need to distinguish themselves from the funeral company professionals with whom they have become so closely associated.[42]

A second, more fundamental concern of the researchers regards a perceived increase in anxiety among younger Sōtō priests over the gap between doctrinal orthodoxy and funeral expediency. As Sasaki notes during one of the roundtables,

> The reason that priests at local temples do not have confidence is that they are taught at the head temple and university that "Real Buddhism is not about conducting funerals, and that there is no independent spirit (アートマン *ātoman*; skt. *ātman*) that is the object of the funeral. For a monk who preaches emptiness to take part in this is strange." This gap causes the priests great distress. Contradictions emerge because priests take the strict doctrine they are taught to the local temples and try to eliminate the idea of a spirit. (Sōtōshū Sōgō Kenkyū Sentā 2003, 283–4)

The concern with priestly confidence is also reflected throughout the *Sōsai* survey, which revealed that less than one-third of the priests think that mortuary rites are consistent with Buddhist teachings. This datum becomes even more significant when one realizes that local sectarian leaders selected specific respondents, skewing the results toward a best-case scenario.[43]

In his contribution to the *Sōsai* volume, "The Dead and the Next World," Sasaki describes what he sees as the fissure between Buddhist doctrine and the day-to-day realities of temples. Citing a similar argument in the Jōdo sect's funerary Buddhism volume, Sasaki notes:

> There are a growing number of young priests who are becoming aware of the gap between the main role of a priest at a temple and the doctrine taught in Buddhist studies. This is becoming a problem for the entire Buddhist world. In other words, as the understanding of Buddhist studies and religious studies at educational organs of different religious or-

42. For details on New Religions and ancestor worship, see Hardacre 1984 and 1988. For more on the connection between priests and the funeral industry, see Rowe 2000 and Suzuki 2000.

43. This bias is something that the researchers themselves are well aware of, admitting in the book that there were a large number of model responses (模範解答 *mohan kaitō*) (Sugawara 2003, 379). One senior researcher confided that he was sure the number of priests who actually think that mortuary rites directly contradict Buddhist teachings is much higher than the 5.2 percent result they determined from the survey.

ganizations grows deeper and deeper, the number of priests who lose confidence in the activities they carry out at their temples will increase. (Sasaki 2003b, 56)

Jōdo Shinshū scholar Ōmura Eishō 大村英昭, who was involved in research projects for both the Sōtō and Jōdo sects, argues that scholarly priests in every Buddhist organization

> have come to place a very low value on the heart-wrenching efforts of priests at local temples (現場 genba), referring to their activities as "diverging from the spirit of the founders." However, I do not think the efforts of the priests at the genba are in vain. Nor do I think that their efforts are a betrayal of the founders of the sect. On the contrary, I think the priests at the genba, from the position of the genba, should establish a "religion of the genba." (Ōmura 2003, 20)[44]

The consistent emphasis on the local temple, or genba, again reveals the centrality of the mortuary problem for the entire sect. Although there is little consensus among scholars even on such fundamental questions as the postmortem fate of the deceased, priestly informants make it quite clear that abstract debate over points of doctrine are of little use to them in dealing with parishioners' questions. While those at the research centers are clearly aware of the funerary realities that local temples face and that, in the end, it is up to the local priest to decide how to deal with such issues in the course of his work, they are still worried that without the proper intellectual and spiritual training, those priests may not be adequately prepared to prevent further erosion of the sect's position in society. Research centers want to help, but they are also walking a fine line between maintaining and propagating acceptable doctrinal interpretations and providing local priests with answers that will satisfy the needs of, for example, a

44. Literally, "the actual place," genba may be represented in colloquial English as "the scene of the action" and is used in Japanese to refer to the site of an accident or the place where actual work takes place. In police dramas and films, the detectives go to the scene of the crime (genba), while the higher-ups issue orders from headquarters. In his work on the Japanese hip-hop scene, Ian Condry notes the way his informants use the term to refer to the actual dance clubs as opposed to the globalized effort to market hip-hop culture. Condry deploys the term both as a way to speak about globalization and as a way to locate a field site when one's research is no longer bounded by a village or specific locale (Condry 2001, 374 and 384). It is worth noting that "genba" is not used by Japanese anthropologists, who prefer the term "field." The use of the term by Buddhists seems consistent with the idea of the site where the actual work of Buddhism takes place.

young man who has recently lost his mother or those of an elderly woman who is worried about how her deceased husband will get along without her in the next world. As a group of Sōtō priests in Shizuoka will demonstrate in the following section, local priests often have a very different idea about the kind of doctrinal help temple priests need.

BOOKS FROM THE PERIPHERY

Although this chapter has focused on the efforts of sectarian researchers to produce a doctrinally consistent and distinctive view of their sects for temple priests, it would be wrong to think that it is only the sect's ostensible center that controls the means of textual production. A publication on funeral customs created by a group of Sōtō priests in Shizuoka prefecture provides a specific, illustrative example of a very different orientation to the role of doctrine in funerary rites.

Conceived in response to the *Sōsai* book discussed above, *Funeral/Memorial Service Customs and Origins* 葬儀・法事のしきたりとその由来 (*Sōgi/hōji no shikitari to sono yurai*; hereafter *Shikitari*) was first published in May 2004 by the Sōtō Sect's Shizuoka Prefecture First Parish Office (曹洞宗静岡県第一宗務所 Sōtōshū Shizuokaken Daiichi Shūmusho). The book was only available through direct order from the publisher, with sales being driven by word of mouth and colorful, one-page flyers. The advertisement copy clearly targets temple priests.

> At long last, the one book you've been eagerly awaiting is finally here! You think you know, but some things are a bit vague. You think you understand, but you could be mistaken. The various customs and origins of Buddhist rites are elucidated here in detail, in the easy to understand explanations you look for in a practical guide. Even if it is just to double check your daily services, this one-of-a-kind volume is extremely convenient.

As with its more "academic" precursor, the intended audience for this volume are local priests who may be lacking the confidence or abilities to provide suitable dharma talks or answer questions at funerals. The advertising for the *Shikitari* book is aimed at that temple priest who, like someone who just cannot lose those unwanted pounds or come up with healthy recipes for the family, needs a little extra help. If this analogy comes across as somewhat flippant, it is not: this is self-help for temple priests.

The introduction to the book lists four main goals: (1) to clarify for priests the origins of various funerary customs; (2) to ensure that priests be able to conduct funerals and memorial services with confidence and sincerity; (3) to provide material for dharma talks at funerals and memorials; and (4) to supply priests with answers to questions regarding customs, offerings, and the like (Editorial board introduction, no page numbers).[45] The introduction also provides three caveats, which most notably include a warning that, since this is not a research book, it does not engage different scholarly interpretations of the historical and doctrinal material at hand. The oversized font and emphasis on straightforward explanations are also suggestive of how the book is to be used, as well as the ways in which the *Sōsai* volume is perceived as deficient. Though not a direct critique of the earlier book, the very production, content, and style of the *Shikitari* volume suggests a great deal about how the *Sōsai* volume was received in local Sōtō circles.

The supervisory editor, Tanaka Ryōshō 田中良昭, who, at the time, was also the assistant head of the Research Center for Sōtō Zen Buddhism and who, we should remember, was intimately involved with the funerary Buddhism project there, summarizes the *Sōsai* book in the following way:

> The result of the *Sōsai* book was to clarify that mortuary rites originally existed as folk beliefs rooted in the simple sentiments, life views, and Japanese ideas of death and spirits. Later, Buddhist meanings were added to create unique rites. Therefore, these practices should not be taken as [examples of] Buddhist doctrine (仏教教理 *Bukkyō kyōri*) but rather as Buddhist culture (仏教文化 *Bukkyō bunka*). (Tanaka 2004, editorial introduction, no page numbers)

He then goes on to admit that the *Sōsai* book failed to sufficiently explore the ways in which custom and accepted practice, in his phrasing, "regionality," remain strongly ingrained in actual funerals.[46] Consequently, the present book aimed to "help Sōtō priests correctly understand the meaning of the 'origins' and 'customs' of mortuary rites, and to carry out the rituals with confidence in order to help them use the funeral as a place to

45. The individual entries are not attributed to any specific writer. At the end of the book there is a list of everyone at the Shizuoka center. Only parish office titles are included; there are no details regarding individual temple affiliation.

46. Tanaka is expressing some of the doubts that many of the researchers at the Research Center felt about the *Sōsai* project: that it did not take into account regional variation and that it did not adequately address the mixing of local custom and Buddhist doctrine, which forms the basis of the sect's funerary rites.

"propagate and edify" (布教教化 fukyō kyōka). He goes on to clarify that, "if you take the *Sōsai* book published by the Research Center for Sōtō Zen Buddhism as principally representing the theoretical side of the sect's mortuary rites, then this book represents the practical application side. Taken together they clarify the entirety of funerals as a form of Buddhist culture" (ibid.). As noted above, sectarian researchers frequently struggle with the tension between popular perceptions and orthodox doctrinal positions. One of their most common responses, as clearly demonstrated by Tanaka's statement above, is to speak of "Buddhist culture," an amorphous field that includes both folk beliefs and Buddhist teachings. Indeed, as Tanaka suggests, the entire *Shikitari* volume is an attempt to clarify the folk (regional) customs that underpin practically every element of the funeral service. This clarification serves two purposes: on the one hand, it allows the sect to embrace those aspects that, though traditional, are not canonical, but, at the same time, it allows them a way to keep it distinct from the perceived (true) Buddhist core of the rite. In this way, Buddhist teachings may be both universalized as a form of culture (that great naturalizing concept) and carefully distinguished from local accretions. The deployment by sectarian researchers of "Buddhist culture" as a catchall term thus allows them and temple priests to embrace both the "pure" doctrine of foundational texts alongside the diverse ways in which Sōtō Zen has been and continues to be practiced and understood by the majority of its followers.[47] I will return to this point later in the chapter. Turning now to the *Shikitari* volume, I would like to consider some examples of this discourse in action.

The book provides priests with a step-by-step explanation (historical, cultural, textual, exegetical), in order, of every ritual facet of wakes, funerals, and memorial services. Topics such as the final water (末期の水 *matsugo no mizu*), shaving the head of the deceased (*teihatsu*), orienting the corpse so that the head points north (北枕 *kitamakura*), incense offerings, the six paths of transmigration (*rokudō*), and "forty-nine-day rice cakes" (四十九餅 *shijūku mochi*) all receive two- or three-page entries that

47. A proper genealogy of the "Buddhist culture" concept as a solution to the folk custom/ Buddhist doctrine "problem," though fascinating, lies beyond the scope of this book. Perhaps not surprisingly, Sasaki Kōkan, former head of Sōtō's Central Research Center, has been trying for years to mediate these binaries in his own work. See, for example, Sasaki 2002, 61–130, and 2004, 33–52. To see examples of how similar relationships have been approached in the study of Buddhism in other countries and time periods, see, for example, Spiro 1970, 140–61; Tambiah 1970, 32–42; Gombrich 1971, 4–8; and Collins 1982, 12–16.

reference Chinese precedents, scriptural sources, and local beliefs.[48] Here, then, is the kind of assistance that temple priests appear to want—a volume that gives them short, easy to understand, informative "blurbs" on every funeral-related subject. This volume provides them not only with answers to difficult questions about specific aspects of mortuary ritual but also a way to deliver responses that are meaningful to the lives of their parishioners. For example, the entry on the coffin (棺 *kan*, or 柩 *hitsugi*) begins with a quotation from the famous novelist Natsume Sōseki 夏目漱石 (1867–1916) on the solemnity of encoffining, proceeds with a one-page discussion of the tradition of Śākyamuni Buddha's golden coffin, adds an aside that there is some scriptural variance regarding the material of the coffin, and details the preparation of Śākyamuni's corpse in oils and five hundred layers of cotton—all to set up the entry's conclusion: "According to the sutras, there is some dispute over whether the Buddha's coffin was of gold or lead, but in either case, Śākyamuni's corpse was placed in a coffin with extreme care and courtesy" (Sōtōshū Shizuokaken Daiichi Shūmusho 2004, 112).[49] Here is a wonderful example of connecting Buddhist scriptural debates to common local practices such as washing and dressing the deceased. Furthermore, it is done in such a way that valorizes a very personal, even emotional, response to the corpse. To further explore the issue of Buddhist culture and better illustrate the differences between the two books detailed above, I will now turn to a close reading of one entry.

Although the question of becoming a Buddha (*jōbutsu*) is not afforded the same attention in the *Shikitari* volume that it receives in the *Sōsai* book, there is a ten-page entry (one of the longest in the book) detailing the bestowing of precepts on the deceased and the related practice of posthumous ordination.[50] What is striking, however, is the increased level of enthusiasm in the *Shikitari* volume regarding that particular passage in the *Brahma Net Sūtra* about joining the ranks of Buddhas.

---

48. In many ways, this book can be seen as a simplified version of Matsu'ura Shūkō's 松浦秀光 definitive work on Zen sect funerals (Matsu'ura 1989).

49. For a more detailed treatment of the textual sources recounting Śākyamuni's cremation, see Strong 2004, chapter 4.

50. There are only four entries out of sixty-six in total that are ten pages or longer: posthumous ordination, memorial tablets (塔婆 *toba*), memorial rites, and the memorial rites to transfer merit to the deceased (追善供養 *tsuizen kuyō*). I would posit that these four areas are where the *Shikitari* writers think temple priests need the most help bridging doctrine with actual mortuary practices.

Since [the Sōtō sect's precepts] are innately pure precepts (自性清浄戒 *jishō seijōkai*) emerging from the brilliance of your own true Buddha nature, from the all-pervasive Buddha nature, if you take the precepts, you are, like that, joining the ranks of the Buddhas. Since these precepts are bestowed according to the great mercy and compassion of the Buddha, just receiving them is sufficient. As proof of this [joining the ranks of the Buddhas], when you receive the precepts, the priest will bestow upon you a lineage chart and the name that identifies you as a disciple of the Buddha, your ordination name. (Sōtōshū Shizuokaken Daiichishūmusho 2004, 58)

In this passage there is no trace of the fundamental doubts raised in the *Sōsai* roundtable regarding the instantaneous efficacy of posthumous ordination. Athough the *Sōsai* researchers complain about widespread misunderstandings of Sōtō doctrine, those working on the *Shikitari* project are more concerned with detailing ways of speaking to parishioners that index Buddhist principles in a simple and reassuring way. In the next example, taken from the same entry, the differences become even more stark. Here, the book addresses the local priest directly, evoking a range of specialized Buddhist concepts and then seamlessly connecting them to popular notions of the soul.

Our sect's funerals (*sōgi*) are not a simple gathering for relatives, friends, and guests to bid farewell to the deceased (告別式 *kokubetsu-shiki*). They are sacred rituals that bestow both the Buddhist precepts and an exposition of the dharma (*indō*) in order to help the deceased be reborn and live on in a Buddhist Pure Land (仏界浄土 *bukkai jōdo*), the world of Buddha. When a person dies and the flesh disappears, it goes without saying that the five senses stop working and memory and consciousness cease, but not everything constituting the person disappears. There is, in the depths of one's personhood, what we should call the fountainhead of life, "Buddha nature" (仏性 *busshō*), "innately pure mind" (自性清浄心 *jishō shōjōshin*), "storehouse consciousness (アラヤ識 *arayashiki*, skt. *ālaya-vijñāna*)," (in conventional terms we would call this the spirit [魂 *tamashi*] or the soul [霊魂 *reikon*]) that remains, that is reborn in the next life, and that continues on forever. (Ibid., 49)

It is worth placing this local approach to an immutable metaphysical essence (*ātman*) next to that of the sect's main researchers noted above.

One could situate this passage from the *Shikitari* volume in two ways. On the one hand, it can be read as a demonstration of precisely the lack of confidence that Sasaki bemoans, as proof of the need to help temple priests overcome the "contradiction" between what they are taught and what they actually do. On the other hand, I believe such a reading projects contradiction where there is none. The overriding concern here is not with whether or not temple priests are denying established doctrine but rather with how to validate and give deeper meaning to individual personhood; with how to better situate Buddhist teachings within broader cultural perceptions.

As scholars have shown, while the issue of no-self is of great significance to a certain segment of elite Buddhists, for most of the Buddhist world, it does not represent a central aspect of the tradition.[51] Temple priests are not operating in some abstract world. In many cases, they are trying to provide a bridge between sectarian teachings and the emotional needs of parishioners. The ideal response to a person's grief rarely depends on a nuanced understanding of the composite, empty nature of the self or Yogācāric categories of consciousness. In addition to their liturgical expertise, priests must be able to address the conditions of the specific individual who has been lost and the pain of those who have lost her. Fulfilling their roles as caretakers for the dead means providing comfort to the living by giving meaning to death—a meaning that makes sense to the family. A priest's ability to tend to the immediate needs of parishioners is of significant concern to researchers at both the center and the periphery. In the *Sōsai* book it manifests as a question of how to provide meaning within a doctrinally consistent framework, while in the *Shikitari* volume, the focus is on making meaning, period.

Beyond instilling the rite with significance (Buddhist or otherwise) in order to console mourners, the priest must also contend with the increased authority of the funeral director. Shibata Yoshinori 柴田芳憲, the main author of the *Shikitari* book, summarizes the importance of Sōtō priests in the following way:

> The role of Sōtō priests during the wake, funeral, and memorial rites is to preside over the rituals as the officiating priest (導師 *dōshi*). It is not to be a character in a funeral director's manual. He should be the great

51. For related examples, see Collins 1982, 12–16 and 65–78; Holt 2009, 177–78; and Schopen 1991.

teacher who bestows religious calm (宗教的安心 *shūkyōteki anjin*) not only on the deceased, but also on the mourning family, the relatives, the guests, the neighbors, the funeral professionals, and all those who attend. (Shibata 2004, 282)

As detailed in chapter 1, the professionalization of mortuary services, particularly over the last five decades in Japan, has led to an increasing encroachment on the priest's ritual authority by funerary workers. Several priests have complained to me about being little more than an employee of the funeral director (葬儀屋 *sōgiya*).[52] The priest must be able to show why a Buddhist funeral is more than simply an opportunity to say goodbye to a relative, friend, or colleague, as well as why it is an essential enactment of core Buddhist principles, a performance of enlightenment that ensures the peaceful repose of the deceased. Thus, the pejorative use of *kokubetsushiki* in the previous passage serves two functions. First, it frames, in a depreciatory way, the increasingly commercialized orientation of funerals and places that trend in opposition to what priests *should* consider the more essential "spiritual" purpose of the funeral proper, or *sōgi*.[53] Second, in drawing a correlation between folk categories of the soul and Buddha nature, the authors emphasize the significance of the definitively Buddhist aspects of the funeral over and above the more secular concerns of "bidding farewell." Here one can see the ways in which local perceptions of the funeral problem both overlap with and diverge from those of the main research center. Both groups are trying to reassert priestly ritual authority through an emphasis on Buddhist concepts, but in the case of *Shikitari* authors, those Buddhist concepts are intimately intertwined with what sect intellectuals would consider folk accretions.

The issue of how priests distinguish themselves from funerary professionals takes us back to the question of priestly confidence that was raised in the *Sōsai* book and survey. In a subsection of the *Shikitari* entry on precepts titled "The Priest's Attitude toward Funerals," the reader is told that Dōgen's words should instill in priests the confidence to conduct funerals and lead the deceased to walk the Buddhist path. The writer then acknowledges that Dōgen vehemently opposed monks conducting funerals

---

52. For more on the growth of funeral professionals in Japan, see Suzuki 2000.

53. Murakami Kōkyō 村上興匡 has argued that the most significant change in Japanese funerals in the postwar period is precisely this shift in emphasis from *sōgi* to *kokubetsushiki* (Murakami 1997).

and memorial services for laity and thought the main activity of a world renouncer should be seated meditation (*zazen*).[54] "However," the writer continues, "Dōgen never opposed dutiful obedience (孝順心 *kōjunshin*) to one's parents and ancestors" (Sōtōshū Shizuokaken Daiichi Shūmusho 2004, 51). This assertion, lacking any citation or textual support, is then followed by a one-paragraph history of Sōtō in which the sect's involvement in funerals is laid squarely at the feet of the second founder, Keizan 瑩山 (1264–1325), and the attempt by his successors to spread Sōtō teachings.[55] Following this explanation is a plea to priests not to neglect Dōgen's teaching of "just sitting" (只管打坐 *shikantaza*) and to sit in meditation each morning, if even for only ten or twenty minutes, to completely become a Buddha oneself (自分自身がほとけになりきる *jibunjishin ga hotoke ni narikiru*).

> If you do this actual training, you will be able to lead funerals with confidence. You will be able to face the altar and, with all your heart, bestow the sixteen precepts (十六条戒授与 *jūrokujōkai juyo*),[56] wave the torch, and guide the deceased to the Buddhist path. If you just try to imitate the actions of a master/teacher, this is nothing more than aping, or playacting. You must have an unwavering faith in your awakening and your confidence as a Sōtō priest and your ability to send the deceased to a Buddhist pure land, to the world of the Buddha. This faith is born naturally from the *zazen* that occurs as part of your daily training. (Ibid., 52)

The imaginative attempt to reposition Dōgen as a supporter of funerals and memorial rites for parents and ancestors sets up an equally innovative approach to seated meditation—it does not matter if you only do a few minutes a day, as long as you try your best. This is the "self-help" aspect of the book I referred to earlier. Rather than seeing these exhortations as

54. The question of Dōgen's position on funerals is not so clear cut. While his own recorded sayings (語録 *goroku*) do not contain funeral sermons, this is not to say that he "vehemently opposed" the practice, but rather that, as Bodiford has shown, "Dōgen's teachings apparently did not include funeral ceremonies" (Bodiford 1993, 191–92).

55. Both Bodiford 1993 and Faure 1987 and 2000 have shown that the portrayal of a purely meditational Sōtō Zen in Dōgen's time that is then compromised by folk practices and esoteric rituals under later leaders is untenable. For an excellent summary, see Ives 1995.

56. Taking refuge in the three jewels, promising to uphold the three ideals of a bodhisattva and observing the ten grave precepts.

further proof of a decline in the dharma, however, I take this passage as a candid attempt to bring significance to the most common practices of temple priests, practices that are often seen as at odds with the writings of sectarian founders.

As suggested above, the readings of Dōgen and Keizan presented in sectarian publications are not historically accurate.[57] Here we should consider "Dōgen" and "Keizan" not as the historical founders of the Sōtō sect in Japan, but rather as metaphors for a kind of "two-Sōtōs" trope: a pure, uncompromising Sōtō sect on the one hand, and an organization that has had to make historical compromises to survive on the other. In a way, one could argue that this binary, and the attempt to overcome it, neatly maps onto the use of "Buddhist culture" to mediate orthodox teachings and folk practices.

BACK TO THE CENTER

The most telling element of this story of local response to the *Sōsai* book is the subsequent reaction of the intellectuals at the main research center. As noted earlier, their initial plan, after finishing the *Sōsai* book, was to turn their attention to parishioner opinion on mortuary practices through extended interviews. This strategy was meant to address various complaints from throughout the sect that the *Sōsai* book focused too much on priests and not enough on the actual mourners. For a number of reasons, in particular the near impossibility of approaching parishioners without going through local temple priests, this field-interview approach was abandoned.[58] Instead, researchers at the Research Center began studying the *Shikitari* book with plans to produce their own version. In perhaps the clearest testament to the persistent struggle to match their own ideas with temple needs, the sectarian researchers at the Research Center are aiming to produce a more academically rigorous work. The researchers think that the Shizuoka priests are on the right track in terms of subject (origins of customs and practices connected to doctrine and Chinese precedents) but not critical enough in their use of sources. For example, one researcher pointed out to me that many entries in the *Shikitari* book made heavy use of Fujii Masao's 藤井正雄 *Dictionary of Buddhist Ritual* (仏教儀礼辞典

---

57. See Bodiford 1993.

58. I was told at several research centers that sects do not have any contact information for parishioners. Researchers are thus entirely dependent on temple priests to provide introductions for interviews and to disseminate surveys as they see fit.

Bukkyō girei jiten, 1977) without ever questioning the quality of his sources. As of the end of 2009, the Research Center had produced reports on seventeen elements of the funeral service (almost all of which appeared in the *Shikitari* volume) and published these in the sect's monthly newsletter *Shūhō*.[59]

The story does not end there. Local priests from Yamanashi prefecture, inspired by the *Shikitari* volume, published a small booklet of cards on funeral themes in 2005, titled *A Manual of Funerary Customs and Buddhist Services* (葬儀の慣習と仏事便覧 *Sōgi no kanshū to butsuji binran*). Consisting of forty-eight flash cards bound by a single ring, the manual includes explanations of "customs" relating to funerals, a set of questions and answers on Buddhist ritual, definitions of basic terms, and advice on dharma talks. Like the authors of the *Shikitari* volume, Abe Toshimasa 阿部俊正, director of Sōtō's Yamanashi Office, argues for the importance of understanding local customs and, what he refers to as, the "simple feelings and world view of the Japanese." Note again the different treatment that key phrase from the *Shushōgi* gets among Sōtō priests who are not involved in roundtable discussions with the sect's intellectual elites: "I think that it is through this simple folk feeling (素朴な民俗の心 *soboku na minzoku no kokoro*) that we will deepen Sōtō sect faith in "joining the ranks of the buddhas" and [becoming a] "disciple of the Buddha."[60] Abe, like the members of the *Sōsai* project, is clearly engaged with fundamental Sōtō sect concepts, but, like his counterparts working on the *Shikitari* volume, he does not appear at all concerned with establishing normative limits for "correct" understanding.

There is far more to the *sōsai mondai* than the commercialization or simplification of funerals. As the different voices above demonstrate, this problem extends to fundamental questions of how best to convey doctrinal tenets and administer to the needs of parishioners. Responses to these questions at times overlap and at times disagree, but, even in the case of disagreement, they highlight, exacerbate, and even create the tensions priests feel over what they do and what they are supposed to do.

The relative ease and low cost of producing quality printed material, along with an increased willingness on the part of local priests to validate their own localized forms of Buddhism, should continue to exert influ-

59. See http://www.sotozen-net.or.jp/gaku/soken/2009center_hou/_SWF_Window.html. Last accessed February 25, 2010.

60. See http://www7.plala.or.jp/shumusho/kakusyudantai/fukyoukyougikai/20050704.htm. Last accessed February 20, 2008.

ence on the central research centers and the public posture of the various sects. Although the long-term effect of such publications on the future of institutionalized Buddhism in Japan is still unclear, there is little doubt that this is where doctrine, regional customs, and sect history are being negotiated and produced at the local and national level.

THE ABCS OF SHINGON GRAVES

To this point I have focused on discussions of funerals and memorial rites primarily among Sōtō and Jōdo sect intellectuals and researchers. In this last section, I want to consider the writings of Shingon researchers and illustrate both how the same sorts of tensions appear in a smaller sect and, more to the point, how these discourses extend to the grave itself.

In 2001, the Edification Center 教化センター of the Buzan branch of Shingon Buddhism 真言宗豊山派 published a hundred-page booklet entitled *Graves* (お墓 *O-haka*) (Shingonshū Buzanha Kyōka Sentā 2001). This was the culmination of a joint project taken up by researchers in various divisions of the sect's General Research Institute (総合研究院 Sōgō Kenkyūin)[61] and was premised on the idea that "Even for those of us in a traditional organization, in order to run temples, it is absolutely necessary to move beyond mere doctrinal understandings and grasp the actual conditions of graves in contemporary Japanese society" (Shingonshū Buzanha Kyōka Sentā 2001, i). As with the research volumes already discussed, this booklet is intended to treat both the doctrinal uniqueness of the sect and the real-world concerns of temple priests and parishioners. The various chapters cover doctrine, history, and customs in an attempt to provide Buzanha priests with a comprehensive set of materials for dealing with graves and the rites that occur there. The individual chapters break down as follows:

1. A doctrinal account of graves.
2. A step-by-step guide that walks priests through the gravestone consecration ritual (石塔開眼作法 *sekitō kaigen sahō*) and the ritual for transferring the contents of a grave (易檀作法 *ekidan sahō*).

---

61. Every one of the seven contributors is a head priest of a temple, and every one (except Okada Hirotaka 岡田弘隆) is listed in the booklet as a researcher at one of the divisions of the General Research Institute: Doctrine (宗学 *shūgaku*), Ritual (事相 *jisō*), Proselytizing (布教 *fukyō*), and Contemporary Edification (現代教化 *gendai kyōka*). Okada is also a lawyer and the member of the Grave-Free Promotion Society quoted in chapter 4.

3. A sample dharma talk for a gravestone consecration service.
4. A five-minute dharma talk entitled "Visiting the grave."
5. A discussion of the history of graves in Japan based on Fujii Masao's *Everything You Wanted to Know About Graves* (Fujii 1991).
6. An article advocating new grave styles, such as eternal memorial graves and scattering ashes, which can meet the changing needs of Japanese society.
7. The A–Z of legal problems surrounding graves—"What every head priest needs to know."
8. A series of legal templates that priests can use at their own temples:
   a. One-page contract for becoming a *danka* and using a temple grave.
   b. Detailed list of rules for using and managing temple graves.
   c. One-page contract for becoming a *danka* and using a communal grave.
   d. Detailed list of rules for using and managing a communal grave.

Note the wide variety of approaches to graves provided in this official, sectarian pamphlet: doctrinal, practical, historical, ethnographic, legal, social, and bureaucratic. Not only is the priestly audience afforded an easy-to-follow overview of core Shingon tenets and a sociocultural history of Japanese graves, but he or she is also provided with detailed ritual manuals, sample contracts, legal advice, and a ready-to-use speech aimed at those "first timers" and priests who are "not used to performing dharma talks" (Nemoto 2001, 32). Because it best demonstrates the larger points I am trying to make about the struggles that sect intellectuals and temple priests are facing in their attempts to match often complex doctrinal concepts with parishioner concerns over the posthumous fate of loved ones, I will now turn to a closer examination of the first chapter of this booklet.

Written by Ōzuka Jishin 大塚慈伸, "Graves From the Point of View of Shingon Doctrine" provides doctrinal background, explication, and justification for the five-tiered grave stone (五輪塔 *gorintō*) favored by the Shingon sect. Using specific texts from the sect's collection of rites (真言宗豊山派作法集 *Shingonshū Buzanha Sahōshū*), Ōzuka details how Shingon ritual, through a series of *mudrās* and *dhāraṇīs* (印言 *ingon*), transforms a lump of stone into a manifestation of the dharma body of Dainichi Nyorai (大日如来; skt. *Mahāvairocana*), invested with the merit of the five elements

(五輪 *gorin*) and the five wisdoms (五智 *gochi*).[62] Thus, he argues, although the grave may look like simply a piece of stone, it is actually an embodiment of Dainichi Nyorai: "The bones buried there are embraced in Dainichi Nyorai's breast," where "If the remains of the deceased are bathed in the power of the sanctified *dharmakāya stūpa* (法身塔 *hosshintō*), the deceased will undoubtedly be freed from the painful sea of life and death to enter nirvana" (Ōzuka 2002, 4). This pattern of step-by-step doctrinal exegesis followed by guarantees of soteriological benefits for parishioner and ancestral remains is repeated throughout the article.

Citing passages from principal esoteric texts such as the *Mahāvairocana Sūtra* (大日経 *Dainichikyō*) and the *Annotations on the Mahāvairocana Sūtra* (大日経疏 *Dainichikyō Sho*), Ōzuka explains that when the officiating priest (阿闍梨 *ajari*; skt. *ācārya*) consecrates (灌頂 *kanjō*) the deceased, he should be contemplating the essential unity of his own body with the five elements of the five-storied gravestone. *Annotations* provides the specific associations the priest is to make first among the five areas of the body, the five colors, and the five elements. The five elements are then connected to the five shapes of the gravestone, and finally, the text tells us which of the five syllables (五字 *goji*) is to be placed in each of these shapes. This string of associations is then connected to what, for Shingon Buddhism, is a key passage of the *Mahāvairocana Sūtra* in which the Buddha *Mahāvairocana* explains the content of his own enlightenment:

我覚本不生	My awakening is originally unborn;
出過語言道	It is beyond language.
諸過得解脱	Obtaining release from all faults,
遠離於因縁	Distantly removed from cause and effect,
知空等虚空	I know that emptiness is itself empty.[63]

Evoking Kūkai's *Principle of Attaining Buddhahood with the Present Body* (即身成仏義 *Sokushin jōbutsugi*), the author then associates the elements with different attributes of the dharma realm/dharma body (法界法身 *hōkai hosshin*; skt. *dharmadhātu dharmakāya*). Therefore, he concludes, the five-tiered gravestone used in Shingon, through its associa-

62. For a general overview of Shingon doctrine, see Hakeda 1972; and Matsunaga and Matsunaga 1974, 177–93.

63. Ōzuka assumes that the person (priest) reading this article will recognize that these five phrases are spoken to the deceased during the consecration of the six elements (六大加持 *rokudai kaji*) as part of the priest's leading of the deceased to the Buddhist path (引導法 *indōhō*).

Fig. 12. Dainichi Nyorai superimposed onto the five-tiered gravestone.
Reprinted with the permission of Bukkyō Dendō Kyōkai and Numata Center
for Buddhist Translation and Research.

tion with the five elements and five syllables, is in fact an instantiation of
the dharma body of Dainichi Nyorai. This union is then put into a more
concrete form using Kakuban's (覺鑁 1095–1143) purported drawing of the
five-tiered gravestone superimposed with Dainichi's body (see fig. 12).[64]

Ōzuka places this image next to a chart he has constructed linking
the five phrases from the *Mahāvairocana Sūtra* quoted above to the five
elements, the five *chakras*/shapes of the gravestone, and the five syllables.
The author's point could not be clearer: via identification with the five
universal elements and five seed syllables, the cosmic Buddha, Dainichi
Nyorai, is identified with the five-storied gravestone. All these transpo-
sitions allow the author to explain that in esoteric thought, the Buddha
is not in some far off place but is inherent in the realities of this world:
"Therefore if the stone is sanctified by the priest with the merit of the

64. These drawings are found in Kakuban's *Gorin kuji myō himitsu shaku* 五輪九字明秘密釈
(*Taishō* [Buddhist Cannon] 2514 (79):11–22), which Hendrik van der Veere translates as "Esoteric Explanation of [the secrets contained in] the 'Wisdom Bearing Sounds' (*myō*) associated
with the Five *Rin* and Nine *Shuji* (esoteric syllables)" (Veere 2000).

dharma realm/dharma body by identifying it with the five syllables and five *chakras*, then it will, without mistake, become a *dharmakāya stūpa* (法身塔 *hosshintō*) that instantiates the reality body of the dharma world" (Ōzuka 2001, 11–12). Furthermore, the author argues, this soteriological efficacy is not limited to gravestones but also holds true for the five-tiered, wooden tablets (五輪卒塔婆 *gorin sotoba*) that are offered (after being purchased from the temple) at graves throughout the year. The article concludes:

> The principle [of Dainichi Nyorai symbolized by the stone marker] means that the ancestors and deceased family members of our followers must by necessity reside as Buddhas and have the "embodied" existence (「よりしろ」的存在 *"yorishiro" teki sonzai*) that is the basis of Shingon doctrine. Therefore, if our parishioners think that graves are simply for burying the ancestors, that they are nothing more than a place for burial, we Shingon priests should try to correct their thinking. We should argue instead that it is precisely because these are graves that have been consecrated according to Shingon doctrine that they are a site where the ancestors will be embraced by the greatest Buddha Dainichi and that they will peacefully attain Buddhahood without any distress. They should be taught of the sublimity and glory of the Shingon sect. (Ōzuka 2001, 15–16)

Tapping into traditional images of what Ryūichi Abé calls "esoteric technology" or what Jacqueline Stone, following Allan Grapard, has termed the "mandalization of the phenomenal world," the author argues for the superiority of Shingon graves (Abé 1999).[65] Here again, a sectarian researcher attempts to connect doctrine to practice in a way that is both normative and that provides temple priests with confidence—in this case, by emphasizing that the general perception of graves as mere storage for the

---

65. Stone, writing in regards to medieval Japan, notes that "Symbols of the sacred realm of Buddhist reality were mapped onto specific features of the phenomenal world via complex sets of correspondences and resemblances, both formal and linguistic, equating, for example, the three pagoda precincts of Mt. Hiei with the threefold truth or the five viscera of the human body with the five wisdom Buddhas. The decoding (actually, encoding) of these resemblances formed the substance of secret transmissions passed down in master-disciple (or father-son) lineages of religious and worldly knowledge, esoteric rites, court precedents, and the arts. These identifications of specific sets of phenomena or activities with Buddhist principles—a paradigm that may in a broad sense be called the "unity of original forms and their manifest traces" (*honji suijaku*)—is proving to have been central to the cognitive, aesthetic, and ideological dimensions of much of medieval Japanese culture" (Stone 2006, 45–46).

ancestors is profoundly mistaken. It is also worth noting here the Shingon equivalent of the doctrinal comfort suggested in the *Shikitari* reading of the *Brahma Net Sūtra*—that one's ancestors "*will* [italics mine] attain Buddhahood without any distress."

A central context for this pamphlet and for the practices of sectarian researchers more broadly involves the ongoing attempt to train temple priests who are thought to lack the doctrinal grounding and self-confidence to maintain sectarian distinctiveness in the face of increased competition on numerous fronts: the popularity of New Religions, the commercialization of funerals, and the deep-rooted effects of the folk beliefs and practices of their temple parishioners. As with the other sects, the funeral problem for Shingon concerns not only the negative public image of priests making money from the bad fortune of others but also the internal issue of priestly confidence and the best way to propagate sect teachings.

It is worth noting that the aim of the Shingon grave pamphlet is far more practical than the *Sōsai* or even the *Shikitari* volume in that it goes so far as to provide model dharma talks, summaries of related laws, and sample contracts. The doctrinal advice, based on core Shingon texts, seems to strike a balance on how to deal with folk aspects of mortuary rites; something missing in the different Sōtō sect positions. There is never any doubt, in any of these publications, that the funeral problem is real and that it must be addressed. Nevertheless, whether inclusive of folk practices or attempting to isolate a normative doctrinal core, all these products of sect research centers posit some sort of disconnect between a given sect's fundamental tenets and the predominant practice of its temple priests.

CONCLUSION

In contrast to the previous four chapters, which primarily dealt with the tangible aspects of funerary Buddhism, this chapter focused on conceptual issues, specifically concerns among sectarian elites and researchers about doctrinal consistency and interpretation. This approach allowed me to situate the *sōsai mondai* in a broader sectarian context by considering how researchers conceive of the problem, develop responses to it, and disseminate their ideas within each sect. There is a notable tendency in the activities of these researchers to extrapolate various aspects of the *sōsai mondai* (changing family structures, loss of parishioners, an increase in *muen* 無縁 graves, and the spreading influence and authority of the funerary industry) into the realm of more existential questions regarding the meaning of Buddhist funerary rites, the role of Buddhism in contemporary Japanese society, and the confidence level of temple priests. In other words, the tangible symptoms of the funerary problem are being taken by these researchers as signs of a deeper doctrinal malaise infecting Japanese Buddhism as a whole.

It should be clear, however, that a focus on doctrine in no way moves us out of the realm of material concerns. The doctrinal aspects of the *sōsai mondai* are just as "real" as the economic. These debates over how to propagate Buddhist teachings, see to the emotional needs of followers, and explain Buddhist ritual (both to parishioners and the priests themselves) strike at the heart of how Japanese Buddhism defines itself today and in the future. Just as competition from New Religions, loss of parishioners, and the collapse of the *ie* 家 system forces priests such as Ogawa and Takizawa into self-reflection about what it means to be Buddhist and what it means to run a temple, philosophical debates over no-self and posthumous ordination among sectarian thinkers implicate institutional structures, educational curricula, and textual production of the sect as a whole. It is no coincidence, for example, that as a result of research into the funeral problem, both the Sōtō and Jōdo sect research centers have begun projects investigating the attitudes, confidence levels, education, and training of temple priests. The Sōtō sect even published a 460-page book on the subject in 2008, *Priests: Their Role and the Issues They Face* (僧侶—その役割と課題 *Sōryo: Sono yakuwari to kadai*), that is almost identical in form and layout to the *Sōsai* volume.

Although at times I have presented the different views on the funerary problem in oppositional terms, it is clearly not that simple. Referring to these centers as essential sites in the production of contemporary Buddhism was not meant to imply a one-sided, top-down model for the way sectarian orthodoxy is disseminated and maintained. The goals of the sects' main researchers in many ways coincide with those of temple priests. Both groups worry that parishioner numbers are dropping, that young people are hardly flocking to temples, and that new burial options in an increasingly commercial funerary market are eroding the social and economic bedrock of temple Buddhism. This is not, then, simply a story of sect leaders and researchers tying the helpless local abbot to the train tracks of doctrinal orthodoxy. As the regional publications of funeral guides for priests in Shizuoka and Yamashina suggest, a closer look reveals priests actually helping out with the knots and suggesting better rope. Yet significant differences do exist. As the back and forth between different Sōtō groups plainly reveals, important debates are still taking place within the sects over the meaning and interpretation of core Buddhist teachings.

Thus, beyond the methodological argument for the need to include research centers in scholarly understandings of how Buddhism in Japan is negotiated, I am also making a larger point about the key elements of that negotiation and what it says about Japanese Buddhism today. The notion that mortuary rites are inconsistent with Buddhist teachings is a definitively modern concern stemming from a combination of drastic social change, twentieth-century institutional structures, and the activities of sectarian researchers and intellectuals.[66] As much as a married, meat-eating, and (relatively) long-haired priesthood served to diminish the perceived gap between the priests and the laity, the impact of Western philological, philosophical, and religious categories on the emergent study of Buddhism in Japan served to produce and expand a gap between a pure doctrinal (now philosophical) tradition and its "degenerated" temple forms. In the postwar period, the effects of a university-educated, scientifically minded group of intellectuals occupying key posts in sectarian research centers has institutionalized these tensions within the various sects. Many of those scholarly categories and assumptions—the Western focus on the individual, no-self as the normative pivot against which all practices are judged, and the isolation of "folk" Buddhism—all inform the practices and perspectives of these research centers today.

Returning to the issues of no-self and posthumous ordination, we can see that the researchers take a stance that precludes any ambiguity or multivalence in the interpretation of these terms. As the discussion of bonds (縁 en) in the previous three chapters has demonstrated, however, temples, particularly those like Tōchōji and Myōkōji that are exploring the social and doctrinal limits of en as part of their development of new burial forms, are dependent on precisely the duality of these concepts—on the flexibility of terms that serve as the basis for both doctrinal and cultural understandings of the world. In taking a normative stance on doctrine, the researchers isolate Buddhist teachings from their cultural context and thus further remove them from the lives of parishioners.

66. This is not to say that similar critiques have not been made against Buddhism before, since clearly they have. But in the same way that modern capitalism is qualitatively different from, for example, the exchange of capital in fourth-century China, the current discourses of Buddhist critique are, in their extent, institutionalization, and broad diffusion, inherently different from earlier forms. I would argue, therefore, that they are modern.

This book opened with a grave and a simple vignette of funerary Buddhism as it is still lived throughout Japan: a summer day, a chorus of cicadas, two generations cleaning a family grave for *o-bon*, and a young boy, self consciously stepping forward alone to address his beloved grandmother, dead and on the other side of the world for almost half his life. Although the scene is bathed in sunlight, there are hints of shadows: abandoned graves; a memorial tablet, toppled and cracked; withered plastic branches; and the implication that someday there will be no one to slake the thirst of the family dead. In the past, there were hardly any abandoned graves here. Then there were a few. Now they stand in silent majority, passing judgment on the living. Underlying this image is the significance of bonds (縁 *en*) between the living and the dead, and the need to maintain those connections across time and space. This story, and the book it introduced, is about the loss of bonds and attempts to maintain them. It is also about the resiliency of bonds and the impossibility of being truly free of the dead.

In 1870, Jules Verne wrote a story about three intrepid travelers, who, along with their two dogs, mount a daring trip to the moon. Tragically, one of the dogs dies along the way, and the group faces the difficult question of what to do with the corpse. When they eventually eject the canine into space, they find to their horror that he is not so easily discarded. He continues along the journey in a tight orbit around the spacecraft. Verne, not without a wicked sense of humor and a fair bit of foreshadowing, named the dog Satellite. Robert Pogue Harrison evokes this story in *Domain of the Dead* to argue for the human need to place corporeal remains in the ground (Harrison 2003). Although Harrison's insights into the role of burial in human identity are fascinating and beautifully described, I believe that in Verne's image of bodies continuously circling one another, we have a particularly apt metaphor for burial and ancestor worship in Japan.

Although we commonly use the term "departed" to refer to the deceased, I would argue that an orbit, rather than a departure, better approximates the full range of Japanese views of the dead. An orbit suggests a certain regularity of proximity and distance; it brings to mind bodies, celestial and ancestral, circling around, in and out of view. For the Japanese, it is an elliptical orbit: The dead are sometimes near, sometimes far, but their return to proximity comes at precise, regular intervals. And yet, orbits, like bonds with the dead, must eventually decay.

This book has focused on the grave as the center of the ancestral orbit. In so doing, it has traced the modern history of why that center is losing its gravitational pull and how, consequently, the economic and social bedrock of temple Buddhism in Japan has eroded to the point where even its continued existence is publicly called into question. In detailing these changes, I have covered a broad range of materials including the social and religious elements of burial and the economic, legal, political, and commercial factors that bear upon the choices people make when they decide how to be buried and memorialized. Buddhist mortuary practices provide scholars with far-reaching insight into religious life as it is lived, institutionalized, debated, advertised, promoted, paid for, legislated, bureaucratized, studied, surveyed, and described by everyone from middle-aged metropolitan housewives to rural priests to sectarian scholarly elites.

What do changing burial practices reveal about contemporary Japanese Buddhism and society? In answering this question, I have taken into account a range of positions and voices: the views of burial society members and parishioners, which stretch from glowing to indifferent; scholarly sectarian attempts to gauge and promote doctrinal orthodoxy; and priestly opinions on everything from the commercialization of the funerary industry and the decline of the parishioner system to the supposed difficulties of squaring Buddhist teachings with temple practice. Here I would like to briefly recapitulate the main arguments of the book.

I began by tracing key themes in the historical development of modern funerary Buddhism to demonstrate how temples came to be the sole source of funerary rites and, in turn, grew dependent on the income from those rites. In the seventeenth century, the temple-certification system, as well as the parishioner system that grew out of it, tied the general population to temples for the next three and a half centuries. The legal changes during the Meiji period, though ending the obligations of the *danka* 檀家 system, also placed the *ie* 家 at the center of government ideology and made memo-rializing the ancestors both an individual and civic duty. The ostensible end of that system in the postwar period, like the end of temple certifica-tion in the early Meiji period, did little to alter the shared trajectory of family graves and temples.

Although there has always been some criticism of funerary Buddhism, including censure of funerary excess in the Tokugawa and Meiji periods, I have shown that it was a confluence of several events in the postwar period that led to the widespread and public criticism we see today. Ur-banization, nuclearization of families, and new living spaces distanced families from communal support networks and the shared ritual knowl-edge they provide. Into this gap stepped funerary professionals, who, in an increasingly commodified ritual market, began unifying all the materials and services and thus exerting control over all aspects of the mortuary process. At the same time, the postwar land reforms made temples more fully dependent on mortuary income, which made them appear complicit in the commercialization of death. The widespread questioning of what were seen as extravagant and outmoded Buddhist funerals in the postwar period was a direct result of this confluence of factors. Critiques of Bud-dhism, however, were not limited to the perception of funerary excess and began to extend to the tradition as a whole. Temple priests recognized these troubling changes in their immediate environs, but their anxiety and self-doubt were made particularly acute by an emerging group of sectarian scholars and researchers focused on the widening criticism. Nevertheless, the *danka*/temple relationship and the obligation for maintaining family graves persisted, supported in no small part by that generation of Japanese who had been raised in pre- and immediate postwar households. It was not until a couple of decades later, with the almost complete commercializa-tion of Japanese society, the nuclearization of now predominantly urban families since the 1980s, and the disappearing wartime generation that the patrilineal values supporting those grave sites came under serious doubt. As I have argued throughout this book, graves were a key site in the broad interrogation of those values, the point at which social norms and Bud-dhist identity could be negotiated.

Although in previous eras, graves were used both to express social class and to exceed it, with the breakdown in the traditional grave system, the new choice-based forms of burial that emerged from the late 1980s pro-vided opportunities for those excluded from that old system. It also al-lowed people to offer a public challenge to established cultural and reli-gious funerary norms.

Readers familiar with twentieth-century Japan will notice that the emergence of new burial forms in the late 1980s corresponds to the death of Emperor Hirohito (1901–89), the bursting of the economic bubble, and the beginning of the so-called lost decade. While it may be tempting to draw connections, I have resisted positing a major rupture in thinking about family and burial that corresponds perfectly to the end of the Shōwa era (1926–89). I have instead tried to argue for continuity across that period. By focusing on the specific individuals and interactions that led to this "grave revolution," I am following recent trends in historical studies of other time periods and rejecting any facile correspondence between era change and social change.

I then detailed the current state of Japanese graves and introduced the concept of *muen* 無縁. Bonds (and loss of said) between the living and the dead are very much at the core of this story. As much as the financial and practical considerations, I believe the fear of *muen* for one's ancestors and for oneself is the driving force behind the development and acceptance of new graves. New family realities mean that more people are in danger of becoming *muen* and thus in need of alternatives. In response, new burial options, which began at a few specific sites, soon spread across the country, appearing at temple, municipal, and commercial graveyards.

Initially aimed at precisely those people who were finding themselves excluded from traditional burial spaces, eternal memorial graves, like any new technology, soon produced unexpected adaptations. Even those groups who had or who could maintain a family grave started to take advantage of the flexibility, low cost, and freedom from obligation of these new sites. They allowed people to forge new bonds, but also, like Tome and Naoko, ritually sever existing ones. Even more striking, in providing grave space to nonparishioners, temples upended over three centuries of postmortem status quo, all in less than two decades. Eternal memorial graves are therefore crucial to understanding both the current state of temple Buddhism and its future. With the potential to rewrite existing funerary rules and reform long-standing relationships, these graves mark the start of what I called the post-*danka* era.

In order to detail the significance of these new graves, I offered an ethnographic case study of Myōkōji that explored two broad-ranging themes: the potential that the Annon grave offered members to contest social norms and the challenge that it presented to temple Buddhism. Naoko and Tome's stories of posthumous divorce via the Annon grave reveal that, while these new graves are certainly conditioned by social changes, they are also the source of many of those changes. As Allison Alexy has demonstrated so clearly, divorce in contemporary Japan has many proximate causes, which may or may not involve an intentional and explicit rejection of the extended-family ideal (Alexy 2008). Naoko and Tome's stories are an example of how eternal memorial graves, as posthumous divorce or revenge, make it possible for individuals to realize their own ideals of family, gender roles, generational relations, and (posthumous) residence.

In the story of the Endōs and, to a certain extent, in Naoko's account of her daughter's pregnancy, we see hints of what eternal memorial graves might come to offer temples in terms of religious affiliation. Religion in Japan is both contextual and practical. Temples, long relying on the tradition of family burial more than on the faith of temple parishioners, find themselves facing a future with neither. Ogawa's criticism of the *danka* system's dependence on obligatory memorial bonds, his conviction that the Nichiren sect should jettison 40 percent of its temples, and his willingness to search outside the sect for a successor illustrate important ways that eternal memorial graves are enabling temple priests to challenge temple and sectarian norms while attracting new clientele.

Tōchōji's En no Kai burial society presented the second ethnographic study of an eternal memorial grave, this time in the heart of Tokyo. Tōchōji's burial site, like that of Myōkōji, provides individuals and families graves without the obligation of becoming parishioners or the need for descendants. In the previous chapter, I focused on the potential for these new graves to challenge social obligations, but this chapter emphasized the vital significance of family bonds. By ensuring that she and her mother would end up together in Tōchōji's eternal memorial grave, Michiko was not so much escaping relationships as she was seeking to maintain them. Tōchōji's attempt to refigure the loss of traditional bonds as the very potential to create unlimited connections is a pivotal response to the *muen* problem. The fact that *en* is not being replaced by something else or being discarded shows how fundamental bonds of attachment are to temple Buddhism. The importance of this argument should have become all the more clear in chapters 5 and 6.

Myōkōji and Tōchōji, though portrayed in part as a contrast between urban and rural, can be considered a two-part amalgamation. It was for this reason that I did not present the two temples in a parallel fashion. By attending to different aspects of each site—Ogawa's background, advertising campaigns by Annex, narratives of control in the stories of Annon members, and ritual services at Tōchōji—I was able to provide a comprehensive picture of contemporary temple realities in the face of changing demographics and shifting social norms. This was not to suggest that

Ogawa is unconcerned with the potential commercialization of Myōkōji membership or that Takizawa's training and background played no part in his decision to create a new type of temple grave at Tōchōji. Rather, the different portrayals of the two main temples treated in this work were designed to emphasize the types of underlying basic concerns that mutually connected these two different sites.

The priests and parishioners at Tōchōji and Myōkōji, regardless of the temples' disparities in size, wealth, sectarian status, organizational structure, and location, share many of the same concerns. Both have struggled to deal with the limits of the parishioner system and traditional family graves that it upholds. Both of their temples have a long-standing dependence on an aging parishioner base, yet both have succeeded in drastically altering the membership structures of their respective temples. Ogawa and Takizawa see eternal memorial graves as a way to revitalize their temples by bringing in a new and diverse membership, and thereby challenging the perception of temples as mere storage facilities for family ancestors. Each temple, then, offers a distinct set of possibilities for what post-*danka* temple membership might look like.

As detailed in chapters 3 and 4, eternal memorial graves and voluntary burial societies signify a remarkable and, for many temple priests, essential challenge to the existing parishioner system. Beyond representing a radically new form of burial based on choice rather than obligation, the members of these new graves offer priests hope of a return to what they see as a more traditional connection to temples; relationships not based solely on mortuary services, but premised on the propagation of Buddhist teachings.

Along these lines, the new graves at Myōkōji and Tōchōji raise the issue of what temple affiliation actually signifies in contemporary Japan: what it means for someone to be a *danka* of a temple, for instance, or to refer to a temple as one's *bodaiji*, and how this differs from being a member (会員 *kaiin*) of a burial society. Do these burial societies represent a break with past traditions, a return to some "golden age" of temple life, or simply an adaptation of the *danka* system, replacing the ideology of the extended family with consumer rhetoric of individual choice? Clearly, Tōchōji and Myōkōji have tapped into the public's fears of *muen*, as well as its ongoing desire to be interred and memorialized at a Buddhist temple free of the traditional restrictions and responsibilities of being a *danka*. Municipal and commercial versions of communal graves exist throughout Japan, but without Buddhist memorial rites they lack the soteriological comfort and stability of temple interment. Of course, as Michiko's responses revealed in chapter 4, the wish to be buried at a temple may involve the simultaneous *desire* for Buddhist memorial services and *belief* that a temple will never go bankrupt. Over the course of my analysis, I have unpacked the ways in which such an ostensibly simple wish is conditioned by complex, historically situated beliefs and socioeconomic forces.

In order to demonstrate broader currents in the devolpment of new burial forms, I also discussed a method of burial that rejects the traditional family grave, thereby precluding the need for Buddhist rituals of death and memorial. The Grave-Free Promotion Society, though not explicitly anti-Buddhist, is nevertheless promoting a form of burial that largely excludes the Buddhist establishment. Though scattering accounts for only a small number of burials each year, it embodies a highly visible and keenly felt affront to Buddhism's monopoly over mortuary rites in Japan. There are important lessons to be learned in the strong reactions the Grave-Free Promotion Society provokes in the Buddhist establishment, from outright rejection to enthusiastic adoption. It is particularly telling that the main Buddhist objection to scattering centers on the perceived danger it poses to the continuity of families—an argument that appeals to the importance of performing memorial services at temples. Here again the emphasis is on the bonds and multigenerational connections so vital to temples such as Myōkōji and Tōchōji.

The second major theme in chapter 5 was the idea of fixity. The eternal memorial graves discussed in this study may signify a new form of burial and a refashioned relationship to temples, but they remain very similar to traditional graves in their offer of a fixed location for regular memorial rites and their reliance on water and stone. The increasingly fraught debate over the fate of contemporary memorial practices is—at bottom—fueled by a deep-seated anxiety over the impending loss of this type of fixity. Whatever its drawbacks, the traditional grave nevertheless derives a substantial portion of its alluring comfort from its claim to concrete, material, rigidity—a quality that eternal memorial graves are also trying to replicate. Scattering, however, rejects this fixity. In its images of claustrophobic, clammy spaces, the Grave-Free Promotion Society equates the traditional grave with a sort of prison. It urges a return to nature as a way of avoiding this posthumous captivity, arguing that by scattering we place the dead in the hearts of the living. I maintain, however, that the lack of fixity is precisely why scattering remains a minority practice.

In the final chapter of the book, I extended the discussion of the funerary problem (葬祭問題 *sōsai mondai*) from temples into the broader institutional structures of the sects themselves. By exploring how sectarian

researcher take up the issue of burial and graves, I argued that debates
over the funerary problem are in fact about the very meaning and future
of Buddhism in Japan. Through readings of sectarian surveys and related
publications that demonstrate the disjunction between the idealized form
of Buddhism held by researchers and the day-to-day realities facing temple
priests, I was able to illuminate the vital role sectarian researchers play
in the maintenance and production of Buddhism in contemporary Japan.
Their fixation on the breach between doctrinally orthodox positions on
no-self on the one hand and the image of temple priests conducting memorial services for individual spirits on the other, appears not to have concerned temple priests or their parishioners. Throughout Asia, Buddhists
have attended to dead spirits without much worry over this supposed contradiction. Why, then, does it appear to be of such great concern now?

To answer that question, I traced the origin of these sectarian researchers. In the Meiji period, Japanese Buddhism encountered Western scholarly
approaches to the tradition, assumptions about the primacy of texts, and
dismissals of "superstitious" rituals. These new ideas were absorbed into
the sectarian educational system and passed on to subsequent generations
of Buddhist scholars. This group included postwar sectarian specialists,
working at newly formed research centers, who were charged with studying and responding to the modern challenges facing the sects. I argued
that these same specialists—while grappling with the realities of temple
life, surveying the inner thoughts of temple priests, and responding to the
various challenges facing the sect—became the source of new doubts about
doctrinal orthodoxy. The concern of scholars about what they perceived as
contradictions in temple practices was transmitted through survey questions and analyses to temple priests in such a way that those scholarly
anxieties in fact came to exacerbate the very "problem" they were lament-
ing. To be sure, many of these problems were not simply a creation of the
research centers: Temples are losing parishioners, non-Buddhist funeral
options are on the rise, and Buddhist funerals are increasingly criticized in
popular discourse as empty ritual forms benefiting no one but the priests
themselves. However, as I demonstrated in chapter 6, researchers tended
to transpose these "concrete" problems into the more intangible realm of
existential crisis.

These researchers have looked to solutions focused on trying to purify
practice and reassert doctrinal norms. Ironically, the successful propagation of those norms hinges on doctrinally based cultural understandings
of relationships that were outlined in previous chapters: between families,
communities, and generations. Chapter 2 cautioned us about the lack of

bonds, chapter 3 demonstrated the ways in which eternal memorial graves could both create and sever bonds, while chapter 4 focused on Tōchōji's efforts to rethink the category of *en*. In turn, chapter 5 emphasized how crucial a multivalent reading of *en* is to the defense of Buddhist burial and memorial in the face of new, non-Buddhist practices.

Though chapter 6 did not focus explicitly on *en*, in exploring the competing approaches to posthumous divorce and no-self expressed in the writings of sectarian elites and local priests, I was able to demonstrate an important tension acting on contemporary Buddhism in Japan. In trying to protect a normative Buddhist core, researchers aim to split doctrinal and cultural readings of the tradition. But as is clearly demonstrated in the varied uses of *en* throughout this book, such a clean break severs precisely those connections so crucial to the ongoing success of temples. Local priests, particularly those regional Sōtō priests publishing their own treatises on burial rites, clearly understand that ritual, doctrine, and cultural practices are not easily divided.

Such tensions point to the larger issue that underscores this book and any project that focuses on contemporary Japanese Buddhism—that doctrine is still being debated among contemporary Buddhists and therefore deserves our attention. This study has not attempted to remove doctrine from center stage, but rather have it share the spotlight with equally significant forces acting on the way Buddhism is lived and propagated today. We need to understand how Buddhist ideals actually play out at temples. The point of this approach is not simply to highlight the supposed contradictions that appear when doctrine and practice meet, but rather to explore the fascinating ways in which this ostensible polarity is negotiated by different groups. In an essay on religion and modernity, Gustavo Benavides writes about the "violent oscillation" (rather than simple contradiction) between religion as ideal and religion as lived (Benavides 2005). While the idea of movement rather than a static opposition appeals to me, in the case of doctrinal ideal and lived reality in contemporary Japanese Buddhism, just how violent this oscillation is depends very much on to whom you are talking. For most temple parishioners and burial society members, practice trumps doctrine. Their religious posture is determined largely by the environment in which they were raised. They are often far more likely to see their activities at graves, family altars, and temples in terms of custom than as "religion" per se. Sectarian researchers are thus faced with the dilemma of having to promote doctrinal orthodoxy to an audience of temple priests who cannot use that orthodoxy to communicate effectively with their followers—priests like Ogawa, who sometimes see that orthodoxy as a burden rather than a path to liberation. Moreover, publishing material aimed at sharpening the doctrinal skills of temple priests may serve to heighten their anxiety over contradictions in the rituals they must carry out on a daily basis. Ultimately, temple priests must negotiate these issues, deciding for themselves how to incorporate the doctrinal tenets of their sects into ritual care of the dead, a process that necessarily involves compromises, consequences, and compensations.

This book has argued that contemporary Japanese Buddhism is best understood in terms of how it attends to the dead; in order for the study of contemporary Japanese Buddhism to become a vibrant field of study, it must approach its subject as a lived tradition, replete with contradictions and the messy turmoil of human lives. The binaries of doctrine and social custom, belief and market forces, or tradition and innovation should not be used to gauge the purity or decline of the tradition, but rather should be taken as ingredients, so to speak; ingredients that, when mixed with human ashes, become capable of telling us more about the current contours and transformations of Japanese Buddhism, about changing Japanese society, and about our approaches to the study of religion.

Jōdo Sect Survey of Funerary Buddhism (1994)[1]

1. When a parishioner dies, who (A) uses what (B) method to contact you?

   (A)   Chief mourner
           Bereaved family member
           Relative
           Neighbor
           Funeral company
           Other

   (B)   Phone call only
           Phone call and temple visit
           Temple visit only
           Other

2. Do you visit the home for the wake or to perform last rites (枕経 makuragyō) (A)? If so, who pays the visit (B)? If not, please explain why (C).

   (A)   I go for both
           Only last rites
           Only wake
           Neither

   (B)   Head priest or the assistant head priest
           A priest from a connected temple
           Other

1. Priest version. Itō and Fujii 1997, 344–47.

3. What standard do you use for giving posthumous names?

    Whether or not they have received precepts
    Contributions (貢献 kōken) to the temple while alive
    Contributions to society
    Following precedents for the mourning family's ancestry
    Posthumous name fee
    Other

4. Do you get asked to perform services for those who are not parishioners (A)? If so, from whom do you get requests (B)? In that case, how do you choose a posthumous name (C)?

    (A)   Often asked
          Sometimes asked
          Rarely asked
          Never

    (B)   Funeral company
          Someone from the area
          Parishioner
          Other

    (C)   From the living name
          Ask their family temple
          A Jōdo sect name
          Other

5. Where do the funerals take place? Put in order from most to least frequent.

    Home
    Temple
    Public facility
    Funeral company hall
    Other

6. Of the following, who does the most in terms of preparation and running the funeral?

Relatives
Neighbors
Funeral company
Other

7. Is the role of the priest in mortuary rites only to participate in the funeral itself? What do you think about the priest's role in the entire funeral?

Only funeral
Not only funeral
Not applicable

8. What things do the mourning family consult with you about? Place in order.

Offering (*fuse*)
Posthumous name
Number of priests
Grave
Dividing the remains (*bunkotsu*)
The Buddhist altar

9. During the funeral or mourning period do you give a dharma talk or explanation of Buddhist teachings (A)? When do you do it (B)?

(A)   Yes
        No

(B)   *Makuragyō*
        Wake
        Funeral service
        At the crematorium during *kotsuage*
        First seventh day of mourning
        During mourning
        End of mourning

10. Have you ever had any problems during a funeral? If so give a concrete explanation.

Mourning family
Funeral company/scheduling
Another temple
No answer

11. Tell us about the timing (A) and location (B) of the interring of a parishioner's ashes.

    (A)   Same day as funeral
           Next day
           First seventh day of mourning
           During mourning
           After mourning period ends

    (B)   Temple graveyard
           Community graveyard
           Cemetery (*reien*)
           Hometown graveyard
           Temple ossuary
           Other

12. When do you conduct mourning period rites for the (A) first seventh day (初七日 *shonanoka*), and (B) the intermediary (中陰 *chūin*) or end of mourning (満中陰 *manchūin*)?

    (A)   Same day as funeral
           Day after the funeral
           Seven days after death
           Other

    (B)   Every seven days
           Only on the fifth or seventh of the seven day periods
           Other

13. Do you have any thoughts about what should be done about the current state of funerals or do you have any doubts? Also, if there is anything, either in the above list of items or not, that has changed considerably from before, please tell us about it.

WORKS CITED

Abé, Ryūichi. 1999. *The Weaving of Mantra: Kūkai and the Construction of Esoteric Buddhist Discourse*. New York: Columbia University Press.

Alexy, Allison. 2008. "Intimate Separations: Divorce and its Reverberations in Contemporary Japan." Ph.D. diss., Yale University.

Anderson, Richard W. 1991. "What Constitutes Religious Activity? (I)." *Japanese Journal of Religious Studies* 18, no. 4:369–72.

Aoki Mitsuo 青木満男. 1994. "Sankotsu no jigyōka to kongo no kadai 散骨の事業化と今後の課題." *SOGI* 21:108–9.

Aoki Shinmon 青木新門. 1996. *Nōkanfu nikki* 納棺夫日記. Tokyo: Bungei shunjū.

Awaya Ryōdō 粟谷良道. 2003. "Minzoku yori shūshi e: Nijū isseiki no kadai 民俗より宗旨へ二十一世紀の課題." In *Sōsai: Gendaiteki igi to kadai*, ed. Sōtōshū Sōgō Kenkyū Sentā, 29–40. Tokyo: Sōtōshū shūmuchō.

Benavides, Gustavo. 1998. "Modernity." In *Critical Terms for Religious Studies*, ed. Mark C. Taylor, 186–204. Chicago: Chicago University Press.

Bernstein, Andrew. 2006. *Modern Passings: Death Rites, Politics, and Social Change in Imperial Japan*. Honolulu: University of Hawai'i Press.

Bodiford, William M. 1992. "Zen in the Art of Funerals: Ritual Salvation in Japanese Buddhism." *History of Religions* 32:146–64.

———. 1993. *Sōtō Zen in Medieval Japan*. Honolulu: University of Hawai'i Press.

———. 1996. "Zen and the Art of Religious Prejudice: Efforts to Reform a Tradition of Social Discrimination." *Japanese Journal of Religious Studies* 23, nos. 1–2:1–27.

Boisvert, Mathieu. 2004. "Pratītya samutpāda (Dependent Origination)." In *Encyclopedia of Buddhism*, ed. R. E. Buswell, Jr., vol. 2, 669–70. New York: McMillan Reference USA.

Bond, George D. 2004. "Arhat." In *Encyclopedia of Buddhism*, ed. R. E. Buswell, Jr., vol. 1, 28–30. New York: McMillan Reference USA.

Borup, Jørn. 2008. *Japanese Rinzai Zen Buddhism*. Leiden: Brill.

Brook, Timothy. 2005. "Institution." In *Critical Terms for the Study of Buddhism*, ed. D. S. Lopez, Jr., 143–61. Chicago: Universtity of Chicago Press.

Bukkyō Taimususha, ed. 1969. *Bukkyō dainenkan* 仏教大年鑑. Tokyo: Bukkyō Taimususha.

Bunkachō 文化庁. 2008. *Shūkyō nenkan* 宗教年鑑. Tokyo: Bunkachō bunkabu shūmuka.

Buswell, Jr., Robert E., ed. 2004. *Encyclopedia of Buddhism*. 2 vols. New York: Macmillan Reference USA.

Butsuji Gaido 仏事ガイド, ed. 2003. *Eitai kuyōbo no hon* 永代供養墓の本. Tokyo: Rokugatsu shobō.

——— 2005. *Eitai kuyōbo no hon* 永代供養墓の本. Tokyo: Rokugatsu shobō.

Cadge, Wendy. 2005. *Heartwood: The First Generation of Theravada Buddhism in America*. Chicago: University of Chicago Press.

Chizan Denbōin 智山伝法院. 1994. *Kyōka shūdan no genjō to kadai* 教化宗団の現状と課題. Tokyo: Chizan Denbōin.

Clarke, Shayne. Forthcoming. *Family Matters in Indian Monastic Buddhisms*. Honolulu: University of Hawai'i Press.

Cole, Alan 1996. "Upside Down/Right Side Up: A Revisionist History of Buddhist Funerals in China." *History of Religions* 35, no. 4:307–38.

Collcutt, Martin. 1986. "Buddhism: The Threat of Eradication." In *Japan in Transition, from Tokugawa to Meiji*, ed. M. B. Jansen and G. Rozman, 143–67. Princeton: Princeton University Press.

Collins, Steven. 1982. *Selfless Persons: Imagery and Thought in Theravāda Buddhism*. Cambridge: Cambridge University Press.

Condry, Ian. 2001. "Japanese Hip-hop and the Globalization of Popular Culture." In *Urban Life: Readings in the Anthropology of the City*, ed. G. Gmelch and W. Zenner, 357–87. Prospect Heights: Waveland Press.

Copp, Paul. 2008. "Notes on the Term 'Dhāraṇī' in Medieval Chinese Buddhist Thought." *Bulletin of the School of Oriental and African Studies* 71, no. 3:493–508.

Covell, Stephen Grover. 2005. *Japanese Temple Buddhism: Worldliness in a Religion of Renunciation*. Honolulu: University of Hawai'i Press.

——— 2008. "The Price of Naming the Dead: Posthumous Precept Names and Critiques of Contemporary Japanese Buddhism." In *Death and the Afterlife in Japanese Buddhism*, ed. J. I. Stone and M. N. Walter, 293–324. Honolulu: University of Hawai'i Press.

Covell, Stephen and Mark Rowe. 2004. "Editors' Introduction: Traditional Religion in Contemporary Japan." *Japanese Journal of Religious Studies* 31, no. 2:245–54.

Cuevas, B., and J. I. Stone, eds. 2007. *The Buddhist Dead: Practices, Discourses, and Representations*. Honolulu: University of Hawai'i Press.

Davis, Winston. 1980. *Dojo: Magic and Exorcism in Modern Japan*. Stanford: Stanford University Press.

Douglas, Mary. 1966. *Purity and Danger: An Analysis of Concepts of Pollution and Taboo*. London: Routledge & K. Paul.

Earhart, Byron. 1989. *Gedatsu-Kai and Religion in Contemporary Japan: Returning to the Center*. Bloomington: Indiana University Press.

Ebersole, Gary L. 1989. *Ritual Poetry and the Politics of Death in Early Japan*. Princeton: Princeton University Press.

Elison, George. 1991. *Deus Destroyed: The Image of Christianity in Early Modern Japan*. Cambridge: Harvard University Press.

Faure, Bernard. 1987. "The Daruma-shū, Dōgen, and Sōtō Zen." *Monumenta Nipponica* 42, no. 1:25–55.

———. 1991. *The Rhetoric of Immediacy: A Cultural Critique of Chan/Zen Buddhism*. Princeton: Princeton University Press.

———. 2000. *Visions of Power: Imagining Medieval Japanese Buddhism*. Princeton: Princeton University Press.

Foulk, T. Griffith. 1993. "Issues in the Field of East Asian Buddhist Studies: An Extended Review of Sudden and Gradual: Approaches to Enlightenment in Chinese Thought." *JIABS* 16, no. 1:93–180.

———. n.d. "The Rise of Zen Studies." Unpublished manuscript.

Fujii Masao 藤井正雄. 1977. *Bukkyō girei jiten* 仏教儀礼辞典. Tokyo: Tōkyōdō shuppan.

———. 1980. *Bukkyō sōsai daijiten* 仏教葬祭大辞典. Tokyo: Yūzankaku shuppan.

———. 1982. "Okotsubotoke no kenkyū お骨仏の研究." In Takaguchi Yasuyuki, *Isshinji fūun oboegaki*. Osaka: Seibundō.

———. 1991. *O-haka no subete ga wakaru hon* お墓のすべてがわかる本. Tokyo: Pureshidentosha.

———. 1995. "Sankotsu to kankyō hogo kisei 散骨と環境保護規制." *Shūkyō Kenkyū* 69:211–32.

———. 1996. "Sankotsu no hōkisei o motomeru tame no shogaikoku jirei 散骨の法規制を求めるための諸外国事例." *Gekkan Jūshoku* 月刊住職 8–9:30–52.

Fujii Masao 藤井正雄 and Hasegawa Shōkō 長谷川正浩, eds. 2001. *Q&A bochi/nōkotsudō o meguru hōritsu jitsumu* Q&A墓地・納骨堂をめぐる法律実務. Nagoya: Shinnihonhōki shuppan.

Gennep, Arnold van. 1960. *The Rites of Passage*. Chicago: University of Chicago Press.

Glassman, Hank. 2001. "The Religious Construction of Motherhood in Medieval Japan." Ph.D. diss., Stanford University.

Gluck, Carol. 1985. *Japan's Modern Myths: Ideology in the Late Meiji Period*. Princeton: Princeton University Press.

Gombrich, Richard. 1971. *Precept and Practice: Traditional Buddhism in the Rural Highlands of Ceylon*. Oxford: Oxford University Press.

Grapard, Allan. 1984 . "Japan's Ignored Cultural Revolution: The Separation of Buddhist and Shinto Deities in Meiji and a Case Study: Tonomine." *History of Religions* 23, no. 3:240–65.

Haga Noboru 芳賀登. 1996. *Sōgi no rekishi* 葬儀の歴史. Tokyo: Yūzankaku shuppan.

Hakeda, Yoshito S. 1972. *Kūkai and His Major Works*. New York: Columbia University Press.

Hara Takahito 原隆仁. 1998. *O-haka ga nai!* お墓がない! Tokyo: Wakō International 和光インターナショナル.

Hardacre, Helen. 1984. *Lay Buddhism in Contemporary Japan: Reiyūkai Kyōdan*. Princeton: Princeton University Press.

———. 1988. *Kurozumikyō and the New Religions of Japan*. Princeton: Princeton University Press.

————. 1997. *Marketing the Menacing Fetus in Japan*. Berkeley and Los Angeles: University of California Press.

Harrison, Robert Pogue. 2003. *The Dominion of the Dead*. Chicago: University of Chicago Press.

Hashizume Shinya. 1996. "Utopias for the Dead-Cities and the Design of Cemeteries in Japan." *Iichiko International* 8:19–39.

Hattori Shōsai 服部松斉. 1956. "Sōsai teigen 葬祭提言." *Kyōka Kenshū* 教化研修 1:54–62.

Hayashi Makoto 林淳. 2002. "Kindai Nihon ni okeru Bukkyōgaku to shūkyōgaku [Tokushū: 'Seikatsu no shūkyō" to shite no Bukkyō] 近代日本における仏教学と宗教学〈〈特集〉「生活の宗教」としての仏教〉." *Shūkyō kenkyū* 宗教研究 76, no. 2:29–53.

Heine, Steven. 2003. "Abbreviation or Aberration: The Role of the *Shushōgi* in Modern Sōtō Zen Buddhism." In *Buddhism in the Modern World: Adaptations of an Ancient Tradition*, ed. Heine, S. and C. S. Prebish, 169–92. Oxford: Oxford University Press.

Himonya Hajime 碑文谷創. 2008. "*Shōhisha no sōgikan wa dō kawatta ka* 消費者の葬儀観はどう 変わったか." *SOGI* 18, no. 4:27–40.

Hiraide Kōjirō 平出鏗二郎. 1902. *Tōkyō fūzoku shi* 東京風俗史. Tokyo: Yasaka shobō.

Hirose Takuji 広瀬卓爾. 1997. "Dainiji ankēto chōsa hōkoku: Gendaijin no sōsai ni taisuru taido 第二次アンケート調査報告—現代人の葬祭に対する態度." In *Sōsai bukkyō: Sono rekishi to gendaiteki kadai*, ed. Y. Itō and M. Fujii, 349–92. Tokyo: Nonburusha.

Holt, John Clifford. 2009. *Spirits of the Place: Buddhism and Lao Religious Culture*. Honolulu: University of Hawai'i Press.

Horton, Sarah J. 2007. *Living Buddhist Statues in Early Medieval and Modern Japan*. New York: Palgrave Macmillan.

Hosono Ungai 細野雲外. 1932. *Fumetsu no funbo* 不滅の墳墓. Tokyo: Ganshōdō shoten.

Hōsunsha 方寸舎. 1898. "Sōgi sagen 葬儀瑣言." *Fūzoku Gahō* 174.

Hozumi Nobushige. 2003. *Ancestor Worship and Japanese Law*. Honolulu: University Press of the Pacific.

Hubbard, Jamie and Paul L. Swanson. 1997. *Pruning the Bodhi Tree: The Storm over Critical Buddhism*. Honolulu: University of Hawai'i Press.

Hur Nam-lin. 2007. *Death and Social Order in Tokugawa Japan: Buddhism, Anti-Christianity, and the Danka System*. Cambridge: Harvard University Press.

Hurvitz, Leon. 1976. *Scripture of the Lotus Blossom of the Fine Dharma*. New York: Columbia University Press.

Inada Tsutomu 稲田務 and Ōta Tenrei 太田典礼, eds. 1968. *Sōshiki muyōron* 葬式無用論. Tokyo: Sōshiki o kaikaku suru kai.

Inoue Haruyo 井上治代. 1990. *Gendai o-haka jijō: Yureru kazoku no naka de* 現代お墓事情—ゆれる家族の中で. Tokyo: Sōgensha.

————. 1993. *Ima sōgi/o-haka ga kawaru* いま葬儀・お墓が変わる. Tokyo: Sanshōdo.

————. 2000. *Haka o meguru kazokuron: Dare to hairu ka dare ga mamoru ka* 墓をめぐる家族論: だれと入るかだれが守るか. Tokyo: Heibonsha.

————. 2003. *Haka to kazoku no hen'yō* 墓と家族の変容. Tokyo: Iwanami shoten.

————. 2008. "'Jumokusō' no hirogari to shimindantai ga unda 'sakurasō' bochi 「樹木葬」の広がりと市民団体が生んだ「桜葬」墓地." *SOGI* 103:89–96.

Inoue Nobutaka 井上順孝, Shimazono Susumu 島薗進, et al. 2004. *Atarashii tsuitō shi-setsu wa hitsuyō ka* 新しい追悼施設は必要か. Tokyo: Perikansha.

Inoue Shōichi 井上章一. 1990. *Reikyūsha no tanjō* 霊枢車の誕生. Tokyo: Asahi shinbunsha.

Intārokku インターロック, ed. 2002. *Shinjidai no o-haka jijō* 新時代のお墓事情. Tokyo: Goma shobō.

Irokawa, Daikichi. 1985. *The Culture of the Meiji Period.* Princeton: Princeton University Press.

Itō Yuishin 伊藤唯真 and Fujii Masao 藤井正雄, eds. 1997. *Sōsai bukkyō: Sono rekishi to gendaiteki kadai* 葬祭仏教: その歴史と現代的課題. Tokyo: Nonburusha.

Ives, Christopher. 1995. "Review of *Soto Zen in Medieval Japan* by William M. Bodiford." *Journal of Japanese Studies* 21, no. 2:521–25.

Ivy, Marilyn. 1995. *Discourses of the Vanishing: Modernity, Phantasm, Japan.* Chicago: University of Chicago Press.

Jackson, Michael. 1998. *Minima Ethnographica: Intersubjectivity and the Anthropological Project.* Chicago: University of Chicago Press.

Jaffe, Richard M. 1997. "The Buddhist Cleric as Japanese Subject: Buddhism and the Household Registration System." In *New Directions in the Study of Meiji Japan*, ed. Hardacre, H. and Adam L. Kern, 670–702. Leiden: E. J. Brill.

———. 2001. *Neither Monk nor Layman: Clerical Marriage in Modern Japanese Buddhism.* Princeton: Princeton University Press.

———. 2004. "Seeking Śākyamuni: Travel and the Reconstruction of Japanese Buddhism," *Journal of Japanese Studies* 30, no. 1:65–96.

Jansen, Marius B. and Gilbert Rozman. 1986. *Japan in Transition, from Tokugawa to Meiji.* Princeton: Princeton University Press.

Jōdoshinshū Honganjiha 浄土真宗本願寺派, ed. 1962. *Matsuji jittai hōkoku chōsasho* 末寺実態報告調査書. Kyoto: Jōdoshinshū honganjiha.

Jōdoshū Henshū 浄土宗編集, ed. 2005. *Jōdoshū shūmon hōsei ruisan* 浄土宗門法制類纂. Tokyo: Jōdoshū Shūmuchō.

Jōdoshū Shūsei Chōsa Kekka Kenkyū Iinkai 浄土宗宗勢調査結果研究委員会, ed. 1991. *Daiyonkai Jōdoshū shūsei chōsa kekka* 第四回浄土宗宗勢調査結果. Tokyo: Jōdoshū Shūmuchō.

Jōdoshū Sōgō Kenkyūjo 浄土宗総合研究所, ed. 1990. *Jōdoshū Sōgō Kenkyūjohō* 浄土宗総合研究所報. Tokyo: Jōdoshū Sōgō Kenkyūjo.

Jones, Andrea Sun-Mee. 2004. "What the Doing Does: Religions, Practice and the Problem of Meaning." *Journal for Cultural and Religious Theory* 6, no. 1:86–107.

Joo, Bong Seok. 2007. "The Arhat Cult in China from the Seventh through Thirteenth Centuries: Narrative, Art, Space and Ritual." Ph.D. diss., Princeton University.

Josephson, Jason Ānanda. 2006. "When Buddhism Becomes 'Religion': Religion and Superstition in the Writings of Inoue Enryō." *Japanese Journal of Religious Studies* 33, no. 1:143–68.

Katō Eiji 加藤栄司. 1993. "Sōsō no jiyū ikō no sōsō 葬送の自由以降の葬送." *Gekkan Jūshoku* 月刊住職 10:61–62.

Kawahashi, Noriko. 1995. "*Jizoku* (Priest's Wives) in Sōtō Zen Buddhism: An Ambiguous Category." *Japanese Journal of Religious Studies* 22, nos. 1–2:161–83.

Kawakita Jirō 川喜田二郎. 1967. *Hassōhō: Kōzōsei kaihatsu no tame ni* 発想法—創造性開発のために. Tokyo: Chūkōshinsho.

Kawano, Satsuki. 2004. "Scattering Ashes of the Family Dead: Memorial Activity among the Bereaved in Contemporary Japan." *Ethnology* 43, no. 3:233–48.

———. 2010. *Nature's Embrace: Japan's Aging Urbanites and New Death Rites*. Honolulu: University of Hawai'i Press.

Kenkyūsha. 1974. *Kenkyusha's New Japanese-English Dictionary*. Tokyo: Kenkyūsha.

Kenney, Elizabeth. 1996/97. "Shinto Mortuary Rites in Contemporary Japan." *Cahiers d'Extrême-Asie* 9:397–440.

———. 2000. "Shinto Funerals in the Edo Period." *Japanese Journal of Religious Studies* 27, nos. 3–4:239–71.

Ketelaar, James Edward. 1990. *Of Heretics and Martyrs in Meiji Japan: Buddhism and Its Persecution*. Princeton: Princeton University Press.

Kitiarsa, Pattana. 1999. "'You May Not Believe, but Never Offend the Spirits': Spirit-medium Cult Discourses and the Postmodernism of Thai Religion." Ph.D. diss., University of Washington.

Klima, Alan. 2002. *The Funeral Casino: Meditation, Massacre, and Exchange with the Dead in Thailand*. Princeton: Princeton University Press.

Komine Michihiko 小峰彌彦. 1995. "Bukkyō wa shizensō o dō kangaeru ka 仏教は自然葬をどう考えるか." *Daihōrin* 62:116–19.

Kretschmer, Angelika. 2000. "Mortuary Rites for Inanimate Objects: The Case of Hari Kuyō." *Japanese Journal of Religious Studies* 27, nos. 3–4:379–404.

LaFleur, William R. 1986. *The Karma of Words: Buddhism and the Literary Arts in Medieval Japan*. Berkeley and Los Angeles: University of California Press.

Langer, Rita. 2007. *Buddhist Rituals of Death and Rebirth: Contemporary Sri Lankan Practice and Its Origins*. Oxford: Routledge.

Lee, Edwin B. 1975. "Nichiren and Nationalism: The Religious Patriotism of Tanaka Chigaku." *Monumenta Nipponica* 30:19–35.

Leighton, Taigen Daniel and Okumura Shohaku, trans. 1996. *Dogen's Pure Standards for the Zen Community: A Translation of Eihei Shingi*. New York: SUNY.

Leve, Lauren G. 1999. "Contested Nation/Buddhist Innovation: Politics, Piety, and Personhood in Theravāda Buddhism in Nepal." Ph.D. diss., Princeton University.

LoBreglio, John. 1997. "The Revisions to the Religious Corporations Law: An Introduction and Annotated Translation." *Japanese Religions* 22, no. 1:38–59.

Lopez, Jr., Donald S. 1995. *Curators of the Buddha: The Study of Buddhism under Colonialism*. Chicago: University of Chicago Press.

Matsunaga, Daigan and Alicia Matsunaga. 1974. *Foundation of Japanese Buddhism*. Vol. 1. Los Angeles: Buddhist Books International.

Matsu'ura Shūkō 松浦秀光. 1985. *Sonshuku sōhō no kenkyū* 尊宿葬法の研究. Tokyo: Sankibō busshorin.

———. 1989. *Zenke no sōhō to tsuizen kuyō no kenkyū* 禅家の葬法と追善供養の研究. Tokyo: Sankibō busshorin.

Mauss, Marcel. 1954. *The Gift: Forms and Functions of Exchange in Archaic Societies*. London: Cohen & West.

Miyazaki Eishū 宮崎英修. 1969. *Fuju fuseha no genryū to tenkai* 不受不施派の源流と展開. Kyoto: Heirakuji shoten.

Mochizuki Shinkō 望月信亨, ed. 1954–1963. 望月仏教大辞典 *Mochizuki Bukkyō Daijiten*, 10 vols. Tokyo: Sekai seiten kankō kyōkai.

Mori Kenji 森謙二. 1993. *Haka to sōsō no shakaishi* 墓と葬送の社会史. Tokyo: Kōdansha.

———. 2000. *Haka to sōsō no genzai: Sosen saishi kara sōsō no jiyū e* 墓と葬送の現在：祖先祭祀から葬送の自由へ. Tokyo: Tōkyōdō shuppan.

Morris-Suzuki, Tessa. 2000. "Ethnic Engineering: Scientific Racism and Public Opinion Surveys in Midcentury Japan." *Positions* 8, no. 2:499–529.

Mullins, Mark, Susumu Shimazono, et al. 1993. *Religion and Society in Modern Japan: Selected Readings*. Berkeley: Asian Humanities Press.

Murakami Kōkyō 村上興匡. 1997. "Sōgi shikkōsha no hensen to shi no imizuke no henka 葬儀執行者の変遷と死の意味づけの変化." In *Sōsai bukkyō: Sono rekishi to gendaiteki kadai*, ed. Y. Itō and M. Fujii, 97–122. Tokyo: Nonburusha.

Murakami Kōshin 村上興進. 2008. *Hōjō o mamoru* 法城を守る. Takasaki: Tendaishū Myōtenji.

Nakajima Takanobu 中島隆信. 2005. *O-tera no keizaigaku* お寺の経済学. Tokyo: Tōyō keizai shinbōsha.

Nakamura Hajime 中村元. 1975. *Bukkyōgo daijiten* 佛教語大辞典. Tokyo: Tōkyō shoseki.

Nemoto Kōei 根本孝英. 2001. "Boseki kaigen kuyō hōwa rei 墓石開眼供養法話例." *Kyōka Sentā Sankō Shiryō 4: O-haka*. Tokyo: Shingonshū Buzanha Kyōka Sentā. 4:31–38.

Nichirenshū Gendai Shūkyō Kenkyūjo 日蓮宗現代宗教研究所, ed. 1989. *Kasochi ji'in chōsa hōkoku: Koko made kiteiru kasochi ji'in, anata wa shitte imasuka?* 過疎地寺院調査報告―ここまで来ている過疎地寺院、あなたは知っていますか? Tokyo: Nichirenshū shūmuin.

Nichirenshū Shūmuin 日蓮宗宗務院, ed. 1974. *Nichirenshū shūsei chōsa hōkokusho* 日蓮宗宗勢調査報告書. Tokyo: Nichirenshū Shūmuin.

——— 2004. *Nichirenshū Shūsei* 日蓮宗宗制. Tokyo: Nichirenshū shūmuin.

Nihon Hōsō Kyōkai 日本放送協会. 1988. *Tera ga kieru: Chūgoku sanchi/furusato kara no hōkoku* 寺が消える―中国山地・ふるさとからの報告. Tokyo: NHK.

———. 2010. *NHK Supesharu: Muenshakai—Muenshi sanmannisennin no shōgeki* NHKスペシャル：無縁社会―無縁死3万2千人の衝撃. Tokyo: NHK.

Noguchi Katsu'ichi 野口勝一. 1898. "Sōshiki no heifū o aratamu beshi 葬式の弊風を改むべし." *Fūzoku Gahō* 風俗画報 172:1–2.

Nojima Hiroyuki 野島博之. 2005. *Shōwashi no chizu: Shōwa no hajimari kara taiheiyō sensō, kōdo seichō jidai made 46 tēma shūroku* 昭和史の地図―昭和の始まりから太平洋戦争、高度成長時代まで46テーマ収録. Tokyo: Seibido shuppan.

Nosco, Peter, ed. 1984. *Confucianism and Tokugawa culture*. Princeton: Princeton University Press.

Ogawa Eiji 小川英爾. 2000. *Hitori hitori no haka: Seija no haka annonbyō* ひとりひとりの墓：生者の墓安穏廟. Tokyo: Daitō shuppansha.

Okada Hirotaka 岡田弘隆. 2001. "O-haka o meguru hōritsu mondai no iroha お墓をめぐる法律問題のいろは." *Kyōka Sentā Sankō Shiryō 4: O-haka*. Tokyo: Shingonshū Buzanha Kyōka Sentā: 69–98.

Ōmura Eishō 大村英昭. 2003. "Sōsai to minzoku no kokoro 葬祭と民俗のこころ." In *Sōsai: gendaiteki igi to kadai* 葬祭―現代的意義と課題, ed. Sōtōshū Sōgō Kenkyū Sentā, 20–39. Tokyo: Sōtōshū shūmuchō.

Ooms, Herman. 1985. *Tokugawa Ideology: Early Constructs, 1570–1680.* Princeton: Princeton University Press.

Ōzuka Jishin 大塚慈伸. 2001. "Shingonshū no kyōri kara mita o-haka to wa 真言宗の教理から見たお墓とは." *Kyōka Sentā Sankō Shiryō 4: O-haka.* Tokyo: Shingonshū Buzanha Kyōka Sentā:1–16.

Ragon, Michel. 1983. *The Space of Death: A Study of Funerary Architecture, Decoration, and Urbanism.* Charlottesville: University Press of Virginia.

Reader, Ian. 1983. "Contemporary Thought in Sōtō Zen Buddhism." Ph.D. diss., Leeds University.

———. 1991. *Religion in Contemporary Japan.* Honolulu: University of Hawai'i Press.

———. 1991b. "What Constitutes Religious Activity? (II)." *Japanese Journal of Religious Studies* 18, no. 4:373–76.

———. 2000. *Religious Violence in Contemporary Japan: The Case of Aum Shinrikyō.* Richmond: Curzon.

Reader, Ian and George Tanabe. 1998. *Practically Religious: Worldly Benefits and the Common Religion of Japan.* Honolulu: University of Hawai'i Press.

Roemer, Michael. 2009. "Religious Affiliation in Contemporary Japan: Untangling the Enigma." *Review of Religious Research* 50, no. 3:298–320.

Rowe, Mark. 2000. "Stickers For Nails: The Ongoing Transformation of Roles, Rites, and Symbols in Japanese Funerals." *Japanese Journal of Religious Studies* 27, nos. 3–4:353–78.

———. 2003. "Grave Changes: Scattering Ashes in Contemporary Japan." *Japanese Journal of Religious Studies* 30, no. 1:185–218.

———. 2004. "Where the Action Is: Sites of Contemporary Sōtō Buddhism." *Japanese Journal of Religious Studies* 31, no. 2:357–88.

———. 2009. "Death, Burial, and the Study of Contemporary Japanese Buddhism." *Religion Compass* 3, no. 1:18–30.

Ryūkoku Daigaku Shūkyōhō Kenkyūkai 龍谷大学宗教法研究会, ed. 1990. *Shūkyōhō kenkyū 10* 宗教法研究 10. Kyoto: Hōritsu Bunkasha.

Sakai Toshihiko 堺利彦. 1903. "Sōshiki kairyō 葬式改良." *Yorozu Chōhō.*

Sasaki Kōkan 佐々木宏幹. 2002. *"Hotoke" to chikara* <ほとけ>と力. Tokyo: Yoshikawa kōbunkan.

———. 2003a. "Sōsai Bukkyō: Kyōgiteki rinen to genba no aida 葬祭仏教―教義的理念と現場の間." *SOGI* 74:49–52.

———. 2003b. "Shisha to raise 死者と来世." In *Sōsai: Gendaiteki igi to kadai,* ed. Sōtōshū Sōgō Kenkyū Sentā, 53–66. Tokyo: Sōtōshū shūmuchō.

———. 2004. *Butsuriki: Seikatsu bukkyō no dainamizumu* 仏力: 生活仏教のダイナミズム Tokyo: Shunjūsha.

Satō Yoshifumi 佐藤良文. 1997. "Jōdoshū ji'in ni okeru sōsai no genjō 浄土宗寺院における葬祭の現状." In *Sōsai bukkyō: Sono rekishi to gendaiteki kadai,* ed. Y. Itō and M. Fujii, 331–47. Tokyo: Nonburusha.

Schopen, Gregory. 1991. "Archaeology and Protestant Presuppositions in the Study of Indian Buddhism." *History of Religions* 31:1–23.

———. 1997. *Bones, Stones, and Buddhist Monks: Collected Papers on the Archaeology, Epigraphy, and Texts of Monastic Buddhism in India.* Honolulu: University of Hawai'i Press.

Scupin, Raymond. 1997. "The KJ Method: A Technique for Analyzing Data Derived from Japanese Ethnology." *Human Organization* 56, no. 2:233–37.

Seneviratne, H. L. 1999. *The Work of Kings: The New Buddhism in Sri Lanka.* Chicago: University of Chicago Press.

Sharf, Robert. 1995. "Sanbōkyōdan: Zen and the Way of the New Religions." *Japanese Journal of Religious Studies* 22, nos. 3–4:417–58.

———. 1999. "On the Allure of Buddhist Relics." *Representations* 66:75–99.

Shibata Yoshinori 柴田芳憲. 2004. "*Henshū kōki* 編集後記." In *Sōgi/hōji no shikitari to sono yurai*, ed. Sōtōshū Shizuokaken Daiichishūmusho, 282–83. Shizuoka: Sōtōshū Shizuokaken Daiichishūmusho.

Shiina Kōyū 椎名宏雄. 2003. "*Motsugo sasō no igi to kadai* 沒後作僧の意義と課題." In *Sōsai: Gendaiteki igi to kadai*, ed. Sōtōshū Sōgō Kenkyū Sentā, 186–203. Tokyo: Sōtōshū Shūmuchō.

Shima Tōru 島亨. 1994. "'Sankotsu' undō e no gimon: Kazoku gensō to kyōdōsei no aida「散骨」運動への疑問: 家族幻想と共同性のあいだ." *Seiron* 11:112–23.

Shimada Hiromi 島田裕巳. 1991. *Kaimyō: Naze shigo ni namae o kaeru no ka 戒名: なぜ死後に名前を変えるのか.* Kyoto: Hōzōkan.

———. 2010. *Sōshiki wa, iranai 葬式は、要らない.* Tokyo: Gentosha shinsho.

Shimazono Susumu 島薗進 1995. "In the Wake of Aum: The Formation and Transformation of a Universe of Belief." *Japanese Journal of Religious Studies* 22, nos. 3–4:381–415.

———. 2001. "'Shūkyō' to 'Religion.'" *Ōfū* 87:51–62.

Shingonshū Buzanha Kyōka Sentā 真言宗豊山派教化センター, ed. 2001. *Kyōka Sentā Sankō Shiryō 4: O-haka 教化センター参考資料4: お墓.* Tokyo: Shingonshū Buzanha Kyōka Sentā.

———. 2003. *Jūshoku no ishiki ni kansuru ankēto chōsa kekka 住職の意識に関するアンケート調査結果.* Tokyo: Shingonshū Buzanha Kyōka Sentā.

Shintani Takanori 新谷尚紀. 1997. "Nihonjin no haka 日本人の墓." *Bukkyō* 38:134–46.

Smith, Robert John. 1974. *Ancestor Worship in Contemporary Japan.* Stanford: Stanford University Press.

Sōgi Reien Bunka Kenkyūkai 葬儀霊園文化研究会. 2000. *Iza to iu toki no sōgi to kuyō jiten イザというときの葬儀と供養事典.* Tokyo: Nihon Bungeisha.

Sōmushō Tōkeikyoku 総務省統計局, ed. 2002. *Nihon tōkei nenkan 日本統計年鑑.* Tokyo: Nihon Tōkei Kyōkai.

Sōsō no Jiyū o Susumeru Kai 葬送の自由をすすめる会, ed. 1991. *'Haka' kara no jiyū: Chikyū ni kaeru shizensō <墓>からの自由: 地球に還る自然葬.* Tokyo: Shakai Hyōronsha.

Sōtōshū Shizuokaken Daiichishūmusho 曹洞宗静岡県第一宗務所, ed. 2004. *Sōgi/hōji no shikitari to sono yurai 葬儀・法事のしきたりとその由来.* Shizuoka: Sōtōshū Shizuokaken Daiichishūmusho.

Sōtōshū Shūmuchō 曹洞宗宗務庁, ed. 1959. *Sōtōshu shūsei hakusho* 曹洞宗宗勢白書. Tokyo: Sōtōshū Shūmuchō.

———. 1985. *Shūmon sōsai no tokushitsu o saguru: Shushōgi to no kanren ni oite* 宗門葬祭の特質を探る一修証義との関連において. Tokyo: Sōtōshū shūmuchō.

———. 1987. *Shōwa 60 nen Sōtōshū shūsei sōgō chōsa hōkokusho* 昭和60年曹洞宗宗勢総合調査報告書. Tokyo: Sōtōshū Shūmuchō.

———. 1991. *Sōtōshū shūsei no ayumi* 曹洞宗宗勢のあゆみ. Tokyo: Sōtōshū Shūmuchō.

———. 1993. *Toshi danshinto no shūkyō ishiki* 都市檀信徒の宗教意識. Tokyo: Sōtōshū Shūmuchō.

———. 1998. *1995 (Heisei 7) nen Sōtōshū shūsei sōgō chōsa hōkokusho* 1995 (平成 7) 年曹洞宗宗勢総合調査報告書. Tokyo: Sōtōshū Shūmuchō.

———. 2001. *Sōtō School Scriptures for Daily Services and Practice.* Tokyo: Sōtōshū Shūmuchō.

———. 2008. *2005 (Heisei 17) nen Sōtōshū shūsei sōgō chōsa hōkokusho* 2005 (平成 17) 年曹洞宗宗勢総合調査報告書. Tokyo: Sōtōshū Shūmuchō.

Sōtōshū Shūsei Chōsaiinkai 曹洞宗宗勢調査委員会, ed. 1984. *Shūkyō shūdan no asu e no kadai* 宗教集団の明日への課題. Tokyo: Sōtōshū Shūmuchō.

Sōtōshū Sōgō Kenkyū Sentā 曹洞宗総合研究センター, ed. 2003. *Sōsai: Gendaiteki igi to kadai* 葬祭: 現代的意義と課題. Tokyo: Sōtōshū Shūmuchō.

———. 2004. *Sōsai ni kansuru ankēto chōsa hōkokusho* 葬祭に関するアンケート調査報告書. Tokyo: Sōtōshū Sōgō Kenkyū Sentā.

———. 2008. *Sōryo: Sono yakuwari to kadai* 僧侶：その役割と課題. Tokyo: Sōtōshū Shūmuchō.

Spiro, Melford E. 1970. *Buddhism and Society: A Great Tradition and its Burmese Vicissitudes.* New York: Harper & Row.

Staggs, Kathleen M. 1983. "'Defend the Nation and Love the Truth.' Inoue Enryo and the Revival of Meiji Buddhism." *Monumenta Nipponica* 38, no. 3:251–81.

Stone, Jacqueline I. 1994. "Rebuking the Enemies of the *Lotus*—Nichirenist Exclusivism in Historical Perspective." *Japanese Journal of Religious Studies* 21, nos. 2–3:231–59.

———. 2004. "By the Power of One's Last Nenbutsu: Deathbed Practices in Early Modern Japan." In *Approaching the Land of Bliss: Religious Praxis in the Cult of Amitābha*, ed. R. K. Payne and K. K. Tanaka, 77–119. Honolulu: University of Hawai'i Press.

———. 2005. "Death." In *Critical Terms for the Study of Buddhism*, ed. D. S. Lopez, Jr., 56–76. Chicago: University of Chicago Press.

——— 2006. "Buddhism." In *Nanzan Guide to Japanese Religions*, ed. L. Swanson and C. Chilson, 38–64. Honolulu: University of Hawai'i Press.

Stone, Jacqueline I., and Mariko Namba Walter, eds. 2008. *Death and the Afterlife in Japanese Buddhism.* Honolulu: University of Hawai'i Press.

Strong, John. 2004. *Relics of the Buddha.* Princeton: Princeton University Press.

Sugawara Toshikiyo 菅原壽清. 2003. "Ankēto chōsa kekka no kaisetsu アンケート調査結果の解説." In *Sōsai: Gendaiteki igi to kadai*, ed. Sōtōshū Sōgō Kenkyū Sentā, 373–407. Tokyo: Sōtōshū Shūmuchō.

Suzuki Hikaru. 2000. *The Price of Death: The Funeral Industry in Contemporary Japan*. Stanford: Stanford University Press.

Swarts, Erica. 2001. "Kaimyō (Japanese Buddhist Posthumous Names) as Indicators of Social Status." Ph.D. diss., Ohio State University.

Swyngedouw, Jan. 1993. "Religion in Contemporary Japanese Society." In *Religion and Society in Modern Japan: Selected Readings*, ed. M. Mullins, S. Shimazono and L. Swanson, 49–72. Berkeley: Asian Humanities Press, 49–72.

Takakusu Junjirō 高楠順次郎, Watanabe Kaikyoku 渡邊海旭, et al. 1924–34. *Taishō shinshū daizōkyō* 大正新修大藏經. 85 vols. Tokyo: Taishō Issaikyō Kankōkai.

Takaguchi Yasuyuki 高口恭行. 1982. 一心寺風雲覚え書き *Isshinji fūun oboegaki*. Osaka: Seibundō.

Tamamuro Fumio 圭室文雄. 1999. *Sōshiki to danka* 葬式と檀家. Tokyo: Yoshikawa kōbunkan.

Tamamuro Taijō 圭室諦成. 1963. *Sōshiki Bukkyō* 葬式仏教. Tokyo: Daihō rinkaku.

Tambiah, Stanley Jeyaraja. 1970. *Buddhism and the Spirit Cults in North-east Thailand*. Cambridge: Cambridge University Press.

———. 1976. *World Conqueror and World Renouncer: A Study of Buddhism and Polity in Thailand against a Historical Background*. Cambridge: Cambridge University Press.

———. 1984. *The Buddhist Saints of the Forest and the Cult of Amulets: A Study in Charisma, Hagiography, Sectarianism, and Millennial Buddhism*. Cambridge: Cambridge University Press.

Tanabe, George. 2008. "The Orthodox Heresy of Buddhist Funerals." In *Death and the Afterlife in Japanese Buddhism*, ed. J. I. Stone, and M. N. Walter, 325–48. Honolulu: University of Hawai'i Press.

Tanaka Hōkoku 田中芳谷, ed. 1960. *Tanaka Chigaku sensei eifu* 田中智学先生影譜. Tokyo: Shishiō bunko.

Tanaka Ryōshō 田中良昭. 2004. "Kanshū ni atatte 監修に当たって." In *Sōgi/hōji no shikitari to sono yurai*, ed. Sōtōshū Shizuokaken Daiichishūmusho. Shizuoka: Sōtōshū Shizuokaken Daiichishūmusho.

Tani Kayoko 谷嘉代子. 1994. "Onna no hi no kai no ayumi kara: Shien no sōsō o motomete 女の碑の会の歩みから一志縁の葬送を求めて." *SOGI* 19:86–8.

Tanigawa Akio. 1992. "Excavating Edo's Cemeteries: Graves as Indicators of Status and Class." *Japanese Journal of Religious Studies* 19, nos. 2–3:271–97.

Teiser, Stephen F. 1988. *The Ghost Festival in Medieval China*. Princeton: Princeton University Press.

———. 1994. *The Scripture on the Ten Kings and the Making of Purgatory in Medieval Chinese Buddhism*. Honolulu: University of Hawai'i Press.

Tipton, Elise. 2008. *Modern Japan: A Social and Political History*. London: Routledge.

Trainor, Kevin. 1997. *Relics, Ritual, and Representation in Buddhism: Rematerializing the Sri Lankan Theravāda Tradition*. Cambridge: Cambridge University Press.

Tsuji, Yohko. 2002. "Death Policies in Japan: The State, the Family, and the Individual." In *Family and Social Policy in Japan: Anthropological Approaches*, ed. R. Goodman, 177–99. Cambridge: Cambridge University Press.

———. 2006. "Mortuary Rituals in Japan: The Hegemony of Tradition and the Motivations of Individuals." *Ethos* 34/3:391–431.

Tsuji Zennosuke 辻善之助. 1983–1984. *Nihon Bukkyōshi no kenkyū* 日本仏教史の研究. 4 vols. Tokyo: Iwanami shoten.

Ueda Noriyuki 上田紀行. 2004. *Ganbare Bukkyō: O-tera renesansu no jidai* 頑張れ仏教-お寺レネサンスの時代. Tokyo: NHK shuppan.

Veere, Hendrik vander. 2000. *A Study into the Thought of Kōgyō Daishi Kakuban: With a Translation of his Gorin kuji myō himitsushaku.* Leiden: Hotei Publishing.

Verne, Jules. 1870. *All Around the Moon.* Project Gutenberg.

Vesey, Alexander M. 2003. "The Buddhist Clergy and Village Society in Early Modern Japan." Ph.D. diss., Princeton University.

Watt, Paul B. 1984. "Jiun Sonja (1718–1804): A Response to Confucianism within the Context of Buddhist Reform." In *Confucianism and Tokugawa Culture*, ed. Peter Nosco, 188–214. Princeton: Princeton University Press.

White, Merry I. 2002. *Perfectly Japanese: Making Families in an Era of Upheaval.* Berkeley and Los Angeles: University of California Press.

Williams, Duncan. 2000. "Representations of Zen: A Social and Institutional History of Sōtō Zen Buddhism in Edo Japan." Ph.D. diss., Harvard University.

———. 2005. *The Other Side of Zen: A Social History of Soto Zen Buddhism in Tokugawa Japan.* Princeton: Princeton University Press.

———. 2008. "Funerary Zen: Sōtō Zen Death Management in Tokugawa Japan." In *Death and the Afterlife in Japanese Buddhism*, ed. J. I. Stone, and M. N. Walter, 207–46. Honolulu: University of Hawai'i Press.

Yamada Shin'ya 山田慎也. 2009. *Gendai nihon no shi to sōgi: Sōsaigyō no tenkai to shiseikan no hen'yō* 現代日本の死と葬儀―葬祭業の展開と死生観の変容. Tokyo: Tōkyō Daigaku shuppankai.

Yamaori Tetsuo 山折哲雄 and Yasuda Mutsuhiko 安田睦彦. 2000. *Sōsō no jiyū to shizensō: Umi yama sora e kaeru tabi* 葬送の自由と自然葬: 海山空へ還る旅. Tokyo: Gaifūsha.

Yamashita Shigeru 山下重人. 1898. "Sōgiron 葬儀論." *Fūzoku Gahō* 174:1–3.

Yampolsky, Philip B., ed. 1996. *Letters of Nichiren.* New York: Columbia University Press.

Yasuda Mutsuhiko 安田睦彦. 1992. "Shizensō no susume 自然葬のすすめ." *Bukkyō* 20:122–29.

———. 1997. "'Sōsō no Jiyū o Susumeru Kai' no ayumi 「葬送の自由をすすめる会」の歩み." *Bukkyō* 38:112–24.

Yasumaru Yoshio 安丸良夫. 1979. *Kamigami no meiji ishin: Shinbutsu bunri to haibutsu kishaku* 神々の明治維新:神仏分離と廃仏毀釈. Tokyo: Iwanami Shoten.

Yifa. 2002. *The Origins of Buddhist Monastic Codes in China: An Annotated Translation and Study of the Chanyuan qinggui.* Honolulu: University of Hawai'i Press.

Yokota Mutsumi 横田睦. 1994. "Igi ari! 'Sōsō no jiyū' 異義あり!「葬送の自由」." *Seiron* 2:250–57.

———. 1996. "Ikotsu wa doko ni demo makeru to shitara dō naru ka?! 遺骨はどこにでも撒けるとしたらどうなるか?!" *Gekkan Jūshoku* 11:56–63.

———. 1997. "Tōtō jitaku no niwa ni ikotsu o makeru jidai ni natta とうとう自宅の庭に遺骨を撒ける時代になった." *Gekkan Jūshoku* 2:60–63.

———. 2000. *O-kotsu no yukue: Kasō taikoku nippon no gijutsu* お骨のゆくえ: 火葬大国日本の技術. Tokyo: Heibonsha.

Zennihon Sōsaigyō Kyōdō kumiai Rengōkai 全日本葬祭業協同組合連合会. 2007. *Daihachikai "Sōgi ni tsuite no ankēto chōsa" hōkokusho* 第8回「葬儀についてのアンケート調査」報告書. Tokyo: Zennihon Sōsaigyō Kyōdō kumiai Rengōkai.

INDEX

Page numbers in *italics* refer to figures.

abandoned graves (*muenbo*): attempts to find living relatives, 47, 47n; consequences of, 46–47; fear of, 49–51, 70, 81, 137–38; gravestones from, 47–48; increase in, 221; loss of revenue from, 47; in municipal graveyards, 47n; reclaiming, 47, 108n; remains turned into statues, 48–49; as symbol of future end of temples, 48, 222. See also *muen* (absence of bonds)

Abe Toshimasa, 211
advertisements, En no Kai, 128–30, 131–32, 137
agency. *See* control, attempts at
agriculture: current state of Japanese, 105; land reforms, 26–28, 103, 142
Akahori Shōmei, 18
Alexy, Allison, 224–25
All Japan Funerary Professional Cooperative Association (Zennihon Sōsaigyō Kyōdō Kumiai Rengōkai), 55
alms (*fuse*), 30, 103, 127, 135
Amida, 60
ancestor worship, 24, 119, 167, 175, 199. *See also* memorial services
ancestral graves: buying, 51; costs, 45n; emergence in Tokugawa period, 22, 161–62; importance, 4, 131; interments, 51–52; laws on ownership and maintenance, 24–25, 51; maintenance costs, 12n; obligations to visit and maintain, 5, 56, 90–91, 108, 223; visiting, 1–2, 6, 6n, 75n, 90–91, 119, 131, 165; women buried with husband's family, 22n, 129. *See also* abandoned graves (*muenbo*)

Annex, 124–26, 128, 129, 140
Annon ("peace and tranquility") grave: changes to traditions, 76–77, 224; communal ossuary, 62, 75–76, 97–98; as community, 86; costs, 75, 109; design, 72–73; female members, 87–98; gravestones, 72–74, *74*; income from, 104; individual graves, 72–74; influence, 59–60; inscriptions, 74, *74*; members, 75–78, 84–85, 110; members' personal narratives, 86–102, 224–25; memorial services, 75–76, 98; name of, 71n, 83; Ogawa on, 69–70; promotion of, 81–82; reasons for development, 69–70, 80, 81, 83, 104, 226; schematic, *99*; site, 71–73, *72*; success of, 59–60, 75–76, 97–98; system, 75–76, 97–98; visitors, 74–75. *See also* Myōkōji
Annon Festival, 82, 109–10
Annon Forest (Mori no Annon), *73*, 73, 83, 98, 100
anonymous deaths, 44
Aoki Mitsuo, 174
Asahi Weekly (*Shūkan Asahi*), 69–70, 81
ash scattering: ambiguities, 176–77; debates on, 156n, 158–60, 161–62, 163; departures from tradition, 175–77; environmental benefits, 153, 156n, 162–64; growing popularity, 36, 153, 158; historical precedents, 156, 161–62, 161n; legality, 153, 155, 156n, 157–58, 176; opposition, 154, 163, 171, 227; preparations, 156–57, 171; public acceptance, 153, 158, 176, 227; regulations, 158–59, 176; revisiting

ash scattering (*continued*)
  sites, 165n, 174; sites, 157, 160, 162–63,
  176; support from Buddhists, 168–70.
  See also Grave-Free Promotion Society;
  natural funerals (*shizensō*)
Association to Reform Funerals (Sōshiki o
  Kaikaku Suru Kai), 35–36
Aum Shinrikyō, 85n, 160, 160n, 182n
Awaya Ryōdō, 199
Azuma Shun'ei, 36

Benavides, Gustavo, 229
Bodiford, William M., 195
bonds (*en*): in Buddhism, 46, 150, 168;
  creating new types, 71, 86, 110, 114,
  120, 225; loss of, 228–29; maintaining,
  150; meaning of term, 45–46. *See also*
  muen
Bone Buddha (*kotsubotoke*) statues, 48–49,
  49
Brook, Timothy, 10
Buddhism: changes in Meiji period, 42, 142,
  222–23; "death" of, 20; decline seen in
  Japan, 7, 20, 103, 105, 140, 222; everyday
  practices, 9; ideal/practical division,
  40–41, 229–30; modernity and, 39–41,
  142; propagation, 147; separation from
  Shinto, 23, 39, 142; statues, 92–93,
  95–96; suppression policies, 23, 27n;
  variations within, 111. *See also* funerary
  Buddhism; temple Buddhism
Buddhist culture, 166–67, 203, 204, 210
Buddhist doctrine: causality, 167, 168;
  codependent origination, 7, 46, 167;
  contradictions in funerary Buddhism,
  6, 7, 180, 196, 200–201, 219, 228; lack
  of interest in, 83–84, 85; mastery over
  death, 95; nonattachment, 114, 169, 170;
  no-self, 6, 7, 194, 207, 219, 228; teaching
  and propagation, 83–86, 179–80, 227–30;
  tensions with practice, 179–80, 179n,
  219, 227–30
Buddhist sects: differences among, 199; identification with, 3–4, 5; in Japan, 3–4n.
  See also sectarian research centers; *and
  individual sects*
Buddhist studies, 40n, 230
Bukkyō Times, 168
burials: cherry blossom, 36–37; contemporary practices, 222; of cremated remains,
  51–52, 156, 192; direct, 36; double-burial
  system, 118; forest funerals, 170–73;

human need for, 221–22; laws on, 24–25,
  24n, 155, 158; traditional practices,
  161–62, 169–70. *See also* graves
burial societies. *See* En no Kai burial society;
  Women's Monument Society (Onna no
  Hi no Kai)

cherry blossom burials (*sakurasō*), 36–37
Chisaka Genbō, 170–71, 172–73
chokusō. *See* direct burials (*chokusō/jikisō*)
Chōshōji, 63
Christians: forest funerals, 171–72n;
  Tokugawa persecution, 21
civil code: current, 25, 51, 52; Meiji, 24–25,
  26, 51
clergy. *See* priests
codependent origination (*engi*), 7, 46, 167
coffins, 205
community: loss of, 127; new sites of, 58, 86
Confucianism, 24, 131
control, attempts at, 94–96, 97, 98–99
corporations for public good (*kōeki hōjin'ei*),
  54
corpses: discarding, 155, 158, 161; liminal
  state, 176. *See also* cremations; death
cremations: forest funerals, 170–73; interment of ashes, 51–52, 156, 192; preva-
  lence in Japan, 152; remains left in crematoria, 158n, 169; traditional practices,
  169–70. *See also* ash scattering
criminal code, 155

Dainichi Nyōrai, 213–15, *215*
Dairenji, 48
danka. *See* parishioners (*danka*)
danka seido. *See* temple parishioner system
  (*danka seido*)
danshinto. *See* temple followers
  (*shinto/danshinto*)
dead: enshrining spirits of, 66, 67; festival of
  (*o-bon*), 1–2, 6, 6n, 51, 119, 140–44, 221;
  Japanese views, 222; separation from living, 176; thirst of, 1–2. *See also* ancestor
  worship; corpses
death: anonymous, 44; impurity, 23n, 65, 67,
  118, 161, 163; mastery over, 95
demographic changes: depopulated areas,
  17–19, 80, 103; effects on funerary Buddhism, 223; nuclear families, 31, 38, 52,
  120; urbanization, 25, 103–4
direct burials (*chokusō/jikisō*), 36, 191–92
discrimination, 193n, 195

divorce: honeymoon, 87n; posthumous, 87–90, 95, 224–25
Dōgen, 197, 208–9, 210
Douglas, Mary, 45

eitai kuyōbo. See eternal memorial graves (*eitai kuyōbo*)
en. See bonds (*en*); *muen* (absence of bonds)
engi. See codependent origination (*engi*)
Enmyōji, 28
En no Kai burial society: advertisements, 128–30, 131–32, 137; bonds created, 120, 225; communal ossuary, 115; criticism of, 131–32; discussion meetings, 130–31, 130n; dual-grave system, 115–18, 119; establishment, 112, 125; fees, 114–15, 127, 133, 133n, 135; goals, 134–35, 146–48, 149–50, 226; growth, 112, 131, 146–47; management company, 124–26, 128; members, 114–15, 120–24, 125–26, 130–31, 141, 145; members' relationship to temple, 136–39, 146–47; memorial offerings, 117–18; memorial services, 115, 137; memorial tablets, 116–17, *117*, 138; memory and memorialization, 118–19; nationalities of members, 114n; parishioners' reactions, 132–36; social implications, 114; staff, 124–28, 129, 130, 131, 137, 140, 148; visiting, 138–39. *See also* Tōchōji
Enryakuji. *See* Mount Hiei Enryakuji Grave Park (Hiezan Enryakuji Dairei'en)
eternal memorial graves (*eitai kuyōbo*): challenges to social norms, 94–95, 96–99, 224; characteristics, 60–65; community sense in, 58; consequences of, 67; costs, 45, 45n, 56–57; development, 4–5, 56, 58–60; differences from traditional burials, 5; early names, 60; ethnographic research, 10; for families, 56; forms, 60, 63; guidebook, 60; implications for temples, 5, 45, 67–68, 102–3, 148, 150–51, 224; individual sites, 62–63, 65; interment methods, 62–63; at Kuonbo, 56–58, 57, 59; locations, 44–45, 45n; maintenance of, 61; in municipal graveyards, 61, 64–65; number of, 60; ossuaries, 59, 61, 62, 63, 75–76, 97–98; parishioners' reactions, 132–34; perceptions of, 60–61; permanence, 63; popularity, 58, 60; priests' relationships with, 150–51; reasons for choosing, 45, 90, 94–102, 110,

129, 130–31, 145–46; relief feelings, 145–46; religious affiliations, 64; religious beliefs and, 90–96, 99, 100–102, 110, 146, 225; religious requirements, 63–64, 63n, 76; as response to *muen*, 44–45, 56, 58, 71, 225; at Shinto shrines, 65–67; societal reasons for development, 69–71, 81, 224; at temples, 45, 56–60, 61–62, 63–64, 115–18, 226–27; in urban areas, 61–62; women's choice of, 45, 59, 129. *See also* Annon ("peace and tranquility") grave
Eternal Tomb (*Fumetsu no funbo*), 49–51, *50*
extended families (*ie*): declining significance, 31, 36, 52; dissolution of system, 25; as ideal, 4, 52; ideology of, 24–25, 35, 52; legal status, 24–25, 52, 222–23; maintenance of family graves, 25, 51–52; as social unit, 22; succession rights, 24–25, 51; women's roles, 88–89, 91–92, 94. *See also* ancestral graves; household succession (*katoku sōzoku no tokken*)

families: eternal memorial graves for, 56; nuclear, 31, 38, 52, 120; values associated with, 4, 131, 165–66. *See also* extended families (*ie*)
family graves. *See* ancestral graves
forest burials, 100, 169–70
forest funerals (*jumokusō*), 170–73
Forest of Rebirth (*Saisei no Mori*), 162–63
Fujii Masao, 70, 82, 158, 210–11, 213
Fumetsu no funbo. See Eternal Tomb
funeral companies (*sōgisha*): control of funeral process, 223; natural funerals offered, 173–74; preparations for ash scattering, 156–57; relations with temples, 38, 126–27, 187, 207–8; rise of industry, 31, 37–38
funeral directors (*sōgiya*), ritual authority, 38, 207–8
Funeral/Memorial Service Customs and Origins (*Sōgi/hōji no shikitari to sono yurai*), 202–11
funerals: arranging, 130–31; commercialization, 208, 223; commodification, 127, 223; contemporary practices, 38, 186–91, 223–24; costs, 30, 34, 38; focus on individual's life, 36; image of deceased, 187–88; offerings to temples, 29–30. *See also* funerary rituals; natural funerals (*shizensō*)

funerary Buddhism: contradictions with doctrine, 6, 7, 180, 196, 200–201, 219, 228; critiques of, 5–6, 30, 31–37, 38, 41–42, 71, 101, 223; declining interest, 140, 191–92, 223; development, 21–25; dilemmas, 6–7, 178–80, 217–18, 227–30; doctrinal implications, 170; educating parishioners and priests, 199–200, 202–10, 212–17; emergence in Tokugawa period, 21–23; ethnographic studies, 8–9; excesses seen, 31–37, 223; importance, 170; lay knowledge of, 144–45, 190–91; in Meiji period, 23–25, 32–35, 222–23; postwar rejection of, 35–37; scholarly study of, 7–9, 15–16; social norms and, 20–21, 94–95, 96–99, 224; status markers, 31–34; surveys on practices, 186–91, 194; tensions between doctrine and practice, 179–80, 179n, 219, 227–30
funerary freedom, 166, 167, 174
funerary rituals: changes in contemporary Japan, 4–5, 36–37; defense of, 166–67; folk practices, 188, 204, 205, 208, 211, 217, 229; *indō* rite, 190–91; interpretations by laity, 190–91, 195–96; memory and memorialization, 118–19; nonreligious, 36, 154, 157, 165, 191–92; priests' roles, 31, 38, 189–90, 207–9; processions, 32–35; protection from malevolent spirits, 118; Shinto, 23; simplification trend, 140; social expression by living, 35; for Sōtō monks, 149. *See also* memorial services
fuse. See alms (*fuse*)
Fūzoku gahō, 32, 34

gaki. See hungry ghosts (*gaki*)
genba (local temple), 201–2
Gennep, Arnold van, 176
GFPS. *See* Grave-Free Promotion Society (Sōsō no Jiyū o Susumeru Kai)
Gokurakuji, 60
Grave-Free Promotion Society (Sōsō no Jiyū o Susumeru Kai): aims, 177; Buddhist members, 169–70; critiques of, 161–62, 163–64, 165–68, 175, 227; environmental platform, 162–64; establishment, 82, 153; ethnographic research, 10–11; Forest of Rebirth, 162–63; influence, 153; manifesto, 155–56; membership, 153; natural funerals performed, 153, 153n, 154–55, 157, 163, 174; publications, 155–57, 161,

174, 175. *See also* natural funerals (*shizensō*); Yasuda Mutsuhiko
grave laws, 24–25, 51, 155, 158
graves: buying, 51–52; communal, 22, 53, 62; contemporary revolution, 71, 223–24; costs, 36, 45n, 52, 54; development of custom, 161–62; double-burial system, 118; fixed locations, 227; of married couples, 22n, 70, 87, 129; negative imagery, 174–75, 227; pamphlet on, 212–17; shortage of available plots, 52–53, 55; types, 52–55. *See also* abandoned graves (*muenbo*); ancestral graves; burials; eternal memorial graves (*eitai kuyōbo*)
Graves (*O-haka*) [Shingon Research Center booklet], 212–17
gravestones: from abandoned graves, 47–48; at Annon, 72–74, 74; height limits, 32; for individuals and couples, 22; Shingon five-tiered, 213–17, 215; significance, 167; at Tōchōji, 115, 118
graveyards: number of, 55; privately managed, 53–54; publicly managed, 47n, 52–53, 55, 61, 64–65. *See also* temple graveyards (*ji'in bochi*)

Harrison, Robert Pogue, 221
Hattori Shōsai, 192–93
Himonya Hajime, 82
Hiraide Kōjiro, 33
Hirohito, Emperor, 224
Hongō Ryōen, 61–62
Hōsenin, Kannon Seien grave, 60
Hosono Ungai, *Eternal Tomb* (*Fumetsu no funbo*), 49–51, 50
household succession (*katoku sōzoku no tokken*), 24–25, 51
hungry ghosts (*gaki*), 46

ie. See extended families (*ie*)
I Have No Grave! (*O-haka ga nai*), 54–55
Ikeda Hayato, 30
Inada Tsutomu, 35–36
individualism, 36, 168–69
Inoue Haruyo, 81–82, 87, 88, 91–92, 91n, 95, 173n
Institute for Zen Studies (Zen Bunka Kenkyūjo), 180
intellectuals, Buddhist: posthumous ordination issue, 195–202; studies abroad,

39–40; studies of mortuary problem, 191–95; Western modernity and, 39–40. *See also* sectarian research centers
Ishihara Shintarō, 157
Ishihara Yūjirō, 157
Ishizaki Yasumune, 167
Isshinji, Bone Buddha (*kotsubotoke*) statues, 48–49, *49*
Itō Yuishin, 178–79n1

Jackson, Michael, 94
Jaffe, Richard M., 39
Japan: constitution, 26, 64; economic development, 30–31; religious affiliations, 3n, 93. *See also* Meiji period; postwar period; Tokugawa shogunate
ji'in bochi. See temple graveyards (*ji'in bochi*)
jikisō. See direct burials (*chokusō/jikisō*)
Jōdo sect: abandoned graves in temple graveyards, 48; eternal memorial graves, 60; intellectuals, 178–79n; surveys, 185, 186–91, 231–34
Jōdo Shinshū sect, eternal memorial graves, 61–62
Jōdoshū Research Institute (JSRI: Jōdoshū Sōgō Kenkyūjo), 11, 182–83
Jōjakkōji, Women's Monument Society grave, 59
JSRI. *See* Jōdoshū Research Institute (JSRI: Jōdoshū Sōgō Kenkyūjo)
jukaishiki. See precept conferral ceremonies (*jukaishiki*)
jumokusō. See forest funerals (*jumokusō*)
Justice Ministry, 155

kaimyō. See posthumous ordination names (*kaimyō*)
kaisō. See ocean scattering (*kaisō*) services
Kakuban, 215
Kannon, 60
Kasahara Kenju, 39
Katō Eiji, 166–67
katoku sōzoku no tokkeni. See household succession (*katoku sōzoku no tokken*)
Kawakita Jirō, 79–80, 79n
Kawanabe Gyōsai, 33
Keizan, 209, 210
Kitabatake Dōryū, 39
Kōanji, 61–62

Kodaira Grave Park's Communal Burial Grave, 65
kōei bochi. See publicly managed graveyards (*kōei bochi*)
Kōeisha, 173–74
kōeki hōjin. See corporations for public good (*kōeki hōjin*)
Kokuchūkai grave, 72, 72n
Komine Michihiko, 167–68
Kuonbo, 56–58, 57, 59

laity. *See* parishioners (*danka*)
land reforms, 26–28, 103, 142
Lotus Sūtra: "Lifespan of the Tathāgata," 71–72n; title inscription on Annon walls, 72

Machida Muneo, 193n
Manual of Funerary Customs and Buddhist Services (Sōgi no shūkan to butsuji binran), 211
married couples, 22n, 70, 87, 129. *See also* divorce
Matsumoto Kōichi, 199
Meiji Civil Code, 24–25, 26, 51
Meiji period: extended-family ideology, 24–25, 35, 222–23; funeral processions, 32–35; funerary Buddhism, 23–25, 32–35, 222–23; religious policies and laws, 23, 27n, 39, 42, 142, 222–23; taxation, 23n, 34n
memorial services: at Annon, 75–76, 98; annual, 6, 52; doctrinal issues, 228; at En no Kai, 115, 137; lack of need for, 175–76; in municipal graveyards, 64–65; offerings to temples, 29–30; at Shōunji *jumokusō* graveyard, 172
memorial tablets (*sotoba*), 75, 116–17, *117*, 138
memory and memorialization, 118–19
min'ei bochi. See privately managed graveyards (*min'ei bochi*)
Miyasaka Yūkō, 162
modernity: Buddhism and, 39–41, 142; mortuary problem and, 219; at Tōchōji, 115–16, 127, 142, 144; urbanization, 25, 103–4
Mori Kenji, 25
Mori no Annon. *See* Annon Forest (Mori no Annon)
Morioka Kiyomi, 81

mortuary problem (sōsai mondai), 6–7, 179, 191–95, 199–202, 210–11, 217–18, 227–30
Mortuary Rites: Contemporary Significance and Issues (Sōsai: Gendaiteki igi to kadai), 194–95, 200–201, 203, 204, 206, 210
Mount Hiei Enryakuji Grave Park (Hieizan Enryakuji Dairei'en), Kuonbo, 56–58, 57, 59
Moyai no Kai, 61
muen (absence of bonds): abandoned graves, 46–47, 137–38, 221; ash scattering as response to, 177; in contemporary Japanese society, 44; eternal memorial graves as response to, 44–45, 56, 58, 71, 225; fears related to, 44, 47, 224; modern and contemporary responses to, 48–51, 120; as positive opportunity, 120; use of term, 46–47
muenbo. See abandoned graves (muenbo)
muen spot, 96–98
Mukō Yama [Burial] Society, 66–67
municipal graveyards. See publicly managed graveyards (kōei bochi)
Murakami Kōkyō, 36
Murakami Kōshin, 28
musical funerals (ongakusō), 36
Myōkōji: daily life, 107–10; danshinto (temple followers), 76–77; graves of parishioners, 108; parishioners, 76–78, 83–85, 104, 108, 226; rebuilding of, 77–78; secular management, 105–6; training sessions, 84–86, 102; visitors, 108–9. See also Annon ("peace and tranquility" grave); Ogawa Eiji
Myōrakuji, 48
Myōtenji, 28
Myōzuiji, 83

Nanjō Bun'yū, 39
Nara Yasuaki, 192, 194
Natsume Sōseki, 205
natural funerals (shizensō): absence of religious elements, 36, 154, 157, 165; Buddhist responses, 154, 164–73; commercialization, 173–74; costs, 173n; definition, 156; distinction from scattering, 174; early, 154–55; number of, 153, 174; opposition, 163, 165–66; promotion of, 152–53, 154, 155–57, 158–61, 164; reasons for choosing, 174–75; religious

freedom issue, 158–60; use of term, 164. See also ash scattering; Grave-Free Promotion Society (Sōsō no Jiyū o Susumeru Kai)
nature, 164. See also forest funerals (jumokusō)
new religious groups, 58, 85n, 102, 103, 185, 199
Nichiren Buddhism Modern Religious Institute (NMRI; Nichirenshū Gendai Shūkyō Kenkyūjo; also referred to as Nichiren Contemporary Religion Research Center), 11, 17, 41, 80, 183
Nichiren sect: priests, 83–84; Risshō University, 78, 79; surveys, 185; training for parishioners, 84–86
Nichiren temples: Annon graves, 83; in depopulated areas, 17–19, 80, 103; eternal memorial graves, 59, 63; number of, 105; study of problems in, 17–20, 105. See also Myōkōji
NMRI. See Nichiren Buddhism Modern Religious Institute
Noguchi Katsu'ichi, 32–33, 34
nonattachment doctrine, 114, 169, 170
no-self doctrine, 6, 7, 194, 207, 219, 228
Nozawa Kiyoshi, 72
nuclear families, 31, 38, 52, 120

o-bon (festival of dead), 1–2, 6, 6n, 51, 119, 140–44, 221
oceans, scattering ashes in, 157, 160, 161, 164, 170, 173, 176–77. See also ash scattering
ocean scattering (kaisō) services, 173
Ogawa Eiji: background, 78–80; chanting of Lotus Sūtra, 71n; children, 81; on contemporary temple Buddhism, 103–7, 111, 225; development of Annon, 71n, 81–83, 226; interviews with potential Annon members, 76–77; letter on Annon, 69–70; management of Myōkōji, 76–78, 83–84, 105–6, 107–10, 111; propagation and teaching, 83–84; public perceptions of, 100; search for successor, 106–7; study of Nichiren temples, 17n; teaching by, 84–86, 147; temple followers and, 76–77
O-haka. See Graves
O-haka ga nai. See I Have No Grave!
Okada Hirotaka, 169–70, 212n
Okamoto Wakō, 121n, 141, 148, 149, 173n

Ōkubo Sengyō, 66–67
Ōmura Eishō, 168–69, 178–79n, 201
ongakusō. See musical funerals (*ongakusō*)
Onna no Hi no Kai. *See* Women's Monument
    Society (Onna no Hi no Kai)
ordination, posthumous, 195–99, 205–6. *See
    also* precepts
Ōta Tenrei, 36
Ōuchi Seiran, 197
Ōzuka Jishin, 213–17

parishioners (*danka*): attracting new, 104,
    146–47; distinction from *danshinto*,
    77–78, 77n; educating about funerary
    Buddhism, 199–200, 212–17; eternal me-
    morial graves for, 63; financial support
    of temple, 5, 22, 135; in future, 104–5,
    226; graves in temple graveyards, 76,
    108; lack of interest in doctrine, 83–84,
    85; of Myōkōji, 76–78, 83–85, 104, 108,
    226; number per temple, 28; obligations,
    54–55, 76, 77–78; relationship to burial
    society members, 76–77; surveys of, 185,
    188–91, 194; temple control over, 21–22,
    23–24n; at Tōchōji, 112, 132–36, 147–48,
    226
posthumous divorce (*shigo rikon*), 87–90, 95,
    224–25
posthumous ordination, 195–99, 205–6
posthumous ordination names (*kaimyō*),
    31–32, 122, 123–24, 125–26, 135, 195–96
postmortem revenge, 96–98
postwar period, 26–31, 35–38, 142
precept conferral ceremonies (*jukaishiki*),
    120–24, *124*
precepts: benefits for laity, 197; posthumous
    ordination, 195–99, 205–6
priests: changes in Meiji period, 39; concerns
    about funeral practices, 200–201; daily
    work at temples, 83–84; education about
    funerary Buddhism, 199–200, 202–10,
    212–17; funeral companies and, 38, 127,
    187, 207–8; funerals of, 149; interviews,
    11; meditation, 209; outside work, 19n,
    28, 29; public perceptions of, 3, 31, 38,
    100, 188, 189–90; roles, 3, 8, 31, 39,
    105, 107, 189–90, 207–9, 218; studies
    abroad, 39–40; surveys of, 185, 186–88,
    190n, 194; teaching and propagation of
    doctrine, 83–86; temple-born, 78–79n;
    temple succession, 79n, 106–7, 148–49;
    tensions between doctrine and practice,

179–80, 227–30; training, 40–41, 107,
    142–43
privately managed graveyards (*min'ei bochi*),
    53–54, 55
processions, 32–35
publicly managed graveyards (*kōei bochi*),
    52–53, 55; eternal memorial graves, 61,
    64–65; religious services in, 64–65

Reader, Ian, 93, 197–98
Reischauer, Edwin, 161n
relics, 170
religious beliefs: authenticity, 101–2;
    eternal memorial graves and, 90–96,
    99, 100–102, 110, 146, 225; in Japan, 93;
    tourism and, 101
Religious Corporations Law, 160, 160n
religious freedom, 26, 154, 158–60
Research Center for Sōtō Zen Buddhism
    (Sōtōshū Sōgō Kenkyū Sentā), 11, 182,
    183–84, 191–95, 210–11
research centers. *See* sectarian research
    centers
revenge, postmortem, 96–98
Rinzai Zen sect, funeral rituals, 170–73, 190
Risshō University, 78, 79, 182
rural areas: depopulation, 17–19, 80, 103;
    land reforms, 26–28, 103, 142
Ryūichi Abé, 216

Sagami Bay, 160, 173
Saisei no Mori. See Forest of Rebirth (*Saisei
    no Mori*)
Saitō Nanako, 154
Sakaguchi Yasuhiko, 105–6, 108–9
Sakai Toshihiko, 32
sakurasō. See cherry blossom burials
    (*sakurasō*)
Sasaki Kōkan, 178–79n, 191, 192, 194, 199,
    200–201, 204n
scattering of ashes. *See* ash scattering
scholars. *See* intellectuals, Buddhist; sectar-
    ian research centers
sectarian research centers: activities, 9–10;
    dilemmas of funerary Buddhism, 6–7,
    178–80, 217–18, 227–30; establishment,
    41; examples, 180–82; goals, 218; rela-
    tions with sects, 183–84; researchers,
    178–79n, 180; research on, 11; roles, 41,
    228; topics, 180, 182–83, 182n; Western
    modernity and, 41. *See also* intellectuals,
    Buddhist; sectwide surveys (*shūsei chōsa*)

sectarian universities, 40–41, 78, 79, 180–82
sects. *See* Buddhist sects
sectwide surveys (*shūsei chōsa*): aims, 191;
history, 185; Jōdo sect, 185, 186–91,
231–34; methods, 187n, 188n; on mortuary practices, 186–91, 194; of parishioners, 185, 188–91, 194; of priests, 185,
186–88, 190n, 194, 231–34; publication of
results, 185–86; questions, 186, 231–34;
Shingonshū Buzanha sect, 187n; Sōtō
Zen sect, 185, 187n, 190n, 194
Shaku Sōen, 39–40
Sharf, Robert, 8–9
Shibata Yoshinori, 207–8
Shienbyō (Mausoleum of Linked Intentions),
59
shigo rikon. See posthumous divorce (*shigo
rikon*)
Shiina Kōyū, 196, 198
Shimaji Mokurai, 39
Shima Tōru, 161–62, 163–64
Shinbo Yoshimichi, 169
Shingon sect: Chizanha temples, 28; eternal
memorial graves, 60
Shingonshū Buzanha sect: Education Center,
212; General Research Institute, 212;
gravestones, 213–17, 215; mortuary prob-
lem, 217; surveys, 187n
Shinkōji, 173n
Shinran, 161
Shinshū (Honganji) sect, intellectuals,
178–79n
Shinshū temples: abandoned gravestones, 48;
incomes, 28–29; number of parishioners,
28
shinto. See temple followers
(*shinto/danshinto*)
Shinto: funerals, 23; separation from Buddhism, 23, 39, 142
Shinto shrines: aversion to death impurity,
23n, 65, 67; enshrining dead spirits,
66, 67; eternal memorial graves, 65–67;
household registration, 23
shizensō. See natural funerals (*shizensō*)
Shōunji, forest funerals, 170–73
Shōwa era, end of, 224. *See also* postwar
period
Shūkan Asahi. See Asahi Weekly (*Shūkan
Asahi*)
shūsei chōsa. See sectwide surveys (*shūsei
chōsa*)

Shushōgi, 197–98
social norms: challenges from eternal memo-
rial graves, 94–95, 96–99, 224; funerary
Buddhism and, 20–21
*Sōgi/hōji no shikitari to sono yurai. See
Funeral/Memorial Service Customs and
Origins*
*Sōgi no shūkan to butsuji binran. See
Manual of Funerary Customs and Bud-
dhist Services*
sōgisha. See funeral companies (*sōgisha*)
sōgiya. See funeral directors (*sōgiya*)
*Sōsai: Gendaiteki igi to kadai. See Mortuary
Rites: Contemporary Significance and
Issues*
sōsai mondai. See mortuary problem (*sōsai
mondai*)
Sōshiki o Kaikaku Suru Kai. *See* Association
to Reform Funerals (Sōshiki o Kaikaku
Suru Kai)
sotoba. See memorial tablets (*sotoba*)
Sōtō Institute for Buddhist Studies. *See*
Research Center for Sōtō Zen Buddhism
(Sōtōshū Sōgō Kenkyū Sentā)
Sōtōshū Sōgō Kenkyū Sentā. *See* Research
Center for Sōtō Zen Buddhism (Sōtōshū
Sōgō Kenkyū Sentā)
Sōtō Zen sect: compromises, 210; Human
Rights Division, 193n, 195; intellectu-
als, 178–79n; monastic training, 142–43;
mortuary problem, 191–95, 199–202;
posthumous ordinations, 195–99;
priests' roles, 218; research centers, 182,
183–84, 191–95; revitalization, 27; rules
for lay funerals, 196n; Shizuoka Prefecture First Parish Office, 202; *Shushōgi*,
197–98; surveys, 185, 187n, 190n, 194;
Yamanashi Office, 211
Sōtō Zen temples: incomes, 27, 29; number
of parishioners, 112, 112n; sutra chanting, 141, 141–42n. *See also* Tōchōji
Stone, Jacqueline I., 95, 216
Stone by the Roadside, A (*Robō no Ishi*)
(Yamamoto Yūzō), 33–34
surveys. *See* sectwide surveys (*shūsei
chōsa*)
sutras, 141, 141–42n. See also *Lotus Sūtra*
Suzuki Eijō, 168

Takeda Shrine, Mahoroba Grave Park, Shrine
of Ancestral Spirits (Soreisha), 65

Takizawa Kazuo: ambivalence about changes to mortuary practices, 127, 140, 150–51; creation of En no Kai, 113–14, 125, 126–27; En no Kai staff and, 127–28, 131–32; on funeral companies, 127; funeral of, 148–50; goals for En no Kai, 134–35, 146–48, 149–50, 226; *o-bon* sermon, 142–44; parishioner's letter and response, 133–36; precept conferral ceremonies, 123; son as successor, 148–49
Tamagawa, Yamanashi prefecture, 162–63
Tamamuro Fumio, 21n, 22n
Tamamuro Taijō, 5, 35, 192
Tanabe, George, 93
Tanaka Chigaku, 72n
Tanaka Ryōshō, 203–4
Tani Kayoko, 59, 82
taxes: exemptions for religious activity, 30n, 38, 64, 105, 125n; in Meiji period, 23n, 34n
temple Buddhism: decline, 48, 222; definition, 4n; family bonds, 150; Ogawa on, 103–7, 111, 225; perceptions of, 5
temple certification system (*terauke seido*), 21–22, 23, 161–62, 222, 223
temple followers (*shinto/danshinto*), 76–77, 77n, 136, 136n
temple graveyards (*ji'in bochi*): eternal memorial graves, 45, 56–60, 61–62, 63–64, 226–27; income, 3, 5, 29, 47; maintenance obligations, 56; obligations of parishioners, 54–55, 76, 108; private management companies, 53; reasons for choosing burials in, 226–27; reclaiming abandoned graves, 47, 108n; security, 55, 226–27; tax status, 64; in Tokugawa period, 162n
temple income sources: alms, 30, 103, 127, 135; funerals, 3, 6, 8, 29–30, 103, 223; grave maintenance fees, 3, 5, 29, 47; land, 26–28, 103; outside work of priests, 19n, 28, 29; parishioner support, 28–29; religious activities, 125
temple parishioner system (*danka seido*), 3, 5, 22, 103, 222, 226. *See also* parishioners (*danka*)
temples: business partnerships, 125, 126; land owned, 26–28; local (*genba*), 201–2; management in postwar period, 26–31; relations with public, 104; in rural areas, 17–19, 80, 103; secular management,

105–6; tax status, 64, 105, 125n; in urban areas, 61–62, 104. *See also* Myōkōji; Nichiren temples; parishioners (*danka*); Sōtō Zen temples; Tōchōji
temple succession, 79n, 106–7, 148–49
Tenrikyō, 102, 102n
terauke seido. *See* temple certification system (*terauke seido*)
Teshima Jirō, 125–26
Tōchōji: eternal memorial grave, 62, 115–18; "First-of-the-Month Service," 120–21; graveyard, 112–13; Hall of Arhats (Rakandō), 116–17, *117*, 118, 119, 138; history, 113; imagery, 115–16; income sources, 125, 134–35; location, 112–13; main hall, 113, 115, 137; memorial services, 115; modernity and tradition at, 115–16, 127, 142, 144; newsletter, 132–36, 132n; *o-bon* services, 140–44; parishioners, 112, 132–36, 147–48, 226; precept conferral ceremonies, 121–24, *124*, 138, *139*; as research site, 113–14; water garden, 115, *116*, 118, 119. *See also* En no Kai burial society; Takizawa Kazuo
Tokugawa shogunate: anti-Christian campaign, 21; class structure, 32–33; decline of Buddhism, 103; family graves, 22, 161–62; funerary Buddhism, 21–23; laws regulating funerary excess, 31–32; temple certification system, 21–22, 23, 161–62
Tokyo. *See* Tōchōji
Tokyo Funeral Company (Tokyo Sōgisha), 37
tourism, 101
Trump, Donald, 107
Tsunoda Tairyū, 196–97

universities, sectarian, 40–41, 78, 79, 180–82
Urakawa Michitarō, 160
urbanization, 25, 103–4
urban temples, 61–62, 104. *See also* Tōchōji

Varanasi, India, 101
Verne, Jules, 221–22

Wakamiya Hachimangū Shrine, 65–67
Wakamiya Mausoleum (Wakamiya Reibyō), 66–67, 66
Welfare Ministry, 55, 153, 155, 158, 160, 176
widows, 59, 81, 129

women: attempts at control, 94–96; divorced
or unmarried, 59, 87–88, 129; eternal
memorial graves chosen by, 45, 59, 129;
marketing to, 129; roles in extended
families, 88–89, 91–92, 94; separate
graves from husbands, 70, 87–90, 129;
widows, 59, 81, 129
Women's Monument Society (Onna no Hi no
Kai), 59, 82

Yamamoto Yūzō, *A Stone by the Roadside*
(*Robō no Ishi*), 33–34
Yanagita Kunio, 33
Yasuda Mutsuhiko: on ancestor worship,
175; at Annon Festival, 82; on commercial ash scattering services, 174; Forest
of Rebirth proposal, 162–63; interviews,

10–11; promotion of ash scattering,
152–53, 154, 157–60, 161; scattering
ceremonies, 154–55. *See also* Grave-
Free Promotion Society (Sōsō no Jiyū o
Susumeru Kai)
Yasukuni Shrine, 67n
Yokota Mutsumi, 158, 160, 163

Zen Bunka Kenkyūjo. *See* Institute for Zen
Studies (Zen Bunka Kenkyūjo)
Zennihon Sōsaigyō Kyōdō Kumiai Rengōkai.
See All Japan Funerary Professional
Cooperative Association (Zennihon
Sōsaigyō Kyōdō Kumiai Rengōkai)
Zen sects. *See* Rinzai Zen sect, funeral ritu-
als; Sōtō Zen sect